W9-BKF-900

The
Band Saw
Book
with 20 Projects

No. 3189
$25.95

The
Band Saw
Book
with 20 Projects

R. J. De Cristoforo

TAB BOOKS Inc.
Blue Ridge Summit, PA

Published by **TAB BOOKS Inc.**
FIRST EDITION/SECOND PRINTING

© 1989 by **TAB BOOKS Inc.**. Reproduction or publication of the content in any manner, without express permission of the publisher, is prohibited. The publisher takes no responsibility for the use of any of the materials or methods described in this book, or for the products thereof.

Library of Congress Cataloging-in-Publication Data

DeCristoforo, R. J.
    The band saw book : with 20 projects / R. J. De Cristoforo.
        p.   cm.
    Includes index.
    ISBN 0-8306-0289-5   ISBN 0-8306-3189-5 (pbk.)
    1. Woodwork.   2.   Band saws.   I. Title.
TT185.D43   1989
684′.083—dc20   89-32260
                                                             CIP

TAB BOOKS Inc. offers software for sale. For information and a catalog, please contact TAB Software Department, Blue Ridge Summit, PA 17294-0850.

Questions regarding the content of this book should be addressed to:

TAB BOOKS INC.
Blue Ridge Summit, PA 17294-0850

Ron Powers: Director of Acquisitions
Kimberly Tabor: Acquisition Editor
Nina E. Barr: Technical Editor
Katherine Brown: Production

Cover photograph courtesy of Delta International Machinery Corporation.

Contents

Introduction

The band saw can cut the fastest and the deepest of any wood-sawing machine. Although it is especially notable for its ability to follow curved lines, the potential of the tool also includes straight sawing, parallel sawing, sawing across, or sawing obliquely to the wood grain. The band saw is an efficient tool for beveling, tapering, forming compound angle joints, cutting narrow slots, and performing many other operations that are routine in a woodworking shop.

A casual research of the machine often leads to the opinion that it is a tool for compound sawing, which makes it possible to produce furniture components like the cabriole leg, and for resawing, which allows sawing thick boards into thin ones.

These features are outstanding and exclusive of the saw and, alone, justify having one, but to limit it to these functions is to ignore other applications that make many woodworking operations easier and faster to accomplish. For example, on a band saw with a 4-inch depth of cut you can produce eight similar components in a single operation by making a pad of ½-inch stock and then sawing as if the assembly was a solid block. Of course, you can increase the number of duplicate pieces if the machine has a 6-inch depth of cut, a capacity that is not uncommon with "small" band saws, or if the pad is composed of thinner material.

The word *small* is a relative term that, in this case, applies to machines that are amply suitable for commercial shops and home workshops. These tools are small only when you judge them against industrial machines that might have more than a 12-inch depth of cut as opposed to a 6-inch cutting depth, or when you judge them against lumber-industry machines that are yards high and can operate with blades that are 12 inches wide. For our purposes, the "small" tool can do big things.

The band saw is not limited to sawing wood. By installing a correct blade, you can use it to saw plastics and plastic laminates; man-made panel materials like particleboard; nonferrous metals such as aluminum, copper, and brass; and with applicable blade-speed adjustment, tough materials like iron and steel.

As for many machines, you can increase the tool's functions or do standard operations more safely, more accurately, or faster, by learning particular techniques and by making jigs and fixtures. Some jigs and fixtures are economical substitutes for commercial accessories and others are just not available from manufacturers. The program is to make, or buy, accessories as you need them. There is little point, except among tool collectors, in adding products that merely take storage space. When you do decide to create an accessory, be as careful with its construction as you should be when producing a project. View the addition as a lifetime tool and work accordingly.

It's always important to me to stress the safety factor of working with tools. They do much for us but are completely disinterested in how they are used. You can abuse them or yourself by ignoring performance procedures; by feeling expert to the point of overconfidence. Expertise does not guarantee safety, a fact reinforced by statistics that prove that as many, or more, professionals are hurt than amateurs. The reason? The casualness that occurs when the expert feels accomplished enough to ignore safety requirements, often to his anguish.

Always remember that the tool is without intellect. It can't distinguish between wood and you. You always must be on guard, aware of your responsibility for safety as well as for quality workmanship. Become acquainted with the tool before you use it by accepting the owner's manual as a bible for the particular unit.

Follow all operating procedures in detail. Do "dry runs," especially when the operation is foreign to you. That is, follow the steps, but with the machine turned off, so you can preview how you must move the wood and how to place your hands for safety.

The band saw has a blade-covering guard that is adjustable vertically to accommodate various stock thicknesses. You must adjust this guard so it barely clears the stock. You will see illustrations throughout this book that seem to ignore the basic safety rule, but that is *not* the way I work. When the guard is shown higher than it should be, please accept that it's so only for clarity in the photographs. Always adjust the guard for maximum blade coverage!

Remember to "measure twice, saw once," and "think twice before sawing."

Chapter 1

The Tool

THE BAND SAW DRIVES A FLEXIBLE, CONTINUOUS-LOOP STEEL BAND WITH CONVENTIONAL-type saw teeth on one edge. The blade rotates in a clockwise direction so cutting in is on a continuous downstroke. This is the family characteristic of the tool regardless of its size or primary function. The largest band saw, which can be stories high, often is called a *band mill*. It has the power to drive exceptionally wide, heavy blades, and lumber mills use it to slice large logs into usable boards or beams.

The term *band resaw* refers to units generally found in millwork factories and in lumberyards, which are used to saw beams or planks into material of lesser thickness. These machines also work with heavy blades although not in the dimensional area of the band mills. Another concept, shown in Figs. 1-1 and 1-2, is the horizontal band saw. It is interesting to know about but is essentially a metal-cutting machine. You can draw comparisons between this tool and a power hacksaw. The category of band saws of most interest to us, like the examples in Figs. 1-3 and 1-4, usually are designated as band scroll saws or, as most catalogs indicate, simply band saws.

The word *scroll* probably enters band-saw terminology because many of the machines can work with blades as narrow as 1/8 inch. This fact means that, while they can't substitute for a jigsaw, they can overlap its functions to a considerable extent.

The jigsaw, shown in Fig. 1-5 is unique in its own right. It works with short, straight blades and operates efficiently with a variety of blades, some of which are hairlike in a cross section. Because the blades can be so slight, the tool is notable for extremely fine kerfs and the minimum radii that blades can turn. It is the one tool that can accomplish the type of intricate sawing demonstrated in Fig. 1-6.

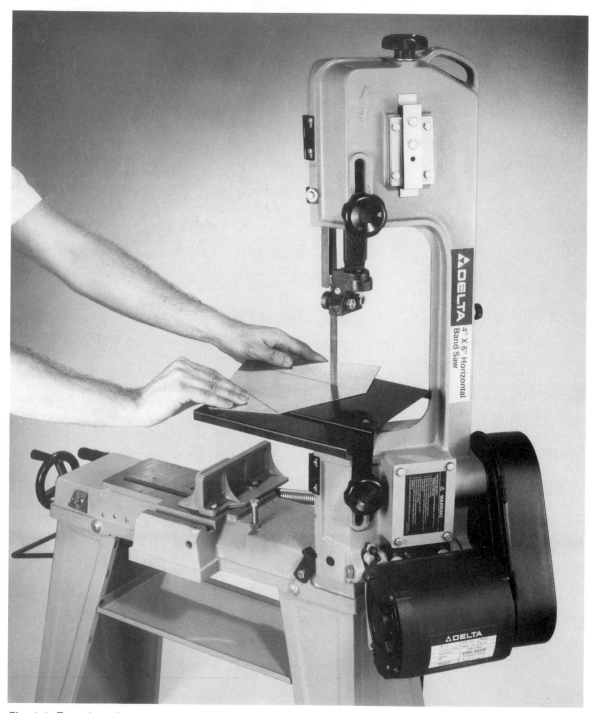

Fig. 1-1. Even though you can use the tool in a vertical position, you call a machine of this type a *horizontal band saw*. The concept has speed ranges in the low fpm area and works with carbon or intermediate-alloy blades to cut all types of metal materials.

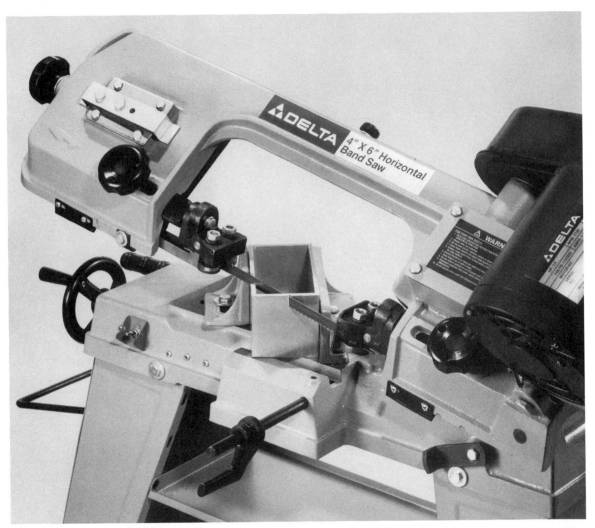

Fig. 1-2. This figure shows the horizontal band saw in its most common position. The machine has various holding devices so materials can be gripped at particular angles. Feed pressure is automatic.

Of course the jigsaw is capable of other chores, but it can't approach the capability of a band saw, which can saw through 6-inch-thick stock like a knife through soft cheese. (See Figs. 1-7 and 1-8.) Even compact, bench-top designs have ample depth-of-cut capacity to saw through a pad of three or four pieces of ¾-inch stock, so you can form several duplicate pieces in a single operation (Fig. 1-9). Being impressed by the tool's cutting speed and depth of cut is a natural reaction to the band saw, but its potential in a woodworking shop is much greater.

THE SIZE OF A BAND SAW

Most catalogs list the size of a band saw as the distance from the blade to the vertical arm of the machine. This dimension relates to the diameter of the wheels (sometimes

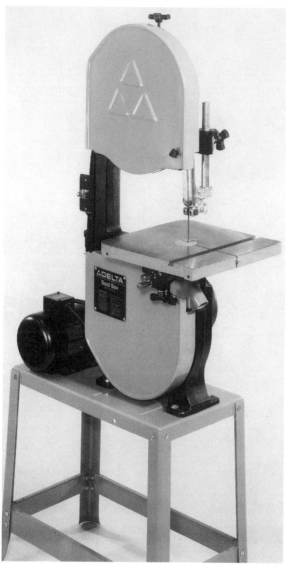

Fig. 1-3. (above) Here is a wood-cutting band saw on an open stand with an exterior motor that connects to the tool's driven pulley by a V-belt. The nozzle under the table allows connection to a vacuum cleaner to minimize sawdust pileup inside the tool.

Fig. 1-4. (right) This tool is the same one shown in Fig. 1-3 but mounted on an enclosed stand and incorporating a speed-reduction unit that provides efficient speeds for sawing nonwood materials. The tool is now a wood/metal band saw.

4

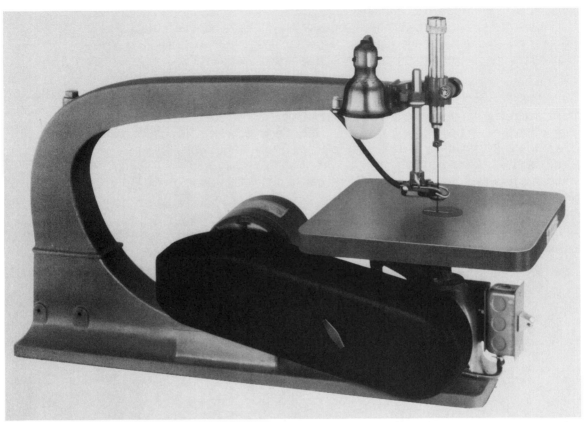

Fig. 1-5. The jigsaw works with short, straight blades that are gripped at each end in upper and lower chucks. Maximum thickness of stock a tool like this can handle is usually about 2 inches.

called *pulleys*) over which the blade travels. So, if the machine has 14-inch-diameter wheels, it is a 14-inch band saw. This concept is hedging just a bit since you must reduce *throat distance* (the line between the "up" side and "down" side of the blade) by the essential safety covering of the blade on the arm side. However, since the necessary reduction is seldom more than ¼ inch or so, it is not a critical factor.

Often, catalogs list size as a combination of throat distance and maximum depth of cut (Fig. 1-10). So, a 10- × -4-inch machine will have 10-inch-diameter wheels and can saw through stock that is not greater than 4 inches thick.

TABLE SIZE

The size of a band-saw table usually is not overly generous. For one thing, its width on the left side can't be more than the blade-to-arm dimension. Also, the tool is not designed for sawing full-size sheets of plywood or other man-made panel materials. Within some plus and minus factors, the table, in width and depth, is equal to the diameter of the wheels. An exception is the Sears/Craftsman 12-inch electronic concept that has an impressive table size of 23 inches × 27 inches (Fig. 1-11). The usual table-size to wheel-diameter characteristic does not restrict normal use of the machine. You can employ certain techniques when you feel a particular procedure will be facilitated through the use of a larger table or an outboard support. We will discuss the solutions to problems of this nature in chapters 2 and 4.

BAND-SAW CONSTRUCTION

Manufacturers have designed most band saws with twin, vertically aligned wheels over which the saw blade travels (Fig. 1-12). A belt or direct electrical current gives power to the lower wheel, while the saw blades turn the upper wheel. So the saw blade can be strained correctly over the wheels and so it will "track" as it should, you can adjust the top wheel vertically and can tilt it forward or backward. We will discuss these factors more in chapter 3.

Fig. 1-6. Because of the extremely fine blades the jigsaw can handle, fine enough to practically turn on themselves, it is notable for sawing intricate scroll work.

Rubber tires cover the rim of the wheels. They might be flat in the contact area or have an inside lip that fits a groove cut into the perimeter of the wheel (Fig. 1-13). In either case, the size of the tires is such that they must be forced over the wheels. No adhesive is used because wear and tear of normal use might call for tire replacement at some time.

Exceptions to the two-wheel design often are found in compact, bench-top units that employ three wheels to rotate the blade (Fig. 1-14). This design permits a lower tool profile while increasing blade-to-arm capacity. Often, the idea permits a larger table for more work support than you would find on compact units of conventional two-wheel design (Fig. 1-15).

Fig. 1-7. One of the outstanding, exclusive features of a band saw is impressive depth of cut. Most available units easily can saw through 6-inch-thick stock.

Band saws have blade guides over and under the table that are adjustable in relation to how you use the blade (Fig. 1-16). You need the guides to prevent the blade from twisting and from being pushed off the wheels during sawing operations. How to situate the guides correctly will be discussed in chapter 3.

It is rare to find a band saw whose table you can't tilt. Usual adjustments allow a full 45-degree tilt to the right and a minimum tilt of 5 to 10 to the left. Without a

Fig. 1-8. Bevel cutting is possible when the machine has a tilting table. This type of cutting often is required for project components. It's also enjoyed by lathe craftsmen who use the idea to reduce the amount of material that they otherwise would have to cut away with lathe chisels.

Fig. 1-9. Even compact band saws can handle stock thicknesses most table saws and radial arm saws can't get through in a single pass. This workbench-mounted example easily saws through three layers of 1-inch material.

tilting table, operations like the cross-bevel cut shown in Fig. 1-17 would not be possible. A unique, exclusive feature that is part of the Sears/Craftsman 12-inch electronic band saw is a tilting head (Fig. 1-18). The concept, like the tilting arbor on a table saw, enables you to make crosscuts and rip-bevel cuts and other chores like compound miters with the workpiece flat on the table. This design gives you better work control, which leads to easier accuracy.

POWER AND SPEED

Most times, the design and size of a band saw dictates its power; that is, the horsepower (hp) of the motor that drives it. Operating with the motor size the manufacturer suggests or supplies is the wise way to go. Overpowering is as negative as underpowering. It would be bad engineering to place a 400 hp engine in a light, subcompact automobile. When there is a choice, a ⅓ hp motor will supply ample

Fig. 1-10. Band-saw capacities are listed as the distance from the blade to the arm and the dimension between the table's surface and the blade guard when it is at its highest point. The former is width of cut; the latter is depth of cut.

power for small band saws in the 14-inch or so range (one that is capable of doing general work in a home workshop or small, commercial cabinet shop). Going to a ½ or ¾ hp motor is not out of the question if your requirements for the tool justify it and you won't harm the tool by the extra "oomph." Consider whether you will be doing considerable resawing of 5- or 6-inch-thick hardwoods, or if you often will create duplicate pieces by sawing through pads composed of six or seven pieces of ¾-inch stock.

Band-saw speeds, although controlled by the rpm of the motor and the diameters of the driving and driven pulleys, are stated in terms of surface feet per minute, or simply, feet per minute (fpm). *Fpm* is the lineal feet traveled by the blade during a specific period of time. Some leeway does exist, however, with adequate speed ranging from 1500 to 3000 fpm, but with the most efficient cutting speed approaching the higher range. This fact, of course, applies to general wood-sawing use.

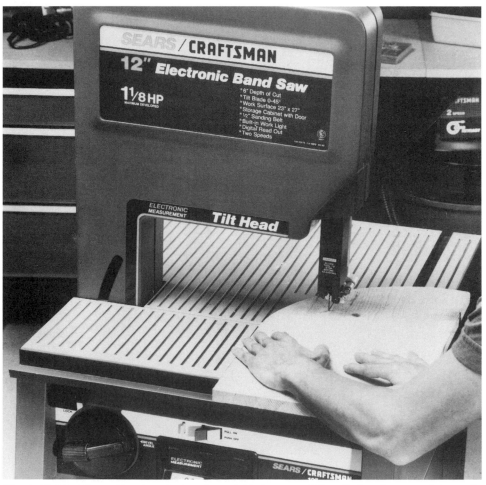

Fig. 1-11. Most times, the size of a band-saw table is compatible with the diameter of the tool's wheels. The Sears/Craftsman 12-inch product is an exception, probably because bevel cutting on the tool does not require a table tilt.

Fig. 1-12. Conventional band-saw design incorporates twin, vertically-aligned wheels. The lower one is powered directly or by belt; the top one idles. It turns because the saw blade is strained over the wheels. The top wheel has its own importance. It is adjustable for correct blade tensioning and tracking.

Is a single speed practical for all band-saw operations? No. For one thing, the speed that is most efficient when using a heavy blade to cut through a dense hardwood is not necessarily the best speed when you wish for the smoothest cut possible and you are using a slight blade to saw through ¼-inch-thick softwood. The band saw also can cut through nonwood materials. While a wood-sawing speed generally is acceptable for cutting a material like aluminum, it doesn't approach being right for something like iron or steel. In the latter cases, you should use blades with hacksawlike teeth and an fpm at snail's pace.

When motor and tool are separate units, you can make speed changes by installing matching-step pulleys. The choice of a low range does not present any hazards, but be sure that the highest range does not exceed what the tool can handle. No guesswork is involved here. The owner's manual will supply pertinent information.

In some not-so-rare cases, the tool might have a built-in speed control. Skil's 10-inch, bench-top model provides any speed from 500 to 2000 fpm merely by turning a dial (Fig. 1-19). The owner's manual lists the most efficient dial settings for sawing wood, as well as materials like plastics and nonferrous metals.

When you mount the Shopsmith band saw on the mother machine (Fig. 1-20), you couple it to the tool's headstock and you control the speed by the speed dial that is standard on the multipurpose tool. The dial is marked for the correct band-saw setting. The available speed range is from 2000 to 3000 fpm. Manufacturers caution owners to adjust the speed dial before connecting the band saw. Going over the correct dial marking would provide motor rpms that are much too high for the mounted tool.

Another example of speed control is found on the Makita model 2114C, 14 inch machine. A built-in 1.8 hp, electronically-controlled motor provides for three settings

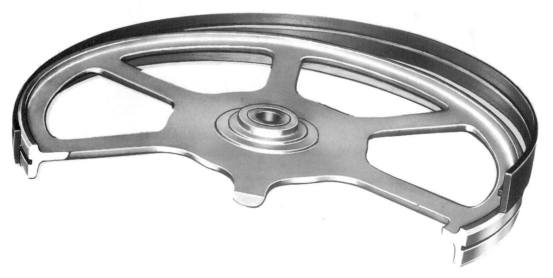

Fig. 1-13. Band-saw wheels are fitted with rubber tires that are stretched into place. This example has a kind of tongue-and-groove design that prevents the tire from slipping. Clean the tires occasionally to prevent buildup of sawdust and other waste particles.

Fig. 1-14. A three-wheel design is an alternate band-saw concept that might be found on bench-top units. The wheels can be small without restricting the tool's width of cut.

and maintains a constant speed despite load variations. You can set a toggle switch at one of three places to supply speeds of 1450, 2200, and 2932 fpm (Fig. 1-21). Thus, you can saw nonwood materials more efficiently.

Some manufacturers offer, at an extra cost, speed controllers that the user incorporates into the machine. These controllers usually are called *speed reducers* since their primary purpose is to slow up the basic blade rotation so metal-cutting blades can be used to saw steel and nonferrous metals like brass and aluminum. Some units reduce to a specific speed; others have controls of some design to provide a range of speeds. You can discover if such an accessory is available by asking a salesperson or by checking the manufacturer's catalog.

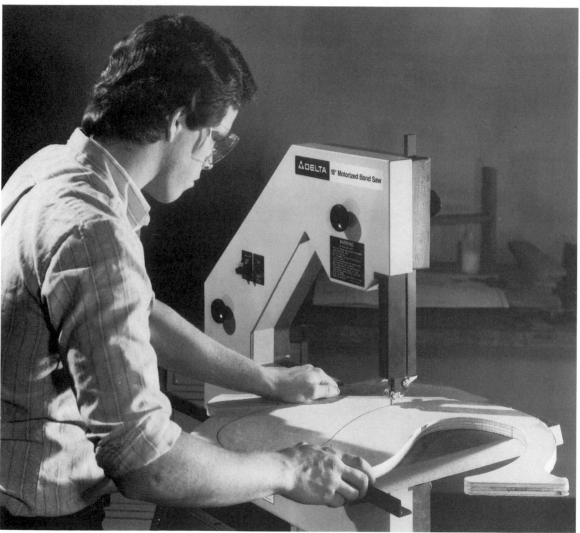

Fig. 1-15. A three-wheel design in effect allows the tool's arm to be further away from the blade; therefore, it often goes along with a table that is larger than a comparable, two-wheel design would allow. The result is a table area that provides additional work support.

BASIC ACCESSORIES

In addition to various saw blades, which are replacement materials rather than accessories, most band saws can be equipped with a miter gauge and a rip fence (Figs. 1-22 and 1-23). The manufacturer might supply one or both of the tools as standard equipment, but usually, the items are optional purchases. In terms of function, since the band saw is an efficient straight cutter as well as a curve cutter, they are necessities. Although you can use a clamped strip of wood as a fence and improvise a miter gauge, adding the equipment that is exactly right for the saw you own is a nice way to go.

You can equip some band saws for sanding, like the Sears/Craftsman unit shown in Fig. 1-24. You would mount a belt of abrasive material over the tool's wheels just like a saw blade, and replace the standard saw guides with a conversion kit that includes a backup for the belt. Because the belts are narrow—½ inch wide is average—some pretty intricate sanding is possible. More information on this band-saw function is given in chapter 12.

Fig. 1-16. Band-saw design must include adjustable side and back guides that will keep the blade from twisting and from being pushed off the wheels during a cut. Although guide positions are standard, how you adjust them can differ from tool to tool—one reason why it's important to study the owner's manual.

Adequate lighting is, of course, important for safety as well as accuracy. Regardless of where you place the machine in the shop, adding a lamp attachment—preferably one mounted on a gooseneck (Fig. 1-25) so you can move it around to provide illumination without work interference—is a wise investment. A few machines such as the Sears/Craftsman tilting-head unit have built-in work lights that the on-off switch controls.

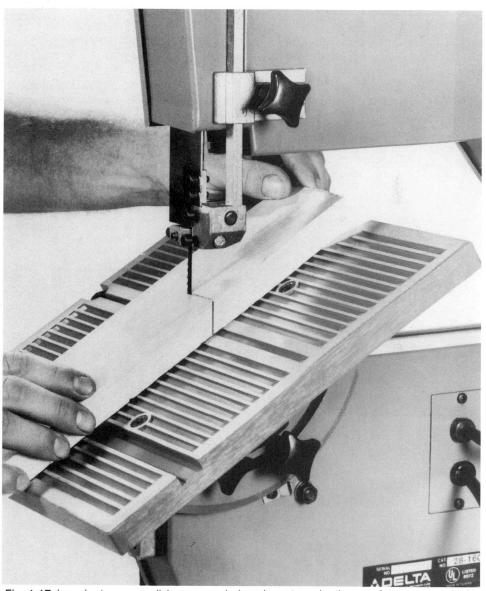

Fig. 1-17. In order to accomplish cross or rip bevels, or to make the cuts for compound miter joints, it's necessary to work with the tool's table tilted. You can tilt most band-saw tables a minimum degree to the left and a full 45 degrees to the right. An adjustable stop allows you to bring the table back to its normal zero position with minimum fuss.

A GLANCE AT SOME CURRENT MODELS

Delta band saws are noted for good design and durability. The 14-inch product is one of the most popular units around for use in commercial shops and home workshops. The unit is available in basic form as a wood-cutting tool or, when equipped with a special speed-control mechanism (Fig. 1-26), as a wood/metal sawing tool. A unique accessory for the wood-cutting edition includes the assortment of parts shown in Fig. 1-27. When you install this "height attachment," you elevate the upper structure of the tool so that its depth of cut increases from 6¼ inches to 12¼ inches. This feature is an interesting idea for anyone concerned with resawing stock that is wider than 6 inches. Blade lengths, of course, must change to 105 inches from the standard 93½ inches.

Fig. 1-18. An exception to the tilt-table rule is found on the Sears/Craftsman electronic band saw. Here, instead of tilting the table, you tilt the band saw. This tilt allows you to do beveling procedures with the work flat on a horizontal table.

The wood-cutting model has a set speed of 3000 fpm. The addition of the speed control provides speeds ranging from 40 to 3000 fpm so that, in addition to wood sawing, the machine can work on materials such as cast iron, stainless steel, alloy steel. Recommended motors include ½ or ¾ hp; usable blade widths run from ⅛ inch to ¾ inch.

Delta also manufactures a 20-inch band saw (Fig. 1-28). Here too, with minimum change in exterior design or overall size, the unit is available as a wood/nonferrous-cutting band saw with speeds of 4500 fpm for wood cutting and 2000 fpm for nonferrous metals, or as a metal-cutting model with a wide, variable speed range of 50 to 4500 fpm. The variable-speed range enables the saw to cut anything from stainless steel to wood. A nice feature is that you can adjust speed with a foot-activated lever.

Fig. 1-19. Skil's bench-top machine provides various speeds that are available merely by turning a dial. It has appropriate speeds for sawing nonferrous metals as well as wood. The speed range is from 500 to 2000 fpm.

Fig. 1-20. The Shopsmith band saw, when you mount it on the basic multipurpose tool, is speed controlled by the dial that is on the tool's headstock. Speed range is from 2000 to 3000 fpm. Be sure the dial is set to ''band saw'' or lower before connecting the extra machine.

An accessory for the machine is a Blade Welder and Flash Grinder (Fig. 1-29). These accessories make it possible to repair blades, make a new blade from bulk stock, or weld a blade after it deliberately has been broken to pass through a workpiece for internal cutting without a lead-in cut from an edge.

The chart shown in Fig. 1-30 is part of the metal-cutting model and serves as an aid to the operator when selecting the correct blade and speed for sawing many ferrous and nonferrous metals, and for nonmetallic materials like plastic laminates, Styrofoam, various plastics, even cardboard, and of course, wood.

Fig. 1-21. The attached motor on Makita's 14-inch band saw is electronically controlled for different speeds. A three-position toggle switch is flicked for fpm settings of 2932, 2200, and 1450. The switch is marked appropriately for sawing wood, plastic, and soft metals.

Ryobi's model BS-50N (Fig. 1-31) is a husky little machine with a big bite. It can slice through wood up to 7 inches thick, and does it with a blade that can be as wide as 2 inches (Fig. 1-32). It is a tool that is ideal for resawing. The unit is not limited to the one application since it can function with a variety of blade widths, going as narrow as ¼ inch. For some reason, Ryobi did not design the table to tilt, maybe because of the company's view of the table's primary function, nor does the table have a slot for a miter gauge. It is, however, supplied with a rip fence. Tracking and blade-tension controls are located on the tool's back and are designed compatibly with the product's overall heftiness. Once adjusted for the blade in use, they hold the setting (Fig. 1-33).

Ryobi offers two other machines that are notable for resawing capability and capacity. The 12½-inch-throat-clearance unit shown in Fig. 1-34 can function with blades up to 3 inches wide and can slice through stock a little better than 12 inches thick. The largest of the trio (Fig. 1-35) does even better. Its distance from blade to arm is almost 22 inches. It can use blades up to 4 inches wide and can resaw stock up to 16 inches thick. These capabilities are impressive for this application. This machine is not a lightweight. It runs with 5 hp and is a hefty, almost 1500 lbs.

An electronically controlled, 1.8 hp motor that maintains constant speed regardless of load variations powers Makita's 2114C machine. A switch on the motor casing (Fig. 1-21) has three positions for speeds of 1450, 2200, and 2932 fpm so you can select an efficient speed for sawing wood, plastics, and soft metals. The tool has a throat clearance of 14 inches and can saw wood up to 7⅛ inches thick. Usable blades run from ¼ to 1 inch wide. A few nice features include a removable safety switch to prevent unauthorized use, a three-position block that allows presetting of three tilt-table angle positions, and ball bearing rollers instead of solid blocks as upper-blade guides. I will demonstrate the rollers in chapter 3.

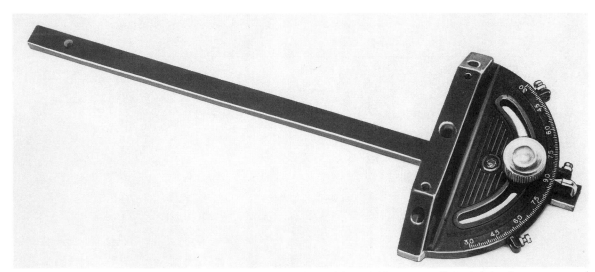

Fig. 1-22. A miter gauge is a valuable accessory for a band saw. It is useful for crosscutting and simple or compound miters. If you have a miter gauge for a table saw you might be able to use it on the band saw, especially if both tools are from the same manufacturer.

The Shopsmith band saw that was shown mounted on the mother tool in Fig. 1-20 can function as an individual tool when you mount it on its own stand (Fig. 1-36). The materials required—stand, motor and pulleys, a special tool-mounting base—are available from the Shopsmith multipurpose tool folks. The machine will operate with blades from ⅛ to ½ inch wide. Throat clearance is about 10½ inches, and depth of cut is 6 inches. The 12-inch-square table tilts 5 degrees left and 45 degrees right and has two grooves perpendicular to each other, so you can use a miter gauge in normal fashion or, with an extension added, as a rip fence. Other features include automatic blade tracking and reversible blade guides that twist the blade to a 30-degree angle from the arm so that you can accomplish crosscutting any length stock that isn't more than 3⅞ inches wide without arm interference.

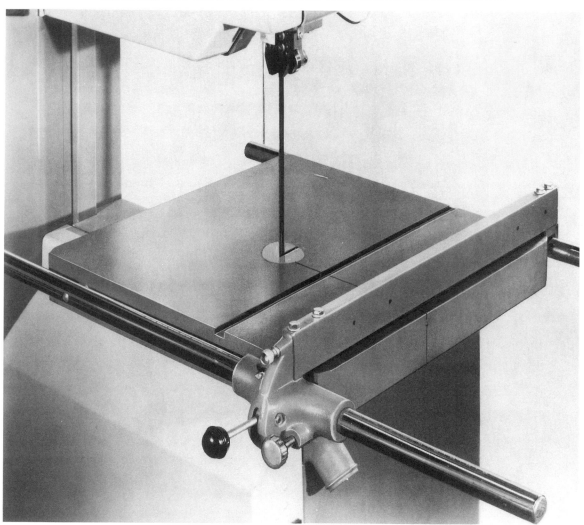

Fig. 1-23. Chances are that if a rip fence is not supplied with the band saw, the tool's table will be organized to accept one as an accessory. A rip fence that you can situate on either side of the blade is as practical an addition as a miter gauge.

The Sears/Craftsman Tilt Head band saw is the first of its kind, not only because the band saw instead of the table tilts for bevel cutting (Fig. 1-37), but because it incorporates the panel shown in Fig. 1-38, which provides electronic measurements for basic tool information. A digital readout will tell the bevel angle, the fpm setting of the blade, the width of the blade, and whether the blade is tensioned correctly. A battery provides power for the display so you can preserve settings when you turn off the tool.

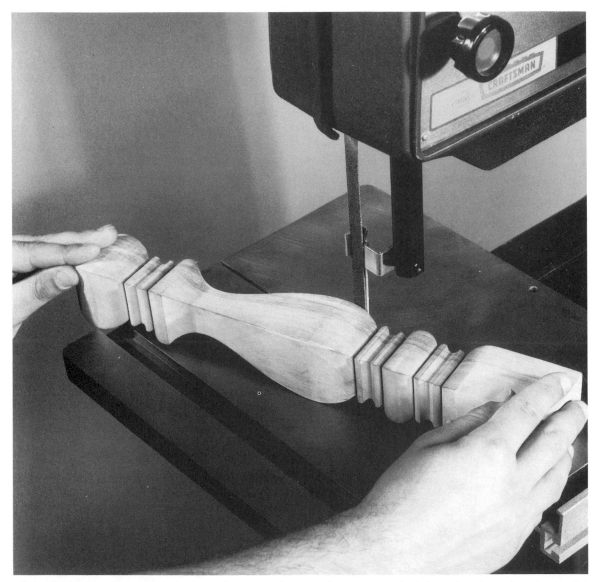

Fig. 1-24. The band saw can be a very efficient sanding machine when you install an abrasive belt and a special platen in place of the saw blade and the standard saw guides. Some machines are supplied with necessary parts; others offer them as optional accessories.

You can set the blade speed for 3000 fpm for routine woodworking, or 1500 fpm when sawing nonferrous metals like copper and brass. Capacities are a 12-inch throat clearance and a 6-inch depth of cut; the generous-size table measures 23 inches × 27 inches. Basic equipment includes a closed stand that provides storage space, a built-in work light, and a sanding belt with the necessary mounting platen. Usable blades run from 1⁄8 to 1⁄2 inch.

The Skil machine displayed in Fig. 1-39 is an example of a new breed of band saws appearing on the market. These saws essentially are made as home-user tools.

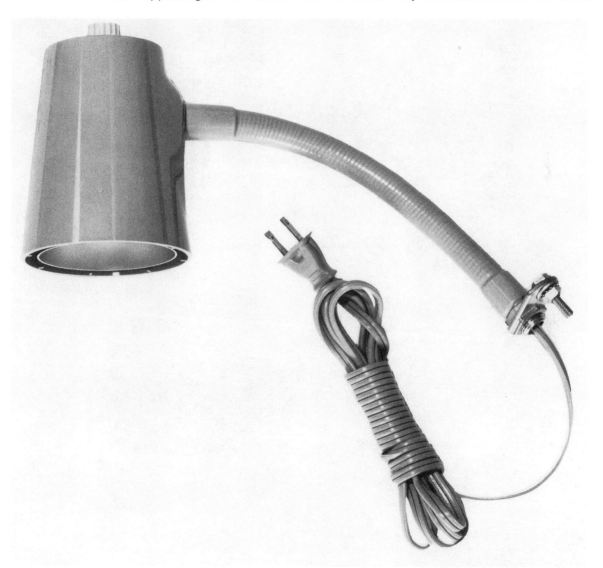

Fig. 1-25. Good lighting is essential for safety as well as accuracy. Even in a well-lighted shop, it's an asset to have an adjustable, tool-mounted lamp so illumination can be directly over the sawing area.

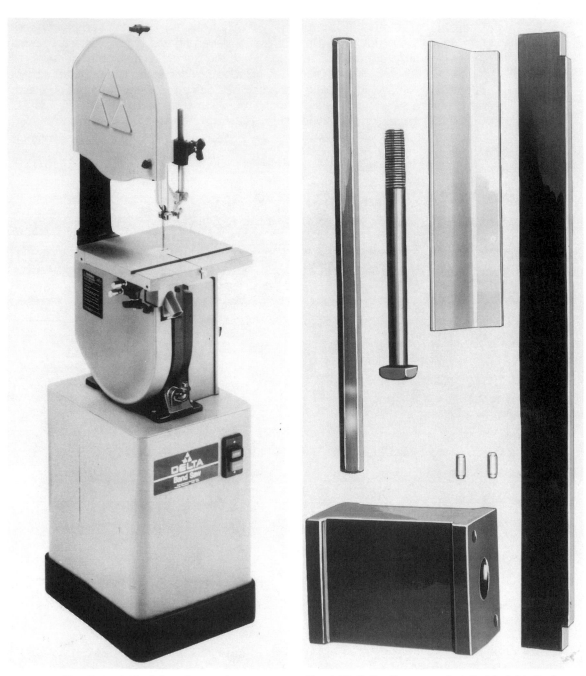

Fig. 1-26. The Delta 14-inch band saw, shown on an enclosed stand and with an installed speed-reduction unit, is a popular choice for commercial, school, and home workshops. It can handle blade widths from ⅛ inch to ¾ inch; depth of cut is 6 inches.

Fig. 1-27. Delta offers a user-installed, height-attachment accessory that increased the tool's depth of cut by 6 inches so you can do conventional sawing and resawing on wood up to 12¼ inches thick.

Fig. 1-28. Delta's 20-inch band saw is an industrial machine that often is found in small shops and school rooms. The tool offers a speed of 4500 fpm for wood cutting and 2000 fpm for sawing nonferrous metals. Depth of cut is better than 13 inches. The table's size is 20 inches × 24½ inches.

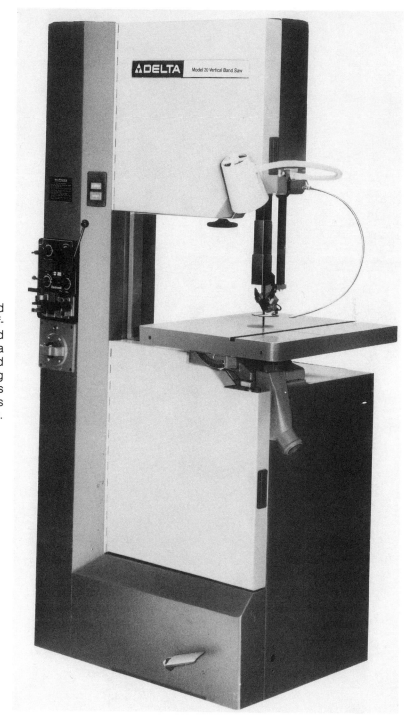

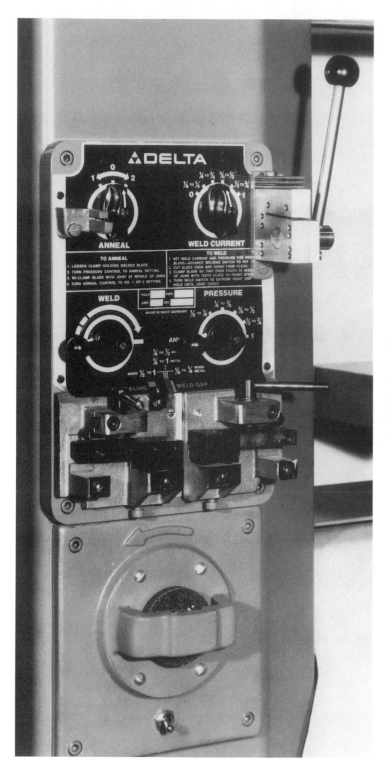

Fig. 1-29. Delta's 20-inch machine also is offered as a variable-speed, metal-cutting tool with speeds that range from a low 50 to a high 4500 fpm. An accessory blade welder and flash grinder allows the operator to repair broken blades or to make new ones from bulk blade stock.

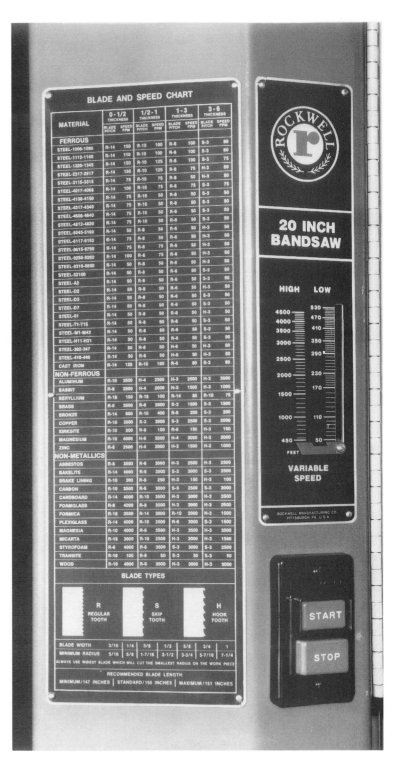

Fig. 1-30. The metal-cutting model displays a chart that suggests correct blade and speed for efficient sawing of various materials. Information on minimum turning radii for various blade widths also is included.

Fig. 1-31. Ryobi's smallest band saw has an attached 15-amp motor and is supplied ready to use as soon as you mount it on a suitable stand. Its throat clearance is almost 10 inches, and it can saw through stock up to 7 inches thick. The table does not tilt, nor does it have a miter gauge groove. It does have a rip fence.

They are designed compactly, with less weight and capacity than the big saws. They are impressive little tools, perfectly capable of performing to band-saw standards. In fact, some of them have built-in features that are lacking in full-size machines. For example, the Skil unit has a knob-controlled, variable-speed mechanism that provides blade speeds of 500 to 2000 fpm. You easily can select an appropriate speed, whether sawing wood or nonferrous metals. A 4-inch depth of cut isn't to be sneezed at, and a ⅝ hp built-in motor provides enough power to drive blades that can range from ⅛ to ⅜ inch. Its cast aluminum, tilting table measures 13 × 14 inches and has perpendicular grooves so you can use the supplied miter gauge routinely or as the backing for a rip fence. Other features include a removable key lock, an outlet to which you can connect a vacuum cleaner, and an optional sander conversion kit that allows you to use the machine as a 1-inch sander/grinder.

Black & Decker's offering in the bench-top band-saw field is of conventional two-wheel design (Fig. 1-40). Its 10-inch table tilts from 0 to 45 degrees, it has a throat clearance of 7½ inches and a depth-of-cut capacity of 3¾ inches, which is enough

Fig. 1-32. The small Ryobi tool shown in Fig. 1-31 has a big bite and power to support it. It can handle blades as wide as 2 inches which makes it a very efficient tool for resawing. It can do more though since blade-width range starts at ¼ inch.

to handle dressed 4-inch stock. A 3.3 amp motor rotates blades that range in width from ⅛ inch to ¼ inch at 650 fpm. Like others of its ilk, it's delivered almost 100 percent assembled (even with the saw blade mounted), so it's ready for use in minutes. Features include a compact miter gauge, a sawdust outlet that you can connect to a vacuum cleaner, and a lockable push-on/push-off switch.

KIT-BUILT BAND SAW

You can build a very respectable band saw, like the examples shown in Figs. 1-41 and 1-42, by working from plans or with kits produced by Gilliom Manufacturing, Inc. Even though you can work from plans and supply your own parts, such as wheels

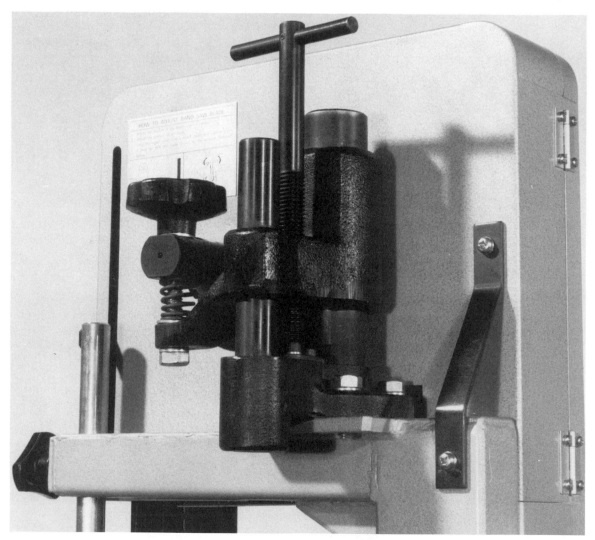

Fig. 1-33. Tension and tracking controls for the Ryobi tool are mounted on the back of the machine. Obviously, they are rugged components, which pretty much describes the tool as a whole.

made of wood, it makes more sense to purchase a kit that, in addition to the plans, supplies all necessary hardware, including aluminum wheels with rubber tires. All you have to supply is the work and necessary wood materials, which consist mainly of ¾-inch plywood and some pieces of hardwood.

The designs are not skimpy. The kit includes most of the features that make the band saw such a versatile machine. Those features include a tilting table with miter-gauge groove and mounting for a rip fence, necessary blade tracking, tensioning, guidance adjustments, etc. Blade speeds are within a good working range which is 2000 or 2100 fpm. Usable blade widths range from ¼ inch to ½ inch. An optional accessory is a speed-reducer jackshaft kit that you can use to reduce blade speed to 175 fpm.

Fig. 1-35. (above) One of the giants in band saws, this concept can work with a blade 4 inches wide to saw stock up to 16 inches thick. Power (5 hp) and weight (1496 lbs) describe this tool as much as a picture does. The table tilts to 45 degrees; a rip fence and auxiliary rear roller for additional work support are supplied.

Fig. 1-34. (left) Ryobi's middle-size saw can work with blade widths of ½ inch to 3 inches. The single-speed tool has better than a 12 inch depth of cut. A rip fence is supplied.

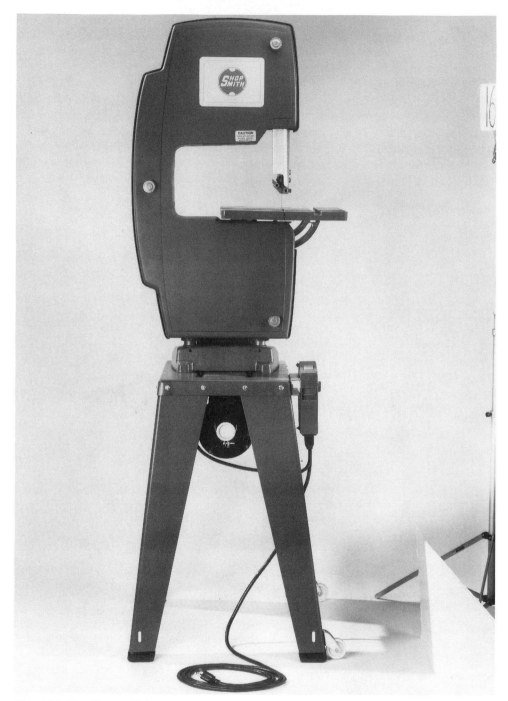

Fig. 1-36. The Shopsmith band saw, when mounted on its own stand and with its own motor, functions very nicely as an individual tool. It's the same tool that mounts on the mother, multipurpose machine. For separate mounting, it requires a special tool-mounting base as well as a stand and motor.

Fig. 1-37. The advantage of the Sears/Craftsman tilt head machine is that you can accomplish beveling procedures with the tool's table in horizontal position. This position helps achieve accuracy since work slippage that can occur on a tilted table is not a factor.

Fig. 1-38. The panel of the front of the tilt-head saw shows digital readouts of electronic measurements of blade speed, blade tilt, and blade tension and width. Accuracy of blade tilt is within half a degree, which is okay for general work. When bevel angles are critical, it's best to make test cuts before sawing good stock.

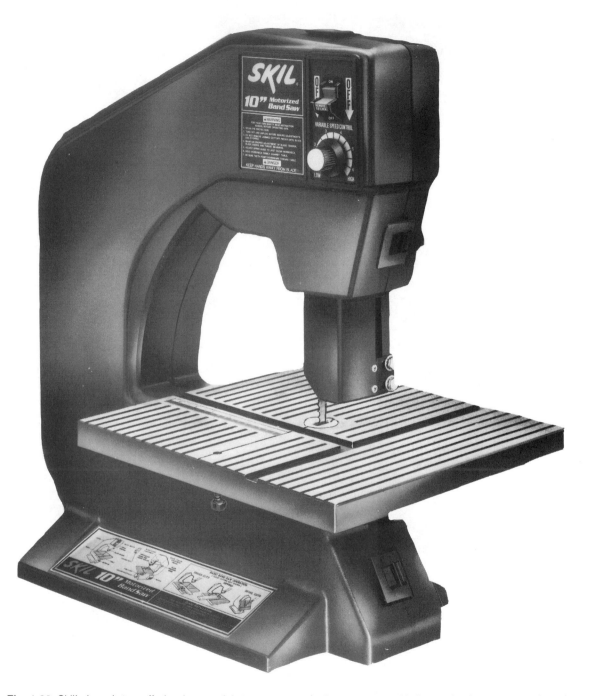

Fig. 1-39. Skil's bench-top offering is one of the compact tools that operates with three wheels so you can increase throat clearance without bulking the tool's height. Blade range is from ⅛ inch to ⅜ inches wide. A knob-controlled, variable-speed mechanism allows speeds of 500 to 2000 fpm.

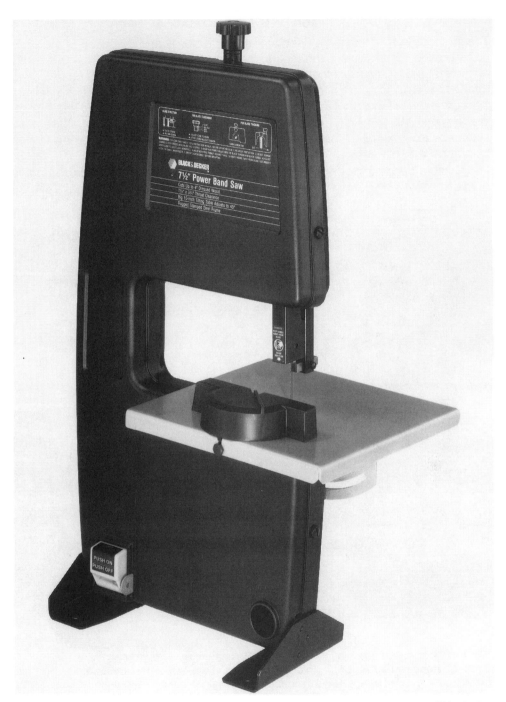

Fig. 1-40. Black & Decker offers a bench-top tool of conventional two-wheel design. This design limits its throat clearance to 7½ inches, but its depth of cut, almost 4 inches, is on a par with other tools of its ilk.

MOUNTING A BAND SAW

The supporting structure for a band saw must be sturdy and designed to minimize tool vibration. Often, unless the tool is designed for floor mounting so the base is an integral part of the machine, the manufacturer offers an optional stand designed for the tool. It's a way to go, but there is a point to be made. As in furniture design, *average* is the criterion that determines the distance from the floor to the tool's table. We're not all tall or short or in between. My opinion is that the height of the table should be approximately the distance from the floor to the operator's elbows when he stands with his arms at his sides.

Custom-building a stand for a tool is not out of line if it adds operating convenience or saves money by using on-hand materials. That is why I have offered

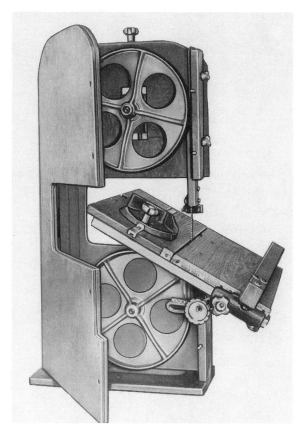

Fig. 1-41. A kit built, 12-inch band saw has a 12¼-inch throat clearance and a 7-inch depth of cut. The design provides for a miter gauge, a rip fence, and a tilting table. You can construct the machine strictly from plans, but it's wiser to buy the kit which provides all the necessary hardware, including aluminum, rubber-rimmed wheels.

Fig. 1-42. You can build the 18-inch, floor-model band saw from a kit. Capacities here are an 18-inch throat clearance and a 12-inch cut depth. Motor recommendation is ½ or ¾ hp. Good plans are provided so the tools are not difficult to fabricate, but slow, careful work is critical for best results.

the stand designs in Figs. 1-43 through 1-45. The projects vary in design because they were made for different machines. One of them should be suitable for a machine you buy, even though you might have to lengthen or shorten the legs a bit to make the tool's table height more convenient for you.

Figures 1-46 through 1-48 also give construction details for the stands. The projects do not have to be pretty, nor do they require intricate joints, but strength is a priority. Use glue in all connections and good-size nails, large wood screws, or lag screws as reinforcement. Adding glue blocks in crucial areas, even though the drawings don't show them, is a good idea.

Fig. 1-43. This figure shows you band-saw stand #1. You can add a door and a shelf easily. Stands can be on casters, but be sure they have a locking feature. You don't want the tool moving about when you are sawing.

Fig. 1-44. This picture is of band-saw stand #2. The height of this stand is about right for a bench-top machine, but check for personal work convenience. It's a simple matter to lengthen or shorten the stand's legs a bit.

Fig. 1-45. Band-saw stand #3 is a shorter stand that suits a machine that is taller than most machines. Be sure to secure the band saw with heavy lag screws or large nuts and bolts.

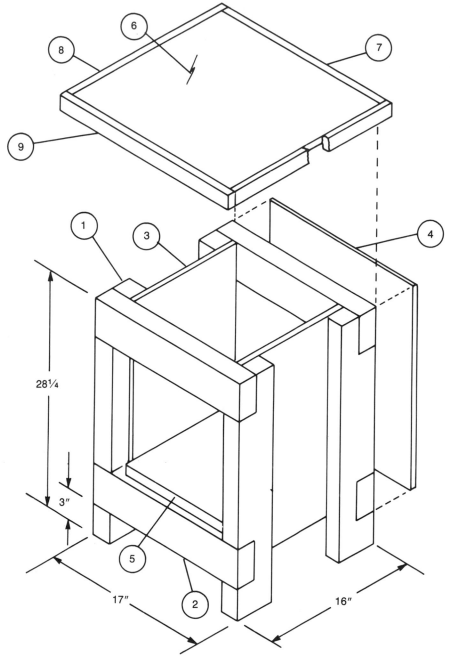

SEE MATERIALS LIST FOR SIZES OF COMPONENTS
(STAND #1)

Fig. 1-46. These construction details are for band-saw stand #1.

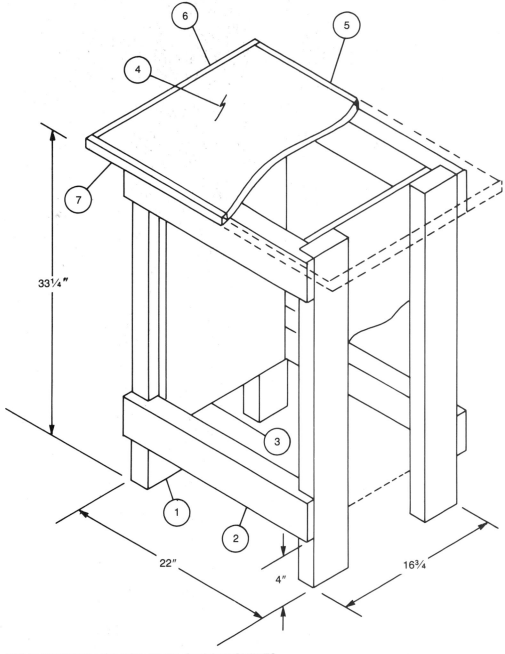

6

5

4

7

33¼″

3

1

2

22″

4″

16¾

SEE MATERIALS LIST FOR SIZES OF COMPONENTS
(STAND #2)

Fig. 1-47. These construction details are for band-saw stand #2.

43

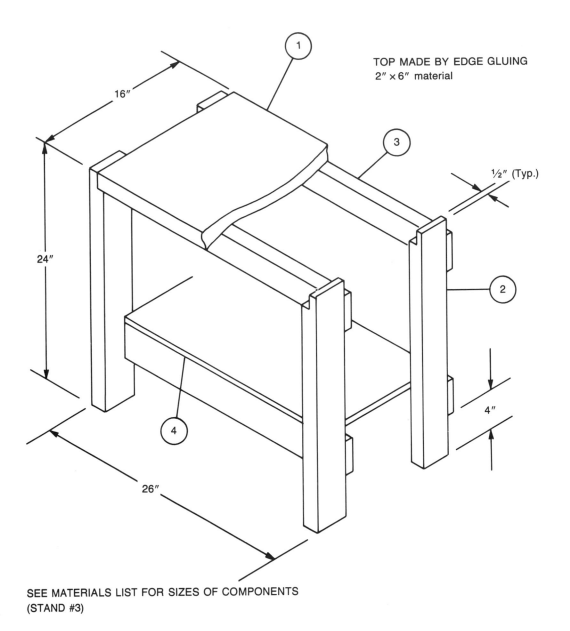

TOP MADE BY EDGE GLUING
2″ × 6″ material

16″

24″

½″ (Typ.)

4″

26″

SEE MATERIALS LIST FOR SIZES OF COMPONENTS
(STAND #3)

Fig. 1-48. These construction details are for band-saw stand #3.

44

Table 1-1. Materials List for Band-saw Stand #1.

Key	Name	No. of Pieces	Size (in Inches)					Material
1	Legs	4	1½	×	3½	×	28¼	Fir
2	Rails	4	1½	×	3½	×	17	Fir
3	Sides	2	½	×	13	×	25¼	Plywood
4	Back	1	½	×	17	×	25¼	Plywood
5	Shelf	1	¾	×	13	×	15¼	Plywood
6	Top	1	¾	×	18½	×	17½	Plywood
7	Trim	1	¾	×	1½	×	18½	Fir
8	Trim	2	¾	×	1½	×	19¼	Fir
9	Trim	1	¾	×	1½	×	20	Fir

Table 1-2. Materials List for Band-saw Stand #2.

Key	Part	No. of Pieces	Size (in Inches)					Material
1	Legs	4	1½	×	3½	×	33¼	Fir
2	Rails	4	1½	×	3½	×	22	Fir
3	Sides	2	¾	×	15¼	×	29¼	Plywood
4	Top	1	¾	×	18½	×	26½	Plywood
5	Trim	1	¾	×	¾	×	26½	Fir
6	Trim	2	¾	×	¾	×	19¼	Fir
7	Trim	1	¾	×	¾	×	28	Fir

Table 1-3. Materials List for Band-saw Table #3.

Key	Part	No. of Pieces	Size (in Inches)					Material
1	Top	1	1½	×	16	×	25	Fir
2	Legs	4	1½	×	3½	×	24	Fir
3	Rails	4	1½	×	3½	×	26	Fir
4	Shelf	1	¾	×	13½	×	23	Plywood

Chapter 2

Blades for
the Band Saw

BAND-SAW BLADES, BECAUSE OF THE WORK THEY MUST DO AND THE FACT THAT THEY must rotate constantly over wheels of rather small radii, are subjected to a considerable amount of stress. Modern metallurgy and operator care with installation and use enables them to endure over a respectable period of operation. It isn't difficult to abuse a blade. Factors that contribute to early breakage and fast dulling often are operational faults. These factors include careless blade tensioning and tracking, incorrectly adjusting the blade guides, attempting to saw curves that are too tight for the blade's width, incorrectly choosing a blade for the job, etc. It often seems a nuisance to change a blade or to recheck blade mounting and guidance, but quality work and blade life depend to a great extent on this kind of attention.

BLADE SIZES

Blade sizes differ in thickness, width, and length. The machine determines the length. There isn't any choice here; you simply obey the manufacturer's instructions. A bit of leeway might exist simply because the adjustment wheel has vertical movement. For example, the standard blade for the Delta 14-inch machine is 93½ inches long, but they can have minimum and maximum lengths of 94 inches and 91½ inches.

A general rule for blade thickness, but not a hard and fast one, has to do with wheel diameter. Theoretically, thickness averages .001 inch for each inch of wheel diameter, so a 14-inch band saw would use blades about .014 inch thick. Since band-saw functions are so varied and there is quite a span in materials it can saw, thinner and thicker blades often are used to achieve optimum band-saw operation.

Blade width is the measurement from the tips of the teeth to the blade's back edge. Manufacturers offer quite a range here, starting at ⅛ inch and going to an extreme of better than 3 inches. Your choice must be compatible with the narrowest and widest blade with which your tool can work. Again, do not use guesswork; literature that comes with the tool will supply the information. A general range will include blade widths of ⅛ inch, ³⁄₁₆ inch, ¼ inch, ⅜ inch, and ½ inch. Some machines can handle blades up to ¾ inch wide; others, at the low end, start with blades of ¼ inch width. It's good practice, especially when doing cutoff work, ripping, and resawing, to use the widest blade the machine allows. The wider the blade, the easier it is to saw straight. You can use some judgement since a narrower blade with less tooth set might produce smoother results than the blade that is theoretically right for the job.

The width of a blade determines its minimum sawing radius (Fig. 2-1). Variances are due to blade style, thickness, and amount of tooth set, but the general rule allows sawing continuously, without backtracking, the given or larger radius that Fig. 2-1 suggests. Trying to force a blade around a tighter turn than its width allows usually results in burn marks, a wider saw kerf, inaccuracy because the blade will twist, and even breakage. Some techniques allow you to ignore the radius rule. I will demonstrate these in the chapter dealing with sawing fundamentals.

TOOTH DESIGN

The most common band-saw-blade teeth are shown in Fig. 2-2. The most popular ones for sawing wood are the regular (or standard) and the skip tooth (or buttress). The blade supplied with the machine probably will have a regular tooth style since it generally is accepted as an all-purpose blade that is efficient for sawing wood and moderately thick nonferrous metals.

The characteristic of the buttress blade is the wide spacing between teeth which promotes effective chip clearance and allows faster cutting of wood, plastics, and nonferrous metals.

With both styles, the thinner blade with light tooth set is the best choice for smooth sawing. Thicker blades with heavy set allow faster sawing and, since they form a wider kerf (Fig. 2-3), they provide more freedom from binding.

For prolonged cutting in thick materials that include wood, plastics, and metal, you should use the hook-tooth blade.

A blade with raker set often is preferred for cutting thicker materials. It has a fast cutoff rate and a uniform kerf. Many operators find it easier with this tooth design to saw contours and to stay close to intricate layout lines. The word *raker* enters the terminology because the tooth that is between the teeth that are bent to the right and the left, has no set at all.

The wave-set blade has the tooth styling found on hacksaw blades. It's the best blade to use for sawing metals—tubing, pipe, sheet stock, structural shapes, and so on. The wave set, especially when the blade has many teeth, practically eliminates the possibility of you stripping teeth when you need to cut thin sections.

All blades are available with various numbers of teeth per inch (tpi). For example, a regular blade might have as few as 8 tpi or as many as 24. A wave-set blade can have as many as 32 tpi. Another specification is "points" per inch (Fig. 2-4). The number of points is always one more than the number of teeth.

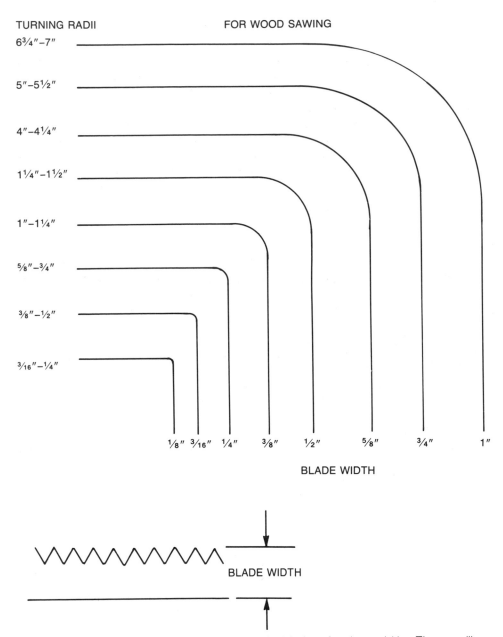

TURNING RADII   FOR WOOD SAWING

6¾″–7″

5″–5½″

4″–4¼″

1¼″–1½″

1″–1¼″

⅝″–¾″

⅜″–½″

³⁄₁₆″–¼″

⅛″ ³⁄₁₆″ ¼″   ⅜″   ½″   ⅝″   ¾″   1″

BLADE WIDTH

BLADE WIDTH

Fig. 2-1. Here you see the typical turning radius for blades of various widths. These radii are not invariable since blade thickness and amount of tooth set are factors that can affect the actual working radius.

Another blade style, a Remington Arms Company product, has no teeth at all; that is, no conventional teeth. Instead, this company coats the edge of the blade with grits of tungsten carbide which solves the problem of sawing materials like reinforced epoxies, phenolics and polyesters, hardened tool steel, low-density

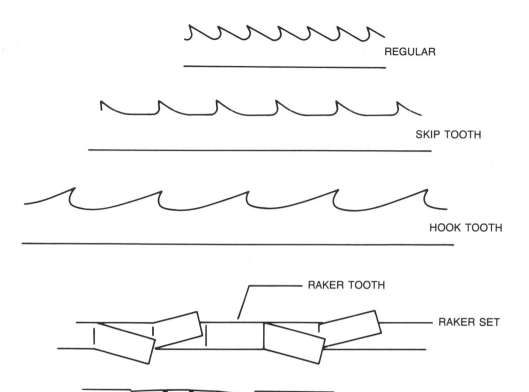

REGULAR

SKIP TOOTH

HOOK TOOTH

RAKER TOOTH

RAKER SET

WAVE SET

Fig. 2-2. This drawing shows the tooth design of various band-saw blades. All styles are available in blades of various width and in a range of number of teeth per inch. The more teeth a blade has, the smoother, but slower, it will cut.

ceramics, and more. The blade material, with a continuous or gulleted edge, is available in bulk coils or as bands that Remington Arms Company custom welds to a particular size. You also can use the toothless blades on wood (Fig. 2-5). While smoothness of cut is excellent, you greatly reduce the speed with which you make the cut.

BLADE SET AND "LEAD"

A saw blade gets through material because its teeth, generally, are bent alternately to the right and the left. This design establishes the width of the groove—the *kerf*—the blade forms which is greater than the blade's thickness (Fig. 2-6). When you move a material squarely into the blade, you would expect that the cut would be on a straight line and 90 degrees to the blade. It's not rare though for a band-saw blade to *lead*, that is, have a tendency to pull to one side or the other of the line you want it to stay on. A natural solution is to change the direction in which you are moving the work to accommodate the blade's fault. If the blade wants to cut to the right, then work-feed direction has to change somewhat to the degree shown in Fig. 2-7. The stronger the lead, the more you must deviate from the ideal feed direction.

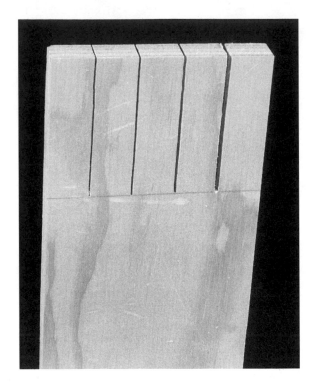

Fig. 2-3. The thickness of a blade and the amount of set determines the width of the kerf. Thin blades with minimum set can't move as freely as blades with heavy set.

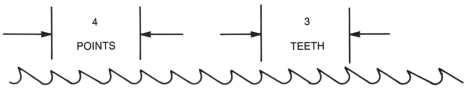

Fig. 2-4. The number of teeth per inch is always one less than the number of points.

One cause of lead that has an easy solution is the incorrect setting of guides so that you push or twist the blade in an off-course direction. The first step, when lead occurs, is to be sure you have installed the guides correctly. This procedure is an alignment factor that I will discuss in chapter 3. If the guides are okay, then it's reasonable to accuse the blade. A bad filing and setting job so the blade, in essence, is sharper on one side might attribute to fault. The blade will lead off toward its sharp side. An operational error might cause lead, like hitting or sawing along the side of a nail or sawing through some tough impurity.

Experienced operators often will correct a slight lead by using a piece of softwood to back up the blade on its good side and very lightly honing the bad side with a fine stone. Both the backup block and the stone must rest solidly on the table, and you must advance the stone so it barely touches the blade. This technique is a negative approach to blade repair since the purpose is to bring both sides of the blade to equal dullness. It is a solution though since it provides more use from a blade that has a bad lead caused by being too heavily set on one side. You should consider the solution temporary. If you constantly must struggle to stay on a pattern line, it will be difficult to work accurately and the guides will wear improperly. The ultimate solution is to recondition the blade or to discard it.

THE WASHBOARD EFFECT

Any blade that is designed for sawing leaves an identifying mark. The band saw's mark is a corrugated surface that can be negligible when you use a slim blade with minimum set, or it can be quite pronounced when the blade is thick and wide and has a lot of set (Fig. 2-8). The set of the blade's teeth primarily causes washboarding, but you should consider other factors that will help to minimize it. Among these other considerations should be mounting the machine to minimize, if not eliminate, vibration, and being fastidious about blade tension and blade-guide position.

Any wood, like fir, that has areas of hard and soft grain will pronounce the washboard effect. It will not be as pronounced on lumber of uniform density.

Fig. 2-5. The toothless blade cuts with hundreds of tungsten carbide particles that are bonded to its edge. It's designed for sawing problem materials, but you can use it on wood. Sawing will be very slow, but the cut edge will be smoother than one you can accomplish with a conventional blade.

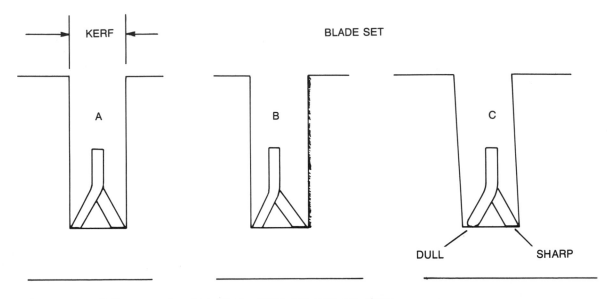

KERF

BLADE SET

A

B

C

DULL   SHARP

A . . . . Optimum results when set is uniform and teeth are sharp
B . . . . Uneven set or a long tooth results in rough cut on one or both sides of the kerf
C . . . . When "lead" exists it is always toward the sharp side

Fig. 2-6. Like most sawing tools, the teeth on band-saw blades are set so the kerf width will be greater than the gauge of the blade. It's not rare for a blade, even a new one, to have "lead."

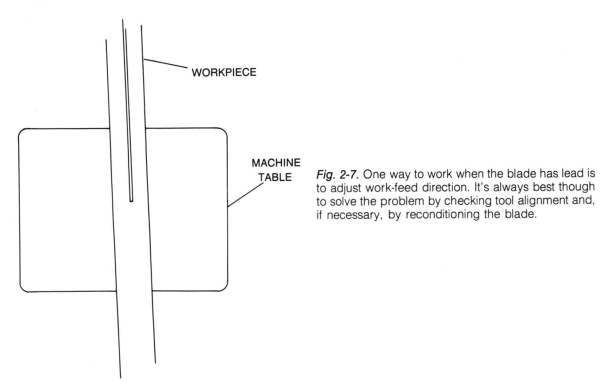

WORKPIECE

MACHINE
TABLE

Fig. 2-7. One way to work when the blade has lead is to adjust work-feed direction. It's always best though to solve the problem by checking tool alignment and, if necessary, by reconditioning the blade.

Generally, when you want smoothest results, you should use a blade that has minimum set. A professional trick that contributes to smoothness is to lightly hone both sides of the blade to reduce sharp tooth points. The blade won't cut as fast as it should, and it won't have as much room in the kerf, but smoothness of cut will improve. When smoothness of cut is not critical, a heavy blade with much set will result in faster sawing. Often, a worker will use such a blade to work faster even though a lesser blade would result in smoother edges (Fig. 2-9).

BLADE SPEEDS

A single-speed band saw will rotate a blade in the range of 2000 to 3000 fpm, which is efficient for sawing wood and many nonwood materials. When the machine adjusts for speed rates, then it is wise to select a speed that is as close as possible to the ideal speed for the job and the blade. Table 2-1 suggests appropriate speeds for popular band-saw blades when you use them to saw hard and soft woods. Table 2-2 supplies information so you can determine fpm speed by checking the diameter of the motor pulley, machine pulley, and the tool's wheels. Table 2-3 provides information so you can determine fpm when you know the rpm of the machine pulley.

BLADE CARE AND STORAGE

A band-saw blade will have a long life if it gets reasonable treatment when you use it and store it. Operationally, you start wrong if you do not select an appropriate blade

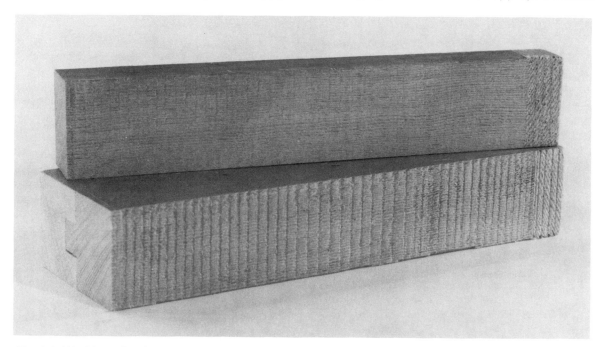

Fig. 2-8. Washboarding is a band-saw blade characteristic. It can be heavy or slight depending on the blade. When the effect is more prominent on one side of the cut, like this example, you can be sure that the blade has a slight kink or that tooth-set is not uniform.

Fig. 2-9. Wide, heavy blades will cut faster and, generally, straighter than the slight ones. Workers often will use a heavy blade to speed production even though a light blade with minimum set would produce smoother results.

Table 2-1. Note that the speeds suggested for popular band-saw blades is within a 2000 to 3000 feet-per-minute range.

TYPE	DESCRIPTION				SUGGESTED SPEED (FPM)	
	Width	Thickness	Kerf	TPI*	Hardwood	Softwood
Woodcutting	3/16"	.020	.045	6	2750	3000
	1/4"	.020	.045	6	2450	2750
	3/8"	.020	.050	5	2150	2450
Combination	1/4"	.025	.045	6	2450	2750
	1/2"	.025	.050	4	2000	2000

*TPI = Teeth Per Inch
Note: Reasonable speed when the combination blades are used on nonwood materials is about 2000 fpm.

Table 2-2. Measuring the diameter of motor pulley, machine pulley, and tool wheel, will reveal the feet-per-minute speed of the blade. Figures are based on a 1725 rpm motor.

Motor Pulley	Tool Wheel	5″	5½″	6″	6½″	7″	8″
			DIAMETER OF MACHINE PULLEY				
2½″	10″	2210	2015	1846	1703	1573	1378
	12″	2635	2402	2201	2030	1875	1643
	14″	3145	2867	2627	2423	2238	1961
2¾″	10″	2418	2210	2028	1872	1742	1508
	12″	2883	2635	2418	2232	2077	1798
	14″	3441	3145	2886	2664	2479	2145
3″	10″	2652	2418	2210	2028	1898	1664
	12″	3162	2883	2635	2418	2263	1984
	14″	3774	3441	3145	2886	2701	2368
3½″	10″	3094	2808	2574	2340	2210	1924
	12″	3689	3348	3069	2790	2635	2294
	14″	4403	3996	3663	3330	3145	2738
4″	10″	3536	3224	2938	2730	2522	2210
	12″	4216	3844	3503	3255	3007	2635
	14″	5032	4588	4181	3885	3589	3145
4½″	10″	3978	3614	3302	3042	2834	2470
	12″	4743	4309	3937	3627	3379	2945
	14″	5661	5143	4699	4329	4033	3515
5″	10″	4420	4030	3692	3406	3146	2756
	12″	5270	4805	4402	4061	3751	3286
	14″	6290	5735	5254	4847	4477	3922

for the job on hand. Important factors include blade width, tooth style, and tpi. A good, general rule is to use the widest blade that will do the job. Use narrow blades when you have to get around tight corners and when following intricate patterns. Sometimes, as any band-saw operator will agree, breaking the rules is permissible. For example, for the smoothest cut possible, you should use a narrow blade in place of a wide blade that would saw easier and faster.

You can avoid premature blade breakage by obeying basic rules. Be careful with alignment and adjustment of blade guides. Rechecking settings during an extended work period is a good idea. Don't force cutting by feeding too fast or insisting that a blade get around a turn that is too tight for its width. Don't set the top guide too high above the work. You should recondition or discard a blade that's worn out. A blade that is running when not in use is still under stress. Turn the machine off when you are not actually sawing. Clean the blades occasionally with a

RPM OF MACHINE PULLEY	BAND-SAW WHEEL DIAMETER		
	10"	12"	14"
10	26	31	37
20	52	63	73
30	79	94	110
40	104	126	146
50	131	157	183
60	158	188	220
70	183	220	256
80	209	251	292
90	236	283	328
100	262	314	366
120	316	377	440
140	368	440	512
160	419	503	586
180	472	565	658
200	524	628	732
250	655	785	915
300	786	942	1098
350	917	1100	1281
400	1048	1256	1464
500	1310	1570	1830

Table 2-3. How blade speed relates to wheel diameter and the rpm of the machine pulley.

soft brush or a lint-free cloth. If you use a solvent, be sure to obey the warnings that are on the container and make sure the environment has good ventilation.

Protective blade storage can be as simple as the ideas shown in Fig. 2-10. The blades are hung full-length over dowels or a half-circle piece whose radius equals that of the tool's wheels. It's a good way to go, but it requires space you might put to better use.

Figure 2-11 demonstrates an improved method. Here, the blade is bent back on itself and then tied in two places. When organized this way, the blade needs about half the space of an unfolded blade.

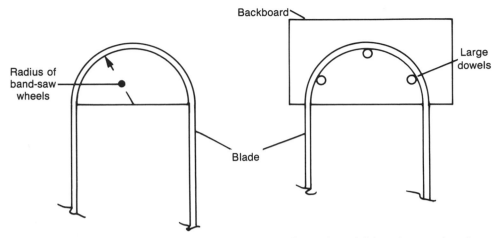

Fig. 2-10. A safe and easy way to store blades is to hang them full length over dowels or a half-circle piece of wood. The problem with the system is the space required.

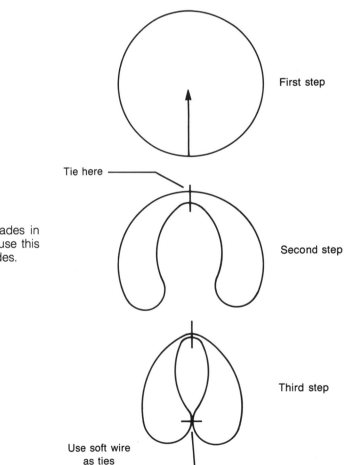

Fig. 2-11. You can fold blades in half. Some manufacturers use this system when shipping blades.

A popular method that minimizes storage space for blades while affording ample protection is to fold them in thirds. The system seems a little complicated but after you practice a bit, you'll see that the blade actually helps you achieve the end result. Start by gripping the blade in both hands as shown in Fig. 2-12. The second step, demonstrated in Fig. 2-13, is to use your thumbs to fold the upper half of the blade down toward the floor while your other fingers twist a bit to turn the teeth outward. Figure 2-14 shows how to let the upper loop fall into the lower one. At this point, bring your hands together so you can trade the loop in one hand for the loop in the other. As you do this, bring the now coiling blade back toward you and it will fall into three uniform loops (Fig. 2-15). Use soft wire to tie the blade so it won't uncoil involuntarily. Although they are not shown in the illustrations, wearing gloves and a face mask when you do the folding makes sense. Also, blades are flexible and

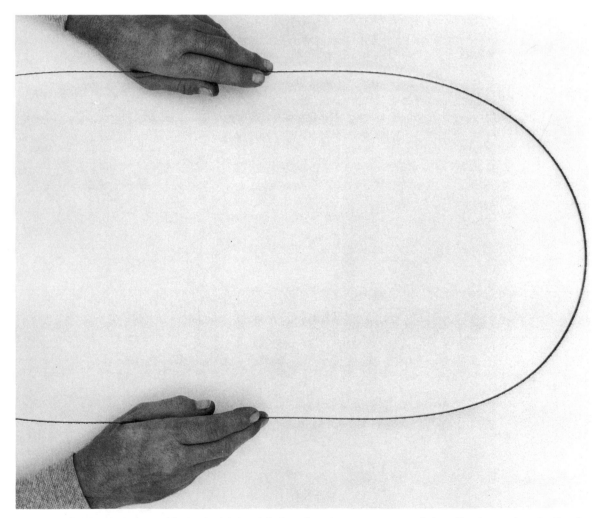

Fig. 2-12. Folding band-saw blades in thirds minimizes the storage space and also affords good protection for the blades. The folding technique starts by holding the blade like this.

have considerable spring, which will be evident when you unfold them. Unfold them carefully, holding them well away from you. Here too, taking the precaution of wearing gloves and a face mask is a good idea.

Be careful not to bend blades anytime you handle them. Check them for bends, kinks, and cracks before you install them.

SHARPENING SAW BLADES

Sharpening band-saw blades is within the scope of small shops, but when you think about the number of teeth on a 90-inch blade with 6 to 8 tpi, you can understand why the chore often isn't recommended as a do-it-yourself activity, and this fact is aside from the expertise involved. A professional sharpener can do the job quicker and probably better than an amateur simply because he has the proper equipment and know-how. A factor to consider is cost. If your equipment includes very wide, heavy blades, blades that are quite expensive to begin with, it will pay you to get them reconditioned. The answer to whether you should have a blade sharpened if the fee is more or as much as the cost of a replacement blade, is obvious.

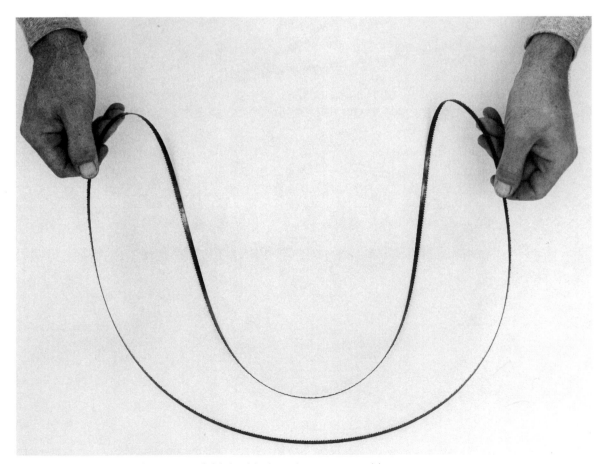

Fig. 2-13. In the second step, you fold the blade to form two equal loops.

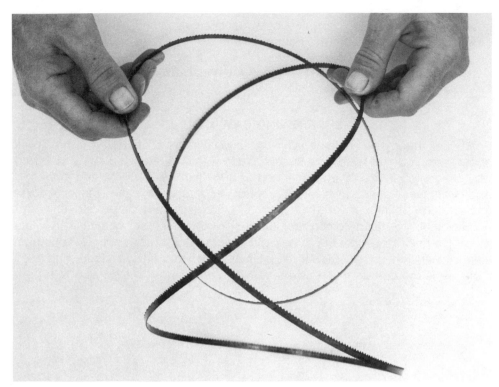

Fig. 2-14. Bring hands together and trade one loop for the other.

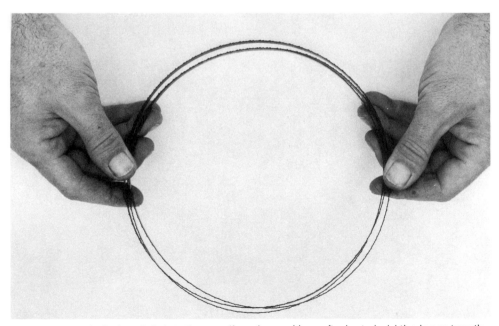

Fig. 2-15. The blade then falls into three uniform loops. Use soft wire to hold the loops together. It's not a bad idea to coat the blades with a film of light oil when storage time will be lengthy.

60

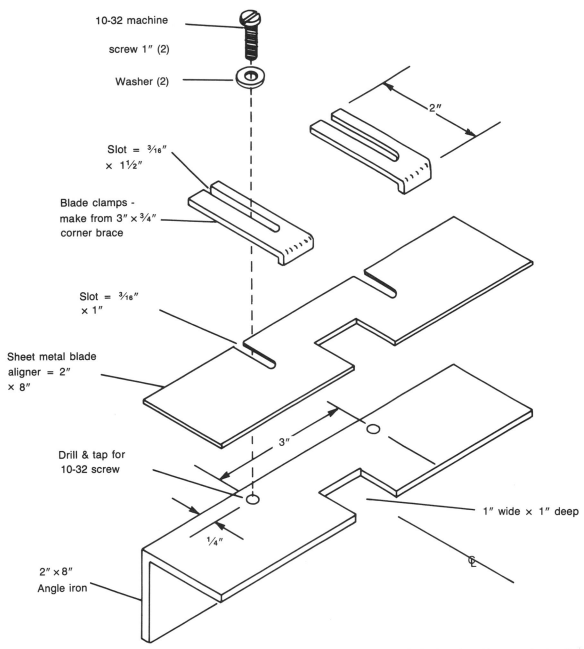

Blade vise (for soldering)

10-32 machine
screw 1″ (2)

Washer (2)

Slot = 3/16″
× 1½″

Blade clamps -
make from 3″ × 3/4″
corner brace

Slot = 3/16″
× 1″

Sheet metal blade
aligner = 2″
× 8″

Drill & tap for
10-32 screw

2″ × 8″
Angle iron

2″

3″

1/4″

1″ wide × 1″ deep

Fig. 2-16. Construction details of a homemade vise that will secure blade ends for brazing. You can fasten the base of the vise to a wooden block which, in turn, you can clamp to a workbench.

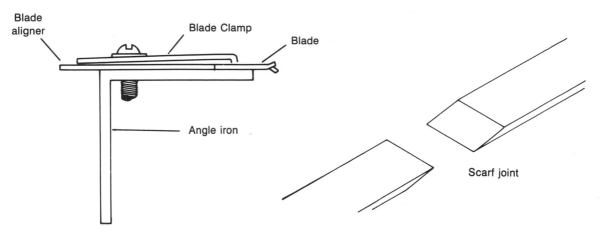

Side view - blade vise in use

Blade aligner

Blade Clamp

Blade

Angle iron

Scarf joint

Fig. 2-17. You cannot repair or make blades from bulk stock casually. The scarf joint must be precise, and you must do the brazing so the connection will be smooth and uniform. Bumps and irregularities will hinder blade performance.

The idea of repairing broken blades that are still in good condition or of assembling blades from bulk, coil stock is another side of the picture. Factory-made blades are usually butt welded, a technique that results in a joint that is clean and smooth. Small shops that are interested in this aspect of band-saw blades can get by with silver brazing.

What is needed, to begin with, is a vise that will hold the blade ends in perfect alignment. These vises are available commercially, or you can make a suitable substitute by duplicating the project that Fig. 2-16 details. You should grind the blade stock, or the ends of the broken blade, square and then bevel it for a distance of one tooth so the "scarf joint" that results will form a single tooth (Fig. 2-17). You do the brazing while the vise holds the blade ends securely and in alignment. The silver brazing method is not difficult and you can do it with an ordinary propane torch. Paint the joint with flux and apply a piece of "solder" at least as large as the lap. With the joint held firmly in the vise, apply heat from the torch and hold it until the solder melts and runs. Remove excess solder by grinding after the joint has cooled. This step is a critical aspect of the operation since the joint must be compatible with the blade's shape and thickness. Kits that include a vise and other essential materials, except for the torch, are available.

Band-saw blade stock, should you choose to make your own blades, is available in 100 foot coils in standard widths, tooth styles, and tpi. A question to ask yourself is whether you will need a number of the same type blades that will be available in a 100 foot coil.

Chapter 3

Adjustments
for Alignment

THE BAND SAW, LIKE ANY POWER TOOL, WILL FUNCTION AS IT SHOULD ONLY IF RELATION-
ships between components receive proper attention. You should check critical
factors when you first use the tool and periodically thereafter since normal use can
disturb original settings. The time and effort required are slight and little enough to
donate for smooth operation and maximum precision. Ignoring essential adjustment
procedures can contribute to many operational faults.

Major adjustments on a band saw have to do with blade tensioning and tracking,
blade-guide settings, and squareness of the table to the side of the blade. The upper
wheel of the machine (Fig. 3-1), which you can raise or lower, tilt forward or backward,
controls both blade tensioning and tracking. *Tension* is the tautness of the blade
when you strain it over both wheels; *tracking* has to do with being certain that the
blade will stay centered on the wheels when it is rotating.

The first step when mounting a blade is to raise the guard to its highest point
and to back off the blade guides so the blade can run freely between them. Lower
the top wheel so you can mount the blade easily and then raise the wheel so the
blade is reasonably tight. Many machines take the guesswork out of tensioning
because they have built-in scales. Adjust the wheel until the indicator on the scale
is at the correct point for the blade in use. The scale will read correctly for average
work and will not be influenced by slight differences in overall blade length. After
you have practiced band sawing, you will find that varying the tension just a bit might
be helpful for particular operations or blades.

When the machine does not have a tension scale, you can make an acceptable
adjustment by manually flexing the blade in the following manner. With the blade
guard at its top-most point, overstress the blade by raising the upper wheel to its
highest situation. Then, while very slowly lowering the wheel, use a finger to press
against the blade at a point midway between the table and guard. When you can

Fig. 3-1. The top wheel of the band saw is the control for correct tensioning and tracking of the saw blade. You may tilt or raise the wheel or lower it by means of a crank or screw or lever—whatever. Consult the owner's manual for information that applies to your tool.

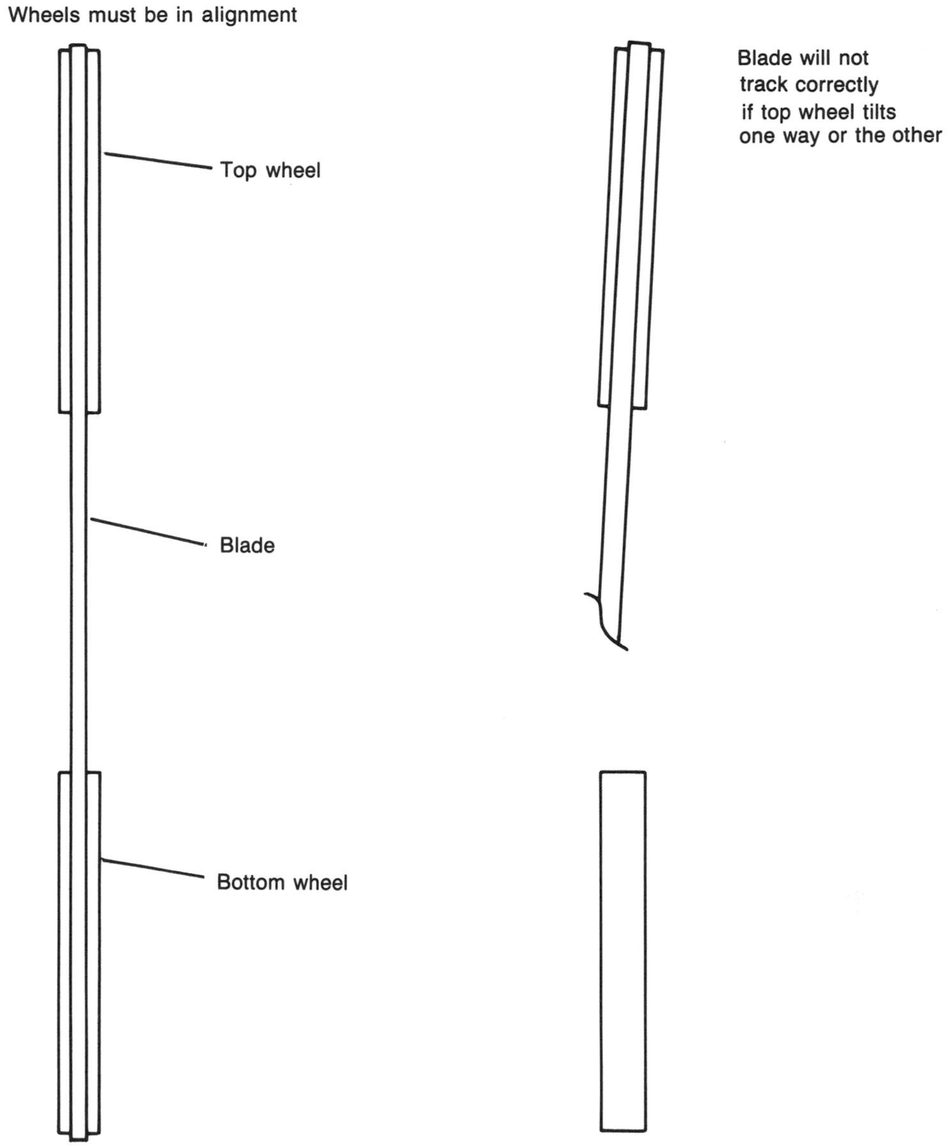

Wheels must be in alignment

Top wheel

Blade

Bottom wheel

Blade will not
track correctly
if top wheel tilts
one way or the other

Fig. 3-2. Tilting the wheel one way or the other moves the blade for centering. Spin the wheel by hand for initial testing! Adjustment procedures do not require power, so keep the tool unplugged as you check the various factors.

flex the blade about ¼ inch with light finger pressure, you can accept that the blade tension can't be too far off a correct adjustment.

A saw blade, after it has been tensioned, should rotate on the center of the upper wheel (Fig. 3-2). This tracking adjustment is important for accurate sawing, maximum blade life, and even for safety since a misaligned blade can move off the wheels.

An adjustment procedure that is appropriate for any band saw is as follows. Be sure that upper and lower blade guides and backups are away from normal blade travel. Then, *by hand*, spin the upper wheel while observing the blade's position on the wheel's rim. Tilt the wheel back if the blade tends to move forward; do the reverse if the blade wants to move to the back rim of the wheel. Make wheel-tilt changes in small degrees while you continue to *hand turn* the wheel. When you feel the blade is tracking correctly, close the machine's wheel covers and flick the switch quickly on and off. If the blade has maintained its position, turn the switch on and allow the blade to run for some seconds while you check its behavior—just to be sure.

After tensioning and tracking, and while guides and backups are away from the blade, it's time to check the normal-use angle between the table's surface and the blade. This angle is a table-position factor that you can check by using a square as shown in Fig. 3-3. If necessary, loosen the table-tilt lock and set the table so the

Fig. 3-3. Check the table for correct zero position after you have adjusted the blade for tension and centering. Do this with upper and lower blade guides backed away from the blade.

angle between its surface and the blade is 90 degrees. Secure the setting and, if one is provided, adjust the stop screw or rod that is located under the left side of the table so you can return the table to neutral position without fuss whenever you have tilted it for a bevel cut. Also, if the machine has a tilt scale, adjust its pointer to read zero. Tilt scales are graduated from 0 to 45 degrees. It's okay to use the scales for approximate settings, but when the cut angle is critical, it's wise to make a test cut before sawing good stock.

BLADE GUIDES

Blade guides are incorporated in band-saw design to provide support on each side of the blade. They help the blade to run faithfully and keep it from excessive twisting when sawing must follow intricate patterns. Guides, as shown in Figs. 3-4 and 3-5, are positioned under and over the table. The guides that are over the table are an integral part of the blade-guard assembly.

Guides are usually short sections of specially-tempered bar stock that slide and that you can lock in housings that straddle the path of the blade. Thus, you can move them horizontally to positions that best suit the blade in use. An unusual blade-guide design is found on the Makita 14-inch band saw (Fig. 3-6). Instead of solid blocks, the guides are bearings that are mounted on eccentric rods which, when turned, move the bearings toward or away from the blade.

In any case, you must position upper and lower guides so the blade will run vertically. Figure 3-7 illustrates the problem that can occur if you do not position the guides correctly. Adjust the guides after the blade has received tensioning and tracking attention. It's best to adjust the top ones first, and then the bottom ones to suit.

Figure 3-8 reveals the correct side and forward guide positions. Be sure the face of the guides is squarely against the side of the blade. Normal use and, sometimes, abuse, might make it necessary to resurface the face of the guides. You can resurface by hand with a fine file or on a grinding wheel. Either way, a final touch with emery paper wrapped around a wooden block will make the bearing surfaces as smooth as they should be.

The clearance that is required between blade and guides is slight, but important. A very simple gauge that you can use is a strip of 20 lb. paper as shown in Fig. 3-9. Press the guide lightly against the paper as you secure its position. This clearance check, of course, is done on both sides of the blade.

BLADE SUPPORT

The blade backup or support bearing, as it is often called, prevents the blade from being pushed too far back during sawing operations. Without the backup, the blade might move backward so its teeth would damage the guides, or the teeth might be damaged. It's not unlikely that the blade might be pushed right off the wheels. Lock the support so there is no contact between it and the back of the blade when the blade is running free (Fig. 3-10). A clearance of about $\frac{1}{64}$ inch is sufficient.

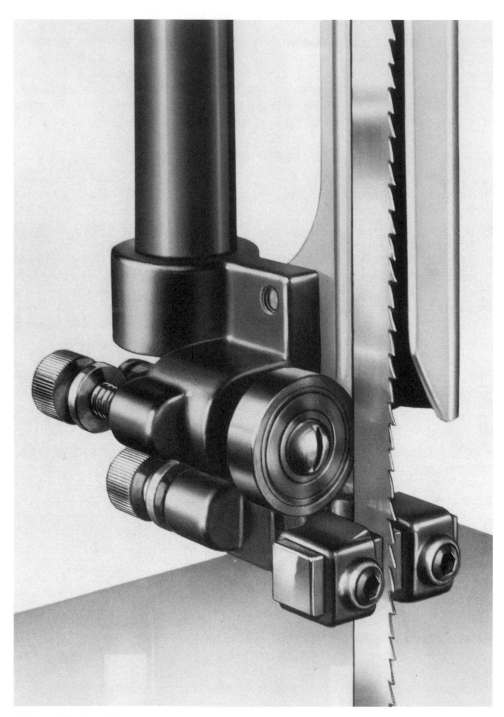

Fig. 3-4. Blade-guidance system consists of twin blocks that straddle the blade and a backup, usually a bearing, that prevents the blade from moving too far back during sawing operations.

LEVELING PIN

Band-saw tables must have slots to allow installation of saw blades. Since the possibility exists that the table might move up or down on either side of the slot, a provision is made for a leveling pin that you install as shown in Fig. 3-11. You can remove the pin by turning it with a wrench or pliers, and you can return it by tapping it, gently, into position. The system of leveling is not standard. Some machines use a screw, others a pivoting strip of metal that is located under the table. Literature that is supplied with the machine will describe the design and instruct how you should use it.

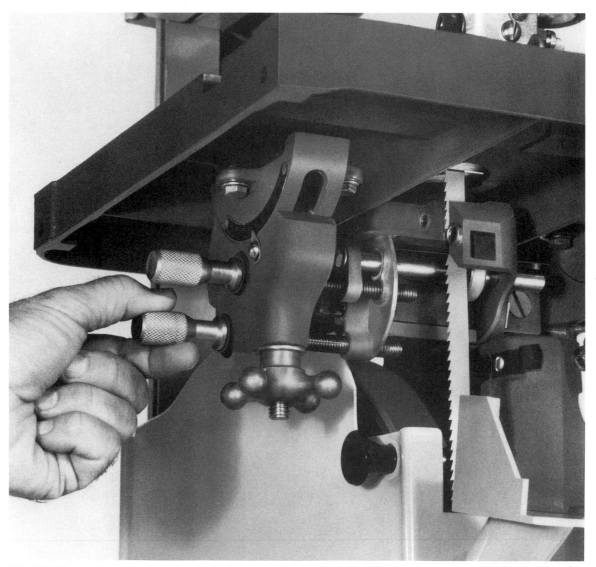

Fig. 3-5. The guidance system is duplicated under the table. Adjust the lower components after the top-side ones are in correct position.

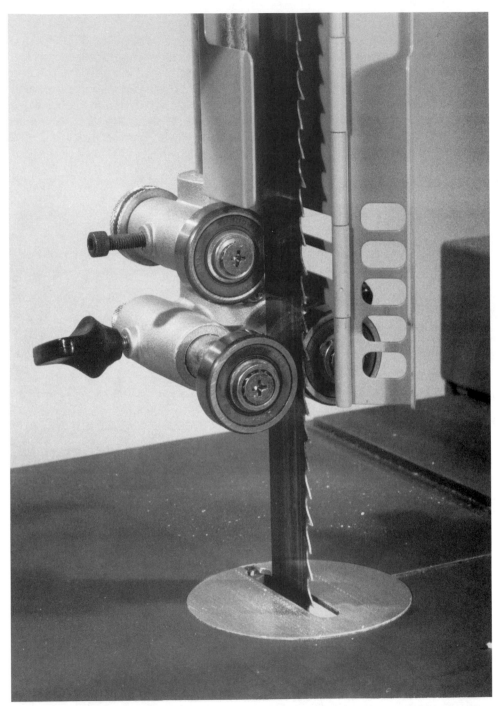

Fig. 3-6. The Makita band-saw guidance system employs bearings instead of blocks. The bearings are mounted on eccentric axles so they can be moved toward or away from the blade.

70

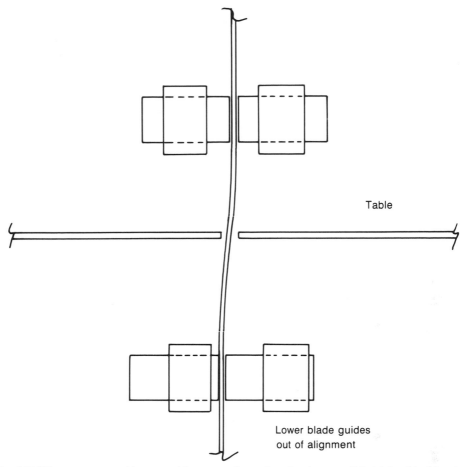

Fig. 3-7. When upper and lower guides are not synchronized, you will twist the blade out of alignment. You will impair accuracy and damage the guides and the blade.

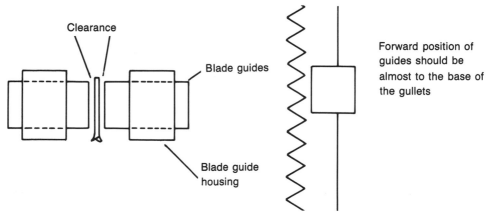

Fig. 3-8. The guides must be square to the blade and positioned to avoid constant contact. The correct forward position will avoid contact with the blade's tooth gullets.

Fig. 3-9. An acceptable method of obtaining clearance between guides and blade is to use a strip of 20 lb. paper as a gauge. Do not force the guides against the paper.

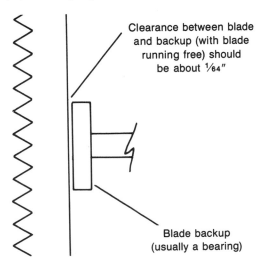

Clearance between blade and backup (with blade running free) should be about 1/64″

Blade backup (usually a bearing)

Fig. 3-10. The backup keeps the blade from moving too far back during sawing. It should not contact the blade when it is running free.

Fig. 3-11. A device is used to ensure that the table surface will stay flat. It might be like the pin shown here or a screw or some other idea. The owner's manual will illustrate it and instruct you on its use.

Chapter 4

Shop Safety

NO ONE USING POWER EQUIPMENT IS IMMUNE FROM DANGER. IF YOU BEHAVE AS IF YOU are immune, you are well on the road toward an accident. We are surrounded by hazards—in the home, in the car, in the garden—wherever we are and whatever the activity. Why is it that some people suffer injuries and others live their entire life whole and happy? The difference might lie in acknowledging that one can be a victim and behaving accordingly. Some people wear seat belts when driving, others don't. Some power-tool operators never lose a degree of fear for the machine; others behave as if bad things can't happen to them or that expertise shields them from injury. It requires little research to discover that professionals as well as amateurs have scars and even missing digits.

One of the problems with safety considerations is that they must come before the activity that interests us—a kind of nuisance bridge. Yet, if you want to get to the other side without the possibility of drowning, you must take the span. Safety factors have to do with the shop in general and with specifics that relate to the tool you are using. It doesn't make sense to ignore them, not when you consider the alternatives.

BAND-SAW SAFETY SPECIFICS

It's a foolish notion that the band saw, or any power tool, is safer to use than another power tool. No power tool is safe. How you behave in the shop, how you maintain it, what your mental attitude is, how you use the tool, are some of the factors to depend on for safety.

Merely working with a damaged or dull blade is risky. A dull cutting edge requires the operator to use more hand pressure to feed stock past the blade, and this sets up the possibility that your hand might slip. Keep blades sharp so you can feed stock with minimum muscle tension.

Blade changing requires you to work with the tool's wheel guards open, and you must manually adjust the top wheel. For this frequent chore and for other tool adjustments, work with the machine unplugged. Check and make adjustments for blade tracking by hand spinning the wheel (Fig. 4-1). When you feel the blade is moving correctly, shut the wheel covers and turn the machine quickly on and off. Then, before working, allow the blade to run free for ten or fifteen seconds to be sure you performed the job correctly.

A frequent check of the blade's condition is good practice. Look for checks or cracks that can be caused by metal fatigue and discard the blade if any appear. A steady clicking sound and radical or eccentric washboarding are warning signals. The blade might be kinked, cracked, or have damaged teeth. If the blade should break during sawing, step quickly away from the machine, turn it off, and wait for the wheels to stop rotating before you open the wheel covers.

GUARD POSITION

When the upper-blade guides are positioned as they should be, about ¼ inch above the surface of the work, the blade guard covers the section of blade that is not in the cut, so a minimum amount of blade is exposed (Fig. 4-2). This position is the ideal position even though many demonstration photos don't show it. The apparent contradiction is for PHOTO CLARITY ONLY. Always work so the guard will provide maximum protection.

HAND POSITION

Most times the operator will stand firmly at the front of the table and slightly to the left of the blade, but this suggestion is not firm since the sawing you are doing might require a change for better hand position and adequate work support. In any event, place your hands well away from the cutting area and avoid having fingers directly in line with the blade (Fig. 4-3). Generally, you will find that using one hand to feed the stock and the other to guide it is an acceptable procedure. But, here too, the pattern you are sawing will influence how you work.

Avoid working on pieces that are small enough to require placing your hands close to the blade. Often, you can saw a small shape on the end or side of a piece that is large enough for safety. Then you can rip it from the base stock. Figure 4-4 shows a band-saw trick that often is used for sawing small pieces. A handscrew or similar device grips the work so hands don't have to come close to the danger area.

SAWING ROUNDS

You can crosscut round stock and small or large dowels, but the action of the blade will tend to spin them in your hands. The safe sawing procedure calls for the use of a V-block as demonstrated in Fig. 4-5. This block allows gripping the material firmly so it can't spin, and your hands will be well away from the blade. I will discuss more techniques that have to do with sawing rounds in the chapter dealing with special applications.

Fig. 4-1. Work with the machine unplugged when organizing blade tension and tracking and when doing other alignment chores. Check for correct blade mounting by hand spinning the top wheel. Good shopkeeping calls for occasionally cleaning the inside of the machine.

WORK SUPPORT

Providing adequate support for the work helps you work safely since you can concentrate on sawing without having to strain to hold the work in position. On the band saw, ripping operations usually require outboard support. Roller-top stands that you can adjust for height are available commercially, or you can custom make one like the unit shown in Fig. 4-6.

The roller used on the prototype is a metal tube that is sealed at each end with wooden discs that are sized for a tight fit (Fig. 4-7), but you can substitute a large round of wood, something in the nature of a closet pole. The axles for the roller are 1/4-inch bolts that turn in oversized holes drilled through the metal support brackets (Fig. 4-8). Since the homemade stand's height is adjustable, it is an all-purpose accessory that can supply outboard support for other machines; for example, table saws and jigsaws. Figure 4-9 provides you with construction details for the stand.

Fig. 4-2. When the upper guides are situated correctly, only about 1/4 inch of the blade will be exposed above the workpiece. This setup is ideal even though it isn't shown so in many of the book's illustrations.

SAFETY ACCESSORIES YOU CAN MAKE

Three items you can construct that are aids to safety and that also can help you work more accurately are on display in Fig. 4-10. These accessories are: a push stick, a spring stick, and a combination pusher hold-down. The push stick, shown in use in Fig. 4-11, lets you make rip cuts without getting fingers close to the saw blade. It should be used regardless of which side of the blade the ripping guide, or rip fence, is situated.

You clamp spring sticks to the saw's table so the unit's fingers, instead of your own, will keep the work in proper position for the cut. The spring pressure should bear against the work in front of the saw blade. If the spring stick applies pressure after the cut, it will tend to close the kerf and bind the blade.

Fig. 4-3. Keeping hands away from the blade and avoiding placement of them on the line of cut are important safety factors. It's difficult to establish a standard since operations might require particular hand positions, but stay safety conscious.

A combination of pusher hold-down, used for ripping operations, holds the work flat on the table while moving it forward for the cut. Because the design has some width, you do not use it when ripping narrow pieces. In such situations, the push stick serves the purpose.

Figures 4-13, 4-14, and 4-15 offer typical designs for the three tools.

GENERAL SHOP-SAFETY CONSIDERATIONS

Proper Attire and Mind-Set

It's reasonable to have a special uniform for shop work. Heavy, nonslip shoes, preferably with steel toes, and tight-fitting shirts and trousers, are a good idea. I don't

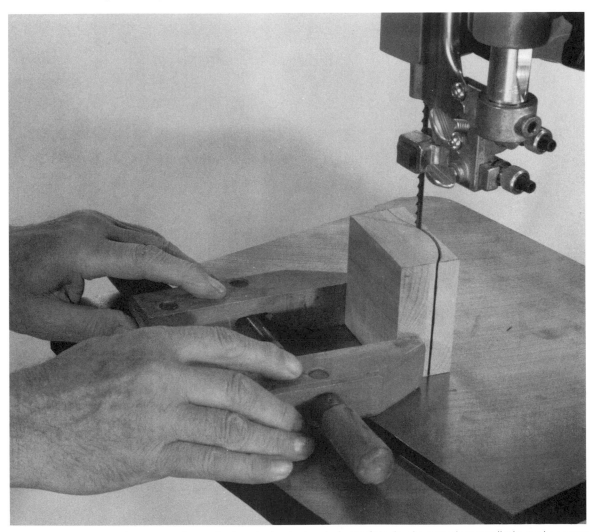

Fig. 4-4. Using a handscrew or other gripping device instead of your hands when sawing small pieces is a neat band-saw technique.

believe in wearing gloves, and a necktie or any loose-fitting clothing that might snag on a tool whether it's idle or in use is a no-no. Jewelry—rings, wristwatches, bracelets, and similar items—are adornments for outside the shop. Worn when working inside the shop, they are hazards. Covering your hair, regardless of its length, is a good idea for safety and protection from dust.

You should treat the shop as if it was a kitchen. You should maintain tables, workbenches, tool surfaces, and the floor in pristine condition. A shop-type vacuum cleaner is a good investment. They are available in various sizes and price ranges, and most will have an exhaust port so the hose can do extra duty as a blower.

Keep the saw's table free of dirt and gum. Often, a cleaning solvent, used according to the instructions on the container, is enough to return the table to proper condition. If not, you can go over the table with a pad sander fitted with a very fine emery abrasive. The weight of the sander will apply all the pressure you need.

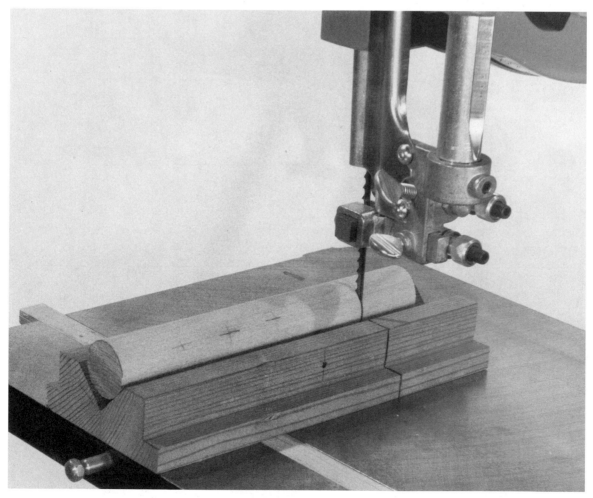

Fig. 4-5. Use a V-block so the action of the saw blade won't cause solid rounds or tubular material to spin in your hands. Attach this homemade accessory to a strip of wood that rides in the table's miter-gauge groove.

Don't force the sander down, just keep it moving. Wipe the table with a lint-free cloth and then apply a generous coating of paste wax. Rub the wax to a fine polish after it is dry. You should repeat the waxing and rubbing frequently so that workpieces will move smoothly and easily when you are sawing.

Protect Eyes, Lungs, and Ears

It's not difficult to convince woodworkers to wear safety goggles or a face mask to protect their vision, but it's often a chore to do the same regarding care of lungs

Fig. 4-6. An outboard-support stand that you can place where needed helps you work with minimum muscle strain. On the band saw, you will use the accessory mostly for long rip cuts. You can buy a stand of this type, or make one, by following our instructions.

and ears. It is a generally accepted fact that headphone-type hearing protectors are as important as any safety device. Motors, saw-blade action, and even many woodworking and metal-sawing operations generate high frequencies. The effects are cumulative; each exposure contributes to possible hearing damage. Good ear protectors will screen out damaging frequencies while still allowing normal conversation and the woodworking noises you should hear.

You should use dust masks for more chores than just sanding. Many routine sawing operations produce waste particles that are best kept from your lungs. Remember that a face mask is only as good as its filter, so be sure to replace the unit as often as necessary.

Good Tool Practice

Get to know all aspects of the machine, which you can do easily by studying the owner's manual. Check particular instructions for mounting, tensioning, and tracking of saw blades. Don't use blades that are wider or narrower for which the

Fig. 4-7. The roller top for the stand can be a length of metal tubing that is sealed at each end with tight-fitting wooden discs, or it can be a ready-made round of wood.

Table 4-1. Materials List for Outboard Support Stand.

Key	Part	No. of Pieces	Size (in Inches)			Material
1	Post	1	1½ ×	2 ×	30	Hardwood
2	Case	2	¾ ×	3½ ×	30	Plywood
3	Case	2	¾ ×	1½ ×	30	Plywood
4	Feet	4	¾ ×	6 ×	11	Plywood
5	Roller support	2	1½ ×	2½ ×	18½	Hardwood
6	Filler	2	½ ×	2 ×	2½	Hardwood
7	Holder	2	⅛ ×	1 ×	4¼	Aluminum
8	Roller	1	1½	O.D. ×	18	Rigid tubing
9	Plug	2	1½ ×	1½ ×	1½	Hardwood

Fig. 4-8. Aluminum brackets support the roller. The hole for the bolt/axle is a little oversize so the roller can rotate freely.

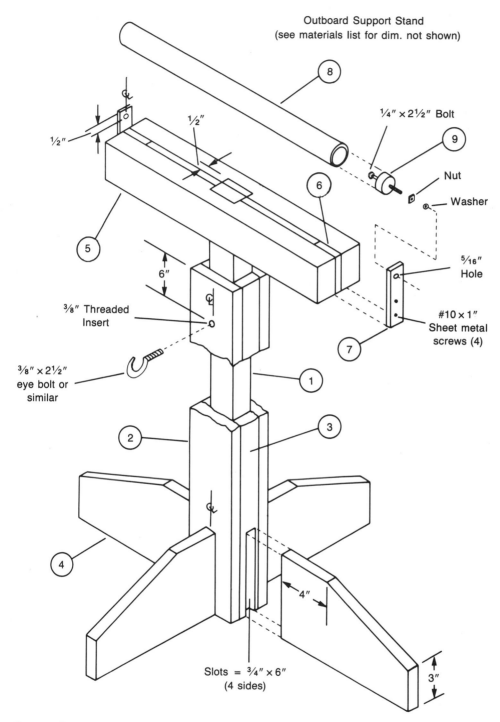

Outboard Support Stand
(see materials list for dim. not shown)

8

¼″ × 2½″ Bolt

9

Nut

Washer

½″

½″

½″

6

5

6″

⅜″ Threaded
Insert

⁵⁄₁₆″
Hole

#10 × 1″
Sheet metal
screws (4)

7

⅜″ × 2½″
eye bolt or
similar

1

2

3

4

4″

Slots = ¾″ × 6″
(4 sides)

3″

Fig. 4-9. These construction details are for an outboard-support stand that you can make. Since its height is adjustable, you can use it for tools other than the band saw.

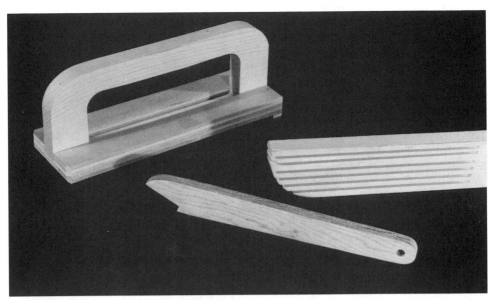

Fig. 4-10. You should make these three important safety tools. From the top, and reading clockwise—combination pusher/hold down, spring stick which is sometimes referred to as a featherboard, and a push stick.

Fig. 4-11. The push stick substitutes for fingers whenever it's necessary to do operations like this ripping chore. Use the pusher to move the work past the blade.

Fig. 4-12. Here is a typical band-saw operation where you can use a spring stick, instead of a hand, to keep work in correct position for the cut. The accessory's fingers must bear against the work in front of the blade.

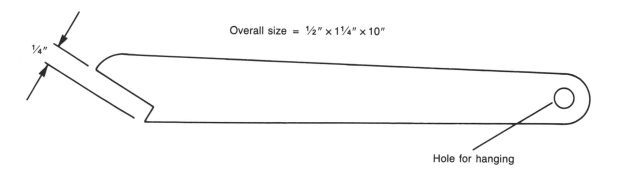

1/4″

Overall size = 1/2″ × 1 1/4″ × 10″

Hole for hanging

Fig. 4-13. This figure shows a typical, easy-to-make push stick. They can be longer, even thinner, or thicker than the sizes suggested. You can make them of plywood or solid stock.

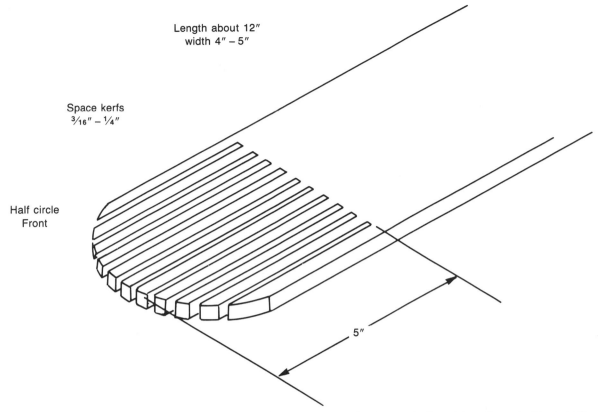

Length about 12″
width 4″ – 5″

Space kerfs
3⁄16″ – 1⁄4″

Half circle
Front

5″

Fig. 4-14. Spring sticks can vary in design and size and you can make them out of hard or softwoods. The length of the fingers when a material like maple or birch is used should be a bit longer than when the project wood is something like pine.

machine is designed. Be sure you have secured the tool to a sturdy bench or stand. Unplug the machine when you change or adjust blades and when you go through alignment checks.

Keep the tool clean inside as well as outside. Don't allow scrap to accumulate on the table. Always wait for the blade to stop running before you remove a workpiece.

Never forget that the tool and the blade it drives can't think for you. There is no way they can distinguish between wood and flesh.

Good Shop Practice

It's never a good idea to overreach, no matter what the operation or the tool you are using. Don't use muscle to support extra-large workpieces. Use outboard supports or ask for extra hands, but be sure to describe the operation and explain how the helper must behave.

Don't work with dull blades. Having to use force to feed stock is a warning to heed. It also might mean that you are trying to cut too fast, an action that can cause harm to you, the blade, and the work.

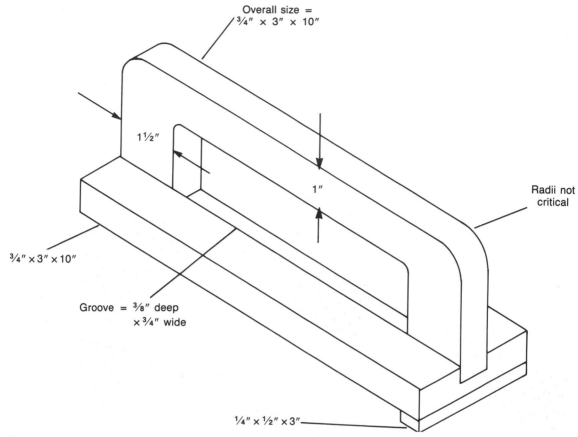

Overall size =
³⁄₄" × 3" × 10"

1½"

1"

Radii not critical

³⁄₄" × 3" × 10"

Groove = ³⁄₈" deep × ³⁄₄" wide

¼" × ½" × 3"

Fig. 4-15. This design is typical for a combination pusher/hold down. You use it for ripping operations and it can work on either side of the blade.

A workshop is not for socializing. You can't visit and work safely at the same time. Warn friends and neighbors not to barge into the shop when they hear machine noise. They might startle you.

Stay alert! The job you are doing must have your complete attention. When you are tired or upset, have taken medicine, or have had an alcoholic drink, substitute television or a good book for woodworking.

Chapter 5

Fundamentals of Sawing

THE BAND SAW'S CUTTING ACTION AND ITS FEATURES ARE EXCLUSIVE. ITS IMPRESSIVE depth of cut allows producing X number of duplicate parts by sawing through a pad composed of individual pieces that are held together with tape or by tack nailing (Fig. 5-1). Another method of duplication is a type of resawing shown in Fig. 5-2 that you do on preshaped pieces. Of course, when the thickness of the stock permits it, you can do this kind of work on other sawing tools, but the band saw's advantage is that you can operate it with blades of minimum thickness. Thus, you minimize waste that relates to the width of the saw kerf.

The tool's blade, with teeth pointing down toward the table, faces forward and cuts constantly in a downward direction. It will not deviate from this mode unless you have neglected blade-guidance adjustments or manipulate the work in a manner that twists the blade or causes it to bind in the kerf. Respectable band sawing does not require a wizard's touch. There is no reason why you can't do a good job the first time you try, if you obey the essential rules of alignment, work with a sharp blade, and accept that you are the guiding force.

HOW WOOD GRAIN AFFECTS BLADE ACTION

You will find that a blade cuts more freely and that it is easier to follow the lines of a pattern when you saw across the grain of the wood. When sawing with the grain, that is, parallel to it, sawing is slower and you must be extra careful with guiding the work since the blade might tend to follow the grain instead of the pattern line. A good way to get the feel, and to understand these basic sawing characteristics, is to make a circular cut in a piece of 1½-inch stock since the blade will encounter all possible grain directions (Fig. 5-3).

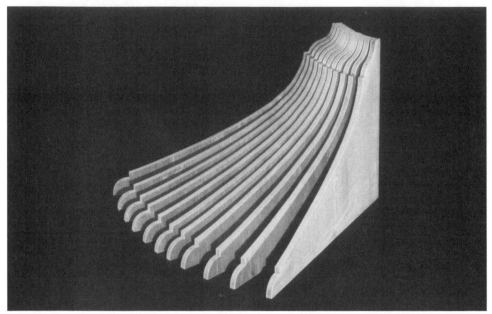

Fig. 5-1. The band saw's depth of cut makes duplication a snap. These eleven pieces of ¼ inch plywood were held together and formed in a single operation—feasible on even the smallest machine.

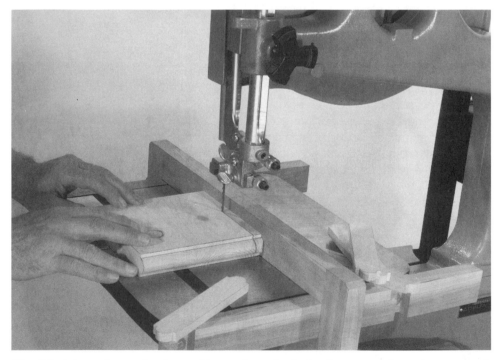

Fig. 5-2. A type of resawing is used to produce duplicates from a preshaped component. Working this way, against a fence, requires that the blade be in good condition, free of "lead."

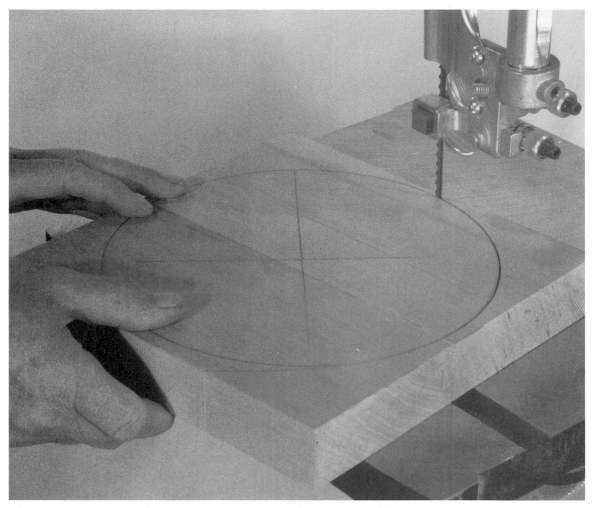

Fig. 5-3. A complete circular cut will acquaint you with how the blade behaves in various grain areas. Making this cut is good practice for a beginner and should be tried on hard and softwoods of various thicknesses.

Results are best when you start the cut in a cross-grain area since entry will be easier and the cut will end in the same area with the blade moving cross-grain where its action is at its best. Avoid starting the cut so that the final phase—the clean-up cut—will be at an angle of 45 degrees to the grain direction. You also will find that starting and ending cuts on the quartering grain will not produce as smooth a job as one that begins in a cross-grain area.

Band-saw cuts are best when they can be continuous. In the case of a circular cut, it's a good idea to start with a piece of wood whose dimensions are a bit greater than the circle's diameter. This size will avoid the runouts and the problem of getting back on the line that occur when the stock is of minimum size (Fig. 5-4).

Using a band saw involves more than cutting circles, so the grain-direction suggestions are not rules that you can't break. The shape of a workpiece often will

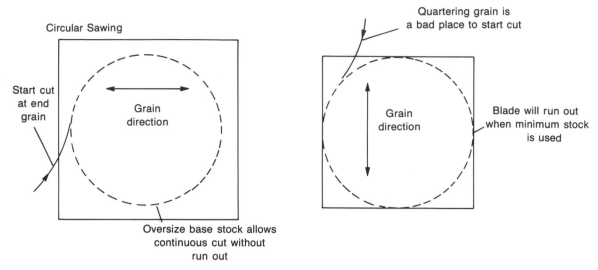

Circular Sawing

Start cut at end grain

Grain direction

Oversize base stock allows continuous cut without run out

Quartering grain is a bad place to start cut

Grain direction

Blade will run out when minimum stock is used

Fig. 5-4. The circular cut exposes the blade to all possible grain conditions. It's always wise to start with an oversize piece so the cut can be continuous. This continuous cut will avoid the roughness that occurs when the blade must run out.

dictate when you must start and end a cut. Observing the cutting line and anticipating how you must move the work to follow the pattern line are primary factors for accurate sawing.

BACKTRACKING

Backtracking, which means moving the work so you can release the blade from a cut you already made, is a factor of band sawing. Two schools of thought exist on how you can accomplish backtracking best. One—turn off the machine and elevate the guides so you can hold the blade in correct position by pressing a piece of soft wood against its teeth while you carefully pull back the work. Two—allow the blade to keep running while you backtrack. Be aware that careless handling of the work can pull the blade off the wheels. Probably, both systems are feasible. When backtracking is short and straight, there is little danger that you might pull the blade, especially if the kerf is wide because of a heavy blade. If you must backtrack on curves and around tight radii, then taking the precaution of system number one is probably wise.

Minimizing Backtracking

Visualizing and planning for the sawing you must do is one way to cut down on backtracking. For example, we offer the "do" and "don't" procedures shown in Fig. 5-5 when the assignment is to form a cutout with sharp corners. In example one, the first cut requires full-length backtracking. The second cut goes to the corner and then you backtrack so the blade can veer off to make the third cut. This procedure removes the bulk of the waste stock and leaves a sharp corner. The final cut is short and straight and removes the waste in the second corner.

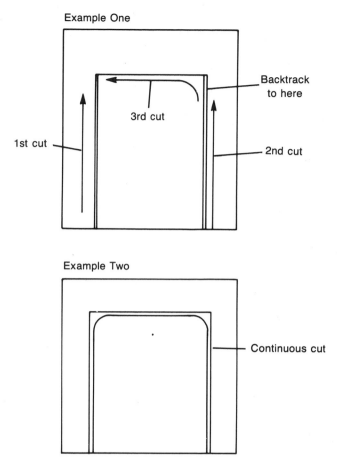

Fig. 5-5. There is always one best way to perform a sawing operation for smoothest results and minimum backtracking. Example two is the least bothersome approach.

In example two, the initial cut is continuous, bypassing both corners. You then use short, straight cuts to clean out the corners; with this method you reduce backtracking to an absolute minimum.

SHORT CUTS COME FIRST

Check the pattern to ascertain what cuts you can make first so you can do major sawing with minimum fuss. In the example shown in Fig. 5-6, the first cut allows you to cut the major portion of the profile without backtracking. The third and fourth cuts, which are short and straight, finish the job.

The examples in Fig. 5-7 also demonstrate how advisable it is to start with short cuts whenever possible. You can see how the need for backtracking would increase if sawing started at other points.

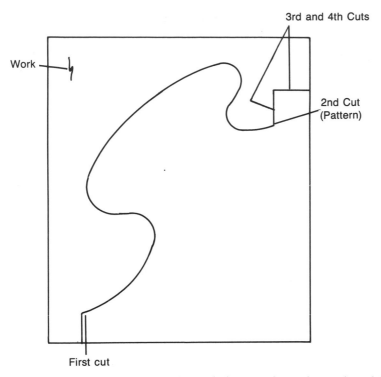

Fig. 5-6. You can see what would happen if you tried to saw the major portion of this profile without the first cut that is suggested. You would have to veer off the line and cut to an edge or backtrack to the starting point.

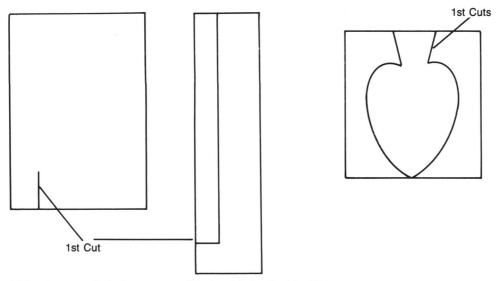

Make short cuts first whenever possible to minimize backtracking

Fig. 5-7. Use preliminary short cuts whenever possible to minimize backtracking. Study the pattern so you can make wise judgements before starting the job.

COMPLEX CUTS

Sometimes the pattern dictates the sequence and number of cuts. Such is the case with the cornice profile shown in Fig. 5-8. It is impossible to make a single, continuous cut to accomplish the job. First cuts, which you should view as complete cuts since they enter and leave the material, begin to remove waste. Second cuts do the same. The final, straight cut removes whatever wood waste remains.

Whenever possible, break up the cutting patterns so a number of shorter cuts will facilitate sawing. The first cut made for the example design shown in Fig. 5-9, establishes the sharp point where the following profile cuts can meet. The last cuts that are straight remove the remaining waste.

Often you can accomplish complex cuts with minimum fuss by first making a continuous cut that follows the pattern as much as possible while bypassing detail points. This cut removes the bulk of the waste stock so it is easier to go back and clean out the areas that remain (Fig. 5-10).

RELIEF AND TANGENTIAL CUTS

You can make relief cuts, like those diagrammed in Fig. 5-11, from the perimeter of a workpiece to the pattern line. They should be as short as possible since you will have to backtrack to move out of them. Most times, you use these cuts so you

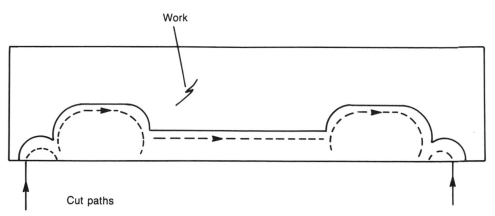

Fig. 5-8. It's often possible to make preliminary cuts that remove waste so backtracking isn't necessary. In some situations, removing waste in pieces is the only way to go.

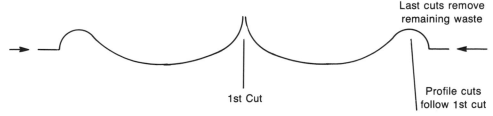

Fig. 5-9. The first, short center cut, allows you to make the profile cuts without complications. There is little backtracking and you can make major cuts continuously.

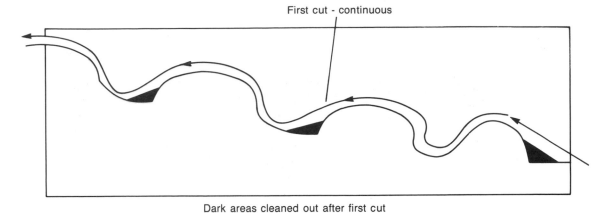

First cut - continuous

Dark areas cleaned out after first cut

Fig. 5-10. When shortcuts are not a solution, it's a good idea to follow the pattern line as closely as possible with a continuous cut, and then return to clean out the problem areas.

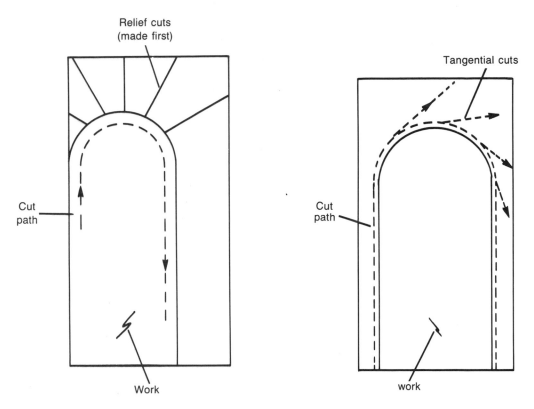

Relief cuts
(made first)

Cut
path

Work

Tangential cuts

Cut
path

work

Fig. 5-11. Relief cuts allow you to get around a curve that is too small for a continuous cut because of the blade's width. The concept is simple. Waste pieces fall away so the blade is not confined in a kerf and so it has more room to turn.

Fig. 5-12. Tangential cutting is another way to coax a wide blade around a tight turn.

can move a blade around a curve that is too tight for a continuous cut because of the blade's width. Because of the relief cuts, individual waste pieces fall away, thus providing more room for the blade to move. The number of initial cuts required will depend on the radius of the curve and the width of the blade.

Tangential cutting (Fig. 5-12) is another band-saw technique that allows a blade to negotiate a turn it can't normally do. The operator leads off the pattern line and saws to the perimeter of the workpiece each time the blade starts to bind. When the waste falls away, the operator returns to where he veered from the pattern line and continues to saw. Like relief cutting, sawing this way simply provides more room for the blade than it would have in a normal kerf (Fig. 5-13).

An alternate method is to make a series of straight cuts tangent to the curve. The idea is to remove as much of the waste as possible so a final cut, on the curved line, can be continuous.

These techniques are for convex curves. You cannot use either of these ideas when the cut is concave and tight. Relief cuts might provide some aid, but the ultimate solution is to work with a narrow blade, sawing as close to the line as possible, and then finishing the job with another tool, for example, a drum sander.

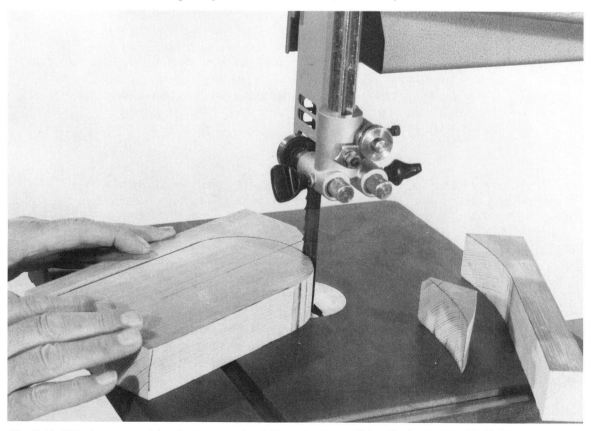

Fig. 5-13. With the tangential technique, cutting follows the line until the blade starts to bind, then it moves to the outside. How often you must move to the outside will depend on the blade's width and, to some extent, the thickness of the stock.

AVOIDING SNARES

Snares or "booby traps," occur in band sawing when you are unable to continue a cut because the work contacts the tool's arm. Backtracking a bit and sawing out to a waste area so you can resituate the work for a different pass direction is a solution, but one that is not always possible because of the pattern that you must follow. The beginner often is frustrated by traps when he doesn't have to be. The experienced band sawer, while accepting them as part of normal procedure, will minimize such episodes by studying the job and determining the best place to start a cut to avoid arm interference. A typical example of "do" and "don't" is detailed in Fig. 5-14. The worker who starts sawing at one point will make the cut easily in a continuous pass. The one who starts without previewing what will happen will find himself trapped.

Traps also can happen on straight cuts and even on small corner cutouts like the example in Fig. 5-15. Note that if you mark the cut required on the wrong side of the stock, you could make the with-the-grain cut, but the tool's arm would interfere with making the final cross-grain cut. If you do the layout on the opposite surface of the work, you easily can make both cuts. Another solution is to make the layout on both surfaces of the stock, then make the second cut after you flip the stock over.

Long notches on very long material pose their own problems, but as always, there is a solution, like the one suggested in Fig. 5-16. The first step is to use the column as a pivot point to make a curved cut to the line of the long dimension. The second full-length cut goes right to the corner and removes the bulk of the waste stock. You now can make a third cut to clean out the corner.

The examples that we have shown are typical but do not cover all possibilities. Experience with the machine will provide necessary education. Most important is the precutting study that will help you judge the best way to complete an assignment.

WORK LAYOUT

A good deal of the work done on a band saw is preceded by marking patterns on the stock. Being careful with how you mark the patterns often can lead to easier sawing, more accurate cutting, and even to saving material. Another consideration is judging the best grain direction of the wood. Whether it runs horizontally, vertically, or obliquely, affects the final appearance of the project. How the grain runs often can affect the strength of a part. For example, cross-grain on a narrow section of a component will not have the strength straight grains provide.

An example of a thoughtful layout is shown in Fig. 5-17, where two identical parts are required. Instead of working with two pieces of wood, a suitably-sized one is selected and marked with a single pattern. After sawing to separate the areas, the marked piece is tack nailed to the unmarked one so a single sawing operation produces duplicates. Parts cut in this fashion should remain locked together until edges are brought to acceptable smoothness by sanding.

Another system that you can use to produce duplicate pieces with a single saw cut is suggested by Fig. 5-18. In this case, the shape required consists of two similar, reversed curves—the classic "ogee" form. It stands, that you must saw very carefully and exactly on the line rather than to either side of it. You easily can correct slight mishaps by joining the pieces after sawing and sanding as if they were a single part.

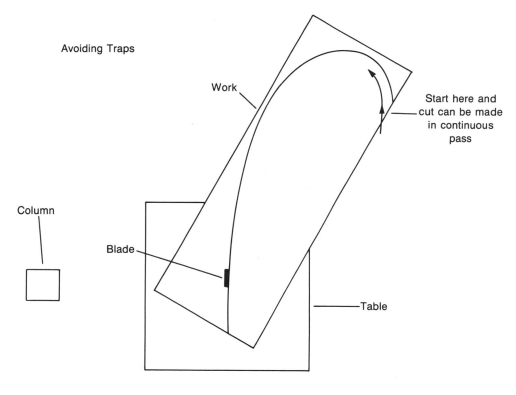

Avoiding Traps

Work

Start here and
cut can be made
in continuous
pass

Column

Blade

Table

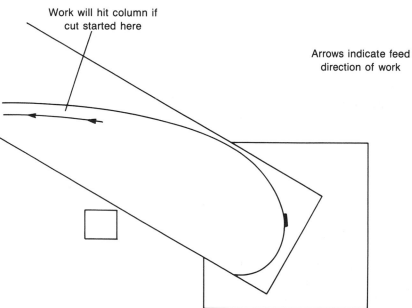

Work will hit column if
cut started here

Arrows indicate feed
direction of work

Fig. 5-14. You can avoid snares simply by studying the pattern and judging the best way to start the cut. When a solution for a continuous cut isn't possible, saw out through a waste area before the work makes contact with the tool's column.

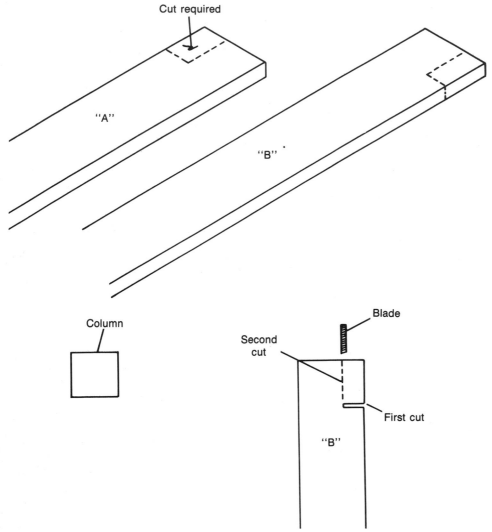

Fig. 5-15. Planning beforehand often provides the solution to a sawing problem. Many times, it's simply a matter of marking the pattern on the "right" side of the stock, or maybe on both sides. The "A" sample will pose problems, but not the "B" sample.

A way to produce a similar ogee shape, while saving material, is shown in Fig. 5-19. In this case, you would glue the section that is separated by the saw cut back onto the base material. It demonstrates, for one thing, how you can produce a component that is wider than the base stock.

Figure 5-20 details a similar idea. Here, the technique is used to produce a component with opposite, similar curves. You would glue the piece that is separated by the saw cut to the straight edge of the base stock. The idea is not limited to producing similar curves since, after you glue the parts together, you can do further sawing on the base piece.

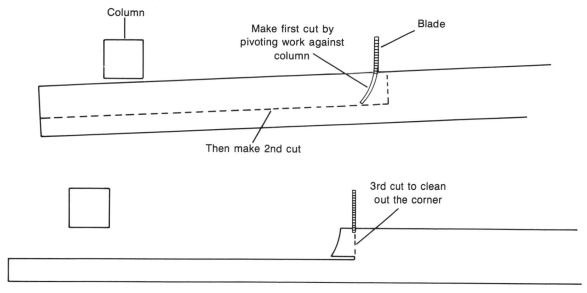

Sawing long notch when column interferes

Column

Make first cut by
pivoting work against
column

Blade

Then make 2nd cut

3rd cut to clean
out the corner

Fig. 5-16. You can form very long notches with hardly any backtracking if you follow this system of sawing.

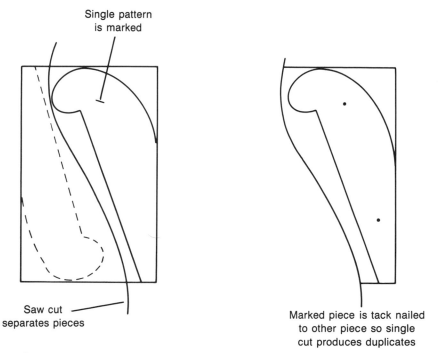

Single pattern
is marked

Saw cut
separates pieces

Marked piece is tack nailed
to other piece so single
cut produces duplicates

Fig. 5-17. Basic band-saw wisdom includes planning for material economy. Working this way saves material and ensures that the parts will be duplicates.

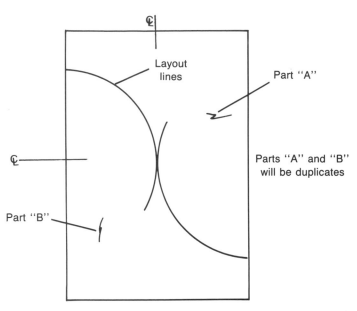

Fig. 5-18. The ogee form provides an example of how a single cut on one piece of wood can provide two similar components. Careful sawing is necessary although you can eliminate little mishaps easily by sanding.

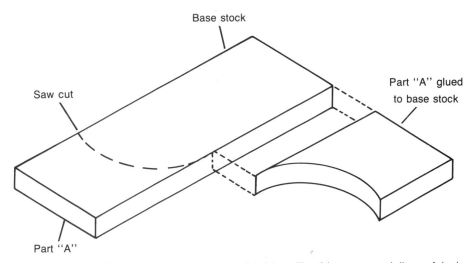

Fig. 5-19. This typical work system saves material. Ideas like this are especially useful when you make projects or components from solid lumber since the material isn't always available in the width you need.

You can produce circular and elliptical forms of almost any size by gluing together individually-sawed segments (Fig. 5-21). Actually, since both forms are symmetrical about a centerline, you can tack nail pieces for similar segments and cut them in pairs. The method is especially useful when the project is made with solid lumber since the material rarely is available in boards more than 12 inches wide.

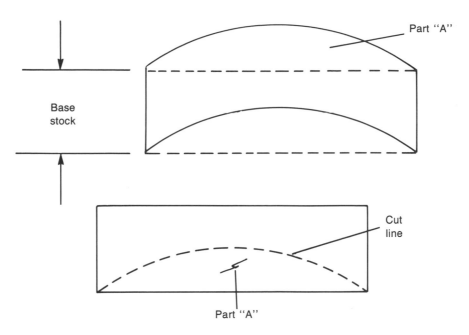

Fig. 5-20. This example shows you how judicious planning can provide a needed component while reducing material requirements.

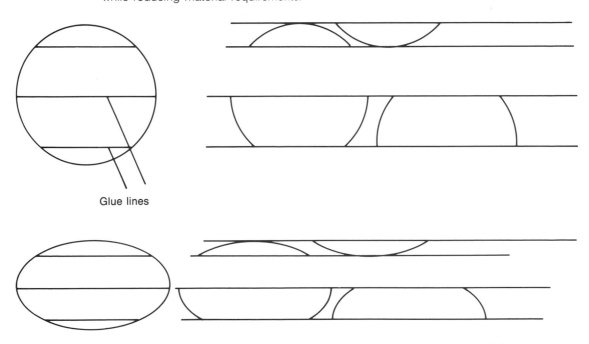

Glue lines

You can form circular and elliptical project components by cutting segments from straight boards

Fig. 5-21. The technique of cutting segments from narrow boards which you then glue together often is used to create large circular and elliptical shapes.

If plywood is the material, then you can form circular parts up to 4 feet in diameter with a single cut. Elliptical forms can be longer if the small diameter is not more than the standard 4 foot width of plywood.

RELIEF AND PATTERN HOLES

It's often possible to predrill material to facilitate sawing or to form tight radii that the blade in use can't get around. The idea is especially used on cutouts typified by the design shown in Fig. 5-22. With corner holes, which you might form with a hand drill or on a drill press, already in the work, you can cut the waste away in a single pass. The holes are a good idea even if the corners must be square since they allow a continuous cut for the major part of the job. It's a simple matter to return and clean out the corners with short, straight cuts.

If you are equipped with a drill press and mortising bits and chisels, you can cut square corners before beginning to saw.

Advantages exist to predrilling holes when you can use them as elements in the design (Fig. 5-23). They can simplify sawing and reduce work time and will offer smooth edges and precise radii. Producing twin components with scalloped edges proves the practicality of predrilling when possible. Drill a board of suitable width on its centerline with equally-spaced holes. A straight saw cut then separates the parts (Fig. 5-24). You can form a large hole with a hole saw chucked in an electric hand drill, or you can use fly cutters turning in a drill press. You must use the latter method very carefully—slowest drill-press speed, hands well away from the cutter, work securely clamped.

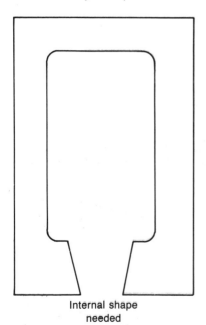

Internal shape
needed

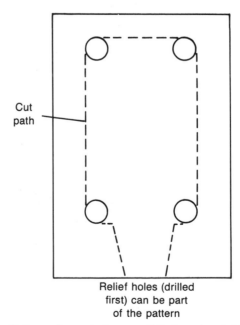

Cut
path

Relief holes (drilled
first) can be part
of the pattern

Fig. 5-22. Predrilled holes often are used to facilitate sawing or to form radii that are too tight for the blade. It's necessary, of course, to be precise when making the layout for the holes.

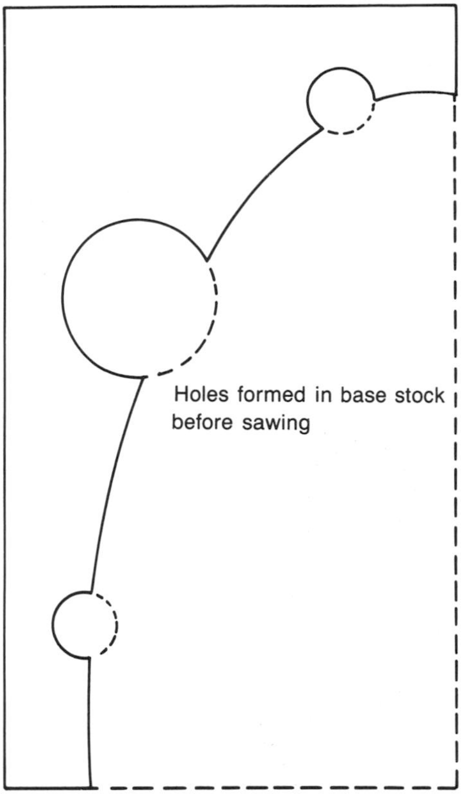

Fig. 5-23. There is nothing amateurish about predrilling small or large holes before sawing if they can be part of the design.

Holes formed in base stock before sawing

SAWING NARROW SLOTS

The method to use when sawing narrow slots will depend primarily on whether the end of the slot will be round or square (Fig. 5-25). If it is square, make the outline cuts freehand, veering toward the opposite corner in a curve the blade in use can manage. You can remove the remaining point by *nibbling*; that is, moving the work into the blade with side-by-side kerfs. Use a file or sandpaper wrapped around a block of wood that will fit the width of the slot to accomplish final smoothing.

The chore is easier if the slot has a round end. First, drill a hole on the centerline of the slot, and then make parallel saw cuts to remove the waste. You can do the sawing freehand or by guiding the work with a fence. When the machine is not equipped with the accessory, you can improvise one simply by clamping a straight piece of wood to the tool's table (Fig. 5-26).

MAKE A FENCE

Straight cutting is as much a part of band-saw work as curve cutting, so a fence is an important accessory. If the tool is not designed for a fence, or if you choose not to buy one, you can construct a unit like the one that is shown mounted in Fig. 5-27, and that is detailed in Fig. 5-28. Establish some essential dimensions by measuring the table on the tool you own, but the concept will be suitable for any band saw.

We will discuss the techniques of straight cutting in the following chapter.

INTERNAL CUTTING

Because band-saw blades are continuous loops, it isn't possible to make an internal cut without a lead-in kerf from an edge of the pattern—not unless equipment is available for welding blades after they have been broken and passed through an entry hole in the work. The procedure is not feasible for small shops especially if the technique is called for rarely. You can, however, work several ways so you can accomplish similar results without special equipment. One of them that has to do with circular cutting is shown in Fig. 5-29. A lead-in cut on a diameter line enters the waste area and then veers to follow the inner circle. You would glue a thin strip of matching wood in place to fill the entry kerf. Finally, smooth inside and outside edges with a drum sander.

Fig. 5-24. A single centerline cut will produce identical pieces with scalloped edges if you prepare the stock by predrilling.

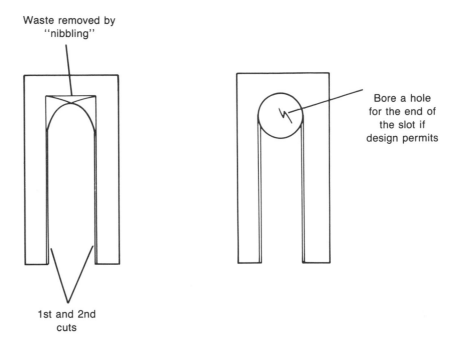

Waste removed by
"nibbling"

1st and 2nd
cuts

Bore a hole
for the end of
the slot if
design permits

Fig. 5-25. You can form narrow slots in these two ways. Both systems require backtracking, but you can accomplish a round-end slot with minimum fuss.

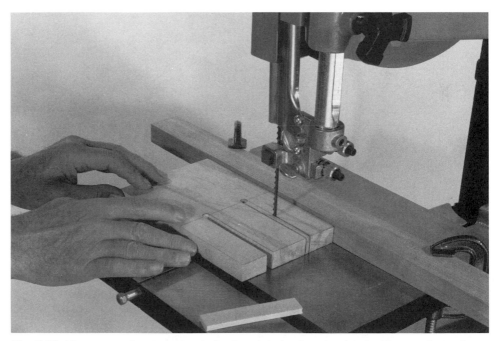

Fig. 5-26. You can make straight cuts for the slots freehand or by working against a fence which, in this case, is just a straight piece of wood. The guard is too high here, as it will be in other photos, but remember—IT'S LIKE THIS FOR PHOTO CLARITY ONLY!

A similar procedure is shown in Fig. 5-30. Here, you make the entry cut tangent to the perimeter of the inner circle so careful cutting will allow you to remove the core in a continuous pass. You can close the kerf slot by gluing in a slim strip of wood, or by coating mating surfaces with glue and then pulling them together with a device like the spring clamp shown in Fig. 5-31, or with a band clamp. The latter idea reduces inside and outside diameters of the project but, because of the slight thickness of band-saw blades, the change is insignificant.

Another idea calls for sawing the project so you reduce it to half increments (Fig. 5-32). You can draw a half circle of the plan on separate pieces, or you can produce half-circle pieces from a solid block after you have halved it with a centerline cut (Fig. 5-33). This technique, if you analyze the shape of the "waste" pieces that result, can lead to material for a series of projects. We will pursue the thought in greater detail in the chapter that deals with projects.

Speaking of "waste" material, it's interesting to note that the castoffs that result from pattern cuts often have interesting shapes and you should not discard them summarily. What further use comes to mind for the "remains" that are displayed in Fig. 5-34?

Fig. 5-27. A rip fence is a valuable band-saw accessory. Most manufacturers provide one with the tool or as an extra-cost accessory. The example shown here is one that you can custom make for the tool you own.

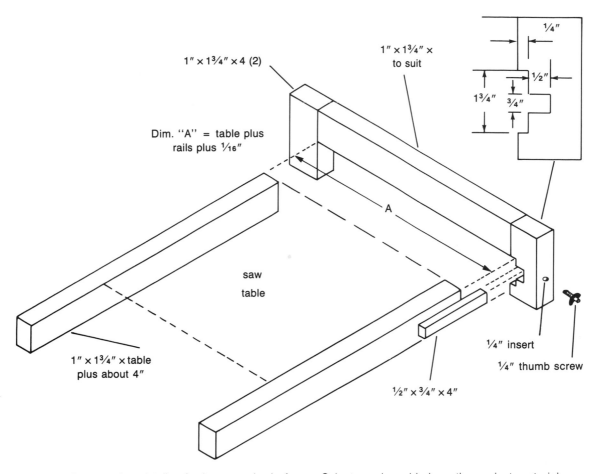

Fig. 5-28. Construction details of a homemade rip fence. Select maple or birch as the project material.

Returning to internal cutouts, another idea to consider when the inside shape doesn't have to be circular is shown in Fig. 5-35. Segmented pieces that are shaped to be appropriate for the form and size of the component or project are perimeter-sawed after you have glued them together to form a solid assembly.

INCREASING TABLE SURFACE

As we noted previously, band-saw table area is rarely overly impressive. So it's up to the operator to increase work support by designing an auxiliary table that he can place on the tool when he needs it (Fig. 5-36). A typical project of this nature is not demanding; it consists of a sheet of cabinet-grade plywood that is rimmed with solid stock and has a substrate structure that fits the dimensions of the machine's table. Construction details of a concept that will do for all band saws are offered in Fig. 5-37. Check the sizes of the parts in the material's list against the dimensions of your machine before cutting to determine if any modifications are in order.

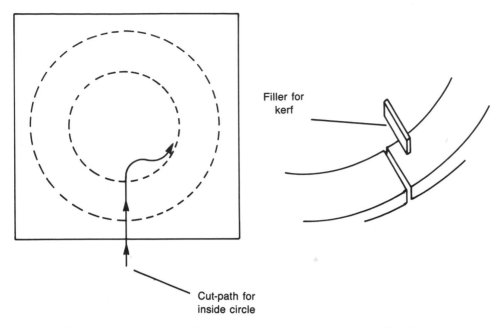

Filler for
kerf

Cut-path for
inside circle

Fig. 5-29. Entry cuts are a way to form inside cutouts on a band saw. The blade can enter on a diameter line and then veer off to follow the inside circumference.

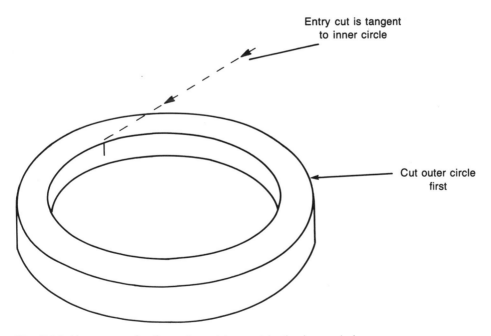

Entry cut is tangent
to inner circle

Cut outer circle
first

Fig. 5-30. You can make the entry cut tangent to the inner circle.

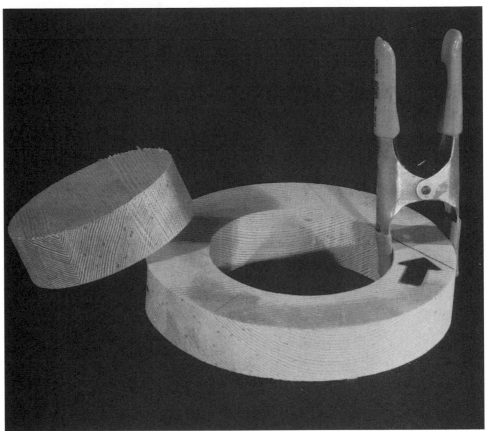

Fig. 5-31. If you make a tangent entry cut, you can close the kerf gap (arrow) with a clamp after coating the mating edges with glue. Alternately, you can fill the kerf with a slim piece of wood.

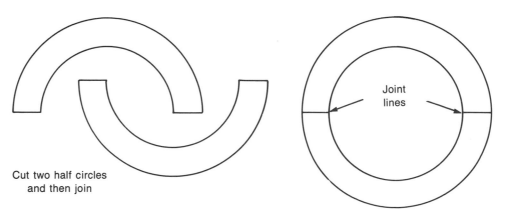

Cut two half circles
and then join

Joint
lines

Fig. 5-32. You can always provide for interior voids by sawing half parts and then joining them together.

Fig. 5-33. Another way to provide for interior voids is to make the circular cuts on a solid block after you have sawed it in half. Save the half cores that remain for possible future use.

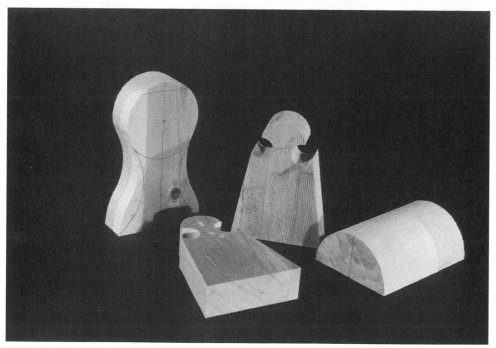

Fig. 5-34. Here are examples of band-saw waste. Why not store pieces like this for additional service?

Fig. 5-35. You also can create internal forms by assembling segments and then sawing the perimeter shape.

Assembly of segments

Circular cut after segments assembly

Fig. 5-36. An auxiliary table will provide nice support when workpieces are oversize. The thickness of the homemade table will lessen the tool's depth of cut, but not significantly.

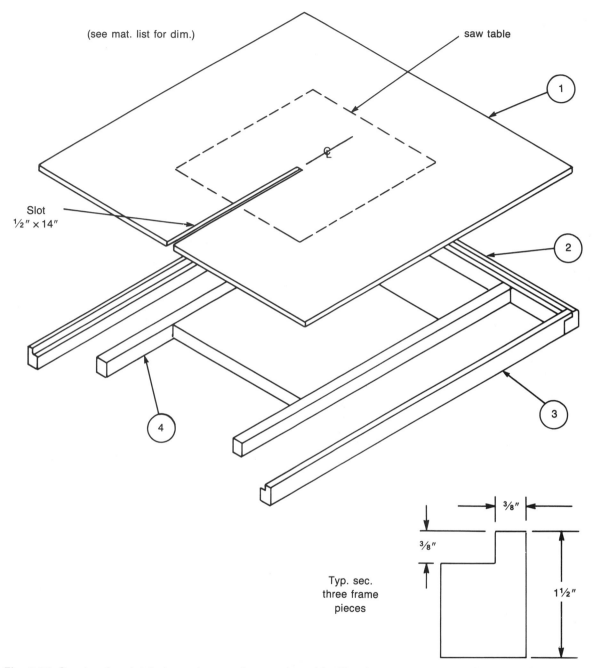

(see mat. list for dim.)

saw table

1

Slot
½″ × 14″

2

3

4

Typ. sec.
three frame
pieces

⅜″

⅜″

1½″

Fig. 5-37. Construction details for a shop-made, oversize table. Check dimensions to see if you need to make modifications because of the table size on your machine. The project is designed so it can be held in place with small C-clamps bearing against the edge of the regular table.

Table 5-1. Materials List for Oversize Table.

Key	Part	No. of Pieces	Size (in Inches)					Material
1	Top	1	⅜	×	30	×	30	Plywood
2	Frame front	1	1	×	1½	×	30¾	Hardwood
3	Frame sides	2	1	×	1½	×	34	Hardwood
4	Clamp ledge	2	1	×	1½	×	30	Hardwood

TROUBLESHOOTING

You can trace "strange" things that can happen during band-saw operations to misalignment, blade problems, operational faults, and so on. It's likely that you will find the cause and the possible solution to the problem by checking the information in Table 5-2.

Table 5-2. Check this information whenever you feel something is wrong with the tool or the operation isn't proceeding as it should or results need attention.

	Problem	Cause	Possible Solution
I N G E N E R A L	Blade moves from cutting line	"Lead"	Recondition or replace blade or try honing lead side
		Blade guide adjustment	Reset guides for the blade in use
		Work handling	Work slowly—use more care when guiding work
		Wood problem—knots—grain structure	Use slow feed—try heavier blade—reduce fpm
		Bad blade	Recondition or replace
	Cuts not square to surface	Misalignment	Angle between table and blade not 90 degrees—reset auto stop
	Blade binds	Radii too small for blade	Change to smaller blade or use relief cuts
	Blade breakage	Forcing cut	Don't feed work faster than the blade can handle
		Radius too small for blade in use	Change to smaller blade or use relief cuts

Table 5-2 (cont.)

Problem	Cause	Possible Solution
Blade breakage	Blade is dull, worn, or damaged	Recondition blade or replace
	Machine setup	Check all alignment factors
Can't backtrack	Work handling	Use care to keep blade in kerf
	Kerf clogged or closed	Clean waste from kerf—keep kerf open with wood splinter
Cut too rough	Character of blade in use	If critical, change to finer blade but cut more slowly
Blade scrapes when running free	Misalignment	Check clearance of blade guides and backup
Blade knocks when running free or cutting	Blade is kinked, bent, or twisted in local area	Remove from machine and straighten if possible or discard
Inconsistent cut quality		
Column interference	Machine has limited width of cut	No cure on some jobs
	Poor planning	Visualize cutting procedure before starting
Bevel cuts not accurate	Misalignment	Check bevel scale and auto stops
	Work handling	Be firm when feeding work—make test cuts
Excessive vibration	Machine organization	Check all alignment factors—check pulleys and belts—be sure machine solidly bolted to bench or stand—uneven floor?
Blade moves off wheels	Machine organization	Check all alignment factors—blade tension—upper wheel tilt
Side of cut is bowed	Blade is too small	Use widest blade available
	Blade tension	Adjust tension for the blade in use
	Work handling	Feed slowly especially on very wide material
Blade moves off line when fence is used	Blade has "lead"	Recondition—hone lead side—replace if necessary
	Dull blade	Sharpen or replace
	Tough, grainy wood	Might be better to do the job freehand
Rough cut	Characteristic of wide blades with heavy set	No cure

(First group label at left: IN GENERAL. Second group label at left: RESAWING.)

Chapter 6

Straight Sawing

BAND SAW" AND "CURVE CUTTING" ARE THOUGHT OF AS ALMOST SYNONYMS, BUT its straight-cutting capabilities are hardly marginal. To think so is to reduce the operational scope of the machine. In fact, on some crosscutting and ripping chores, it can outshine other tools like table saws and radial arm saws. For one thing, even a bench-top concept with its 4-inch depth of cut can handle thicker stock than the average table saw. While cutoff length is limited by the distance from blade to arm—without special techniques that is—ripping distance is unlimited. It might seem picayune, but another plus factor is minimal waste because band-saw blades are comparatively thin..

You can do crosscutting and ripping freehandedly, but working with guides such as a miter gauge and rip fence makes these chores easier to do and will ensure accuracy. Since guided cutting does not allow any manual feed-direction adjustment for lead, it is critical for the blade to be in prime condition. Only if the blade has uniform and sufficient set can you expect it to cut straight in work-guided situations.

CROSSCUTTING

Crosscuts are made across the grain of the wood, usually to establish the length of a component, as opposed to ripping which is done with the grain to provide a specific board width. The standard guide for crosscutting is a miter gauge which, of course, requires that the table have a slot for the gauge's bar to ride in. Some of the techniques that follow will demonstrate how to gauge cutoffs even if the table is not designed with a slot.

Crosscutting is done by holding the work firmly against the miter gauge and flat on the table as you move gauge and work as a unit past the blade (Fig. 6-1).

A slow feed is recommended since even a perfect blade, especially a narrow one, can wander off course if you force it. Saw teeth are designed to cut just so fast; insist on more, and you invite trouble.

You can use conventional miter-gauge accessories like the hold-down clamp assembly shown in Fig. 6-2 to keep the work in perfect position for the cut. Allow the gauge to guide the cut. Keep your hands to the right of the blade; using one hand at the free end of the work to help guide it is a very bad practice. When the cut is complete, allow the machine to stop before you remove the cutoff. As usual, the guard must be close to the work—*not* the way it appears in the photos.

A standard sawing trick used on the band saw as well as other machines is to reverse the position of the miter gauge when sawing wide material (Fig. 6-3). Always make sure the gauge will have a secure position throughout the pass. If the width of the workpiece leads you to believe otherwise, then it's best to do the job freehandedly.

Little room exists between the blade and the miter-gauge slot even on large machines, but you can provide more by making the slotted table extension that is shown in Fig. 6-4. The idea also offers a means of providing a slot for a table that lacks one. You can make the extension by working from the plan in Fig. 6-5. You

Fig. 6-1. You can do accurate crosscutting with a miter gauge so long as the saw blade is in prime condition. Be sure the table slot and blade are parallel and that the angle between miter-gauge head and blade is 90 degrees.

easily can mount the accessory if the regular table already has holes in it. If not, you can drill special holes, or simply use small C-clamps to secure the project. Be sure surfaces of extension and saw table are on the same plane.

Crosscutting Long Work

Like any machine, the band saw is not perfect. Its fault is the limited distance between the blade and arm. If the machine is a 10-inch version, you can't make an 11-inch cutoff, not in normal fashion anyway. The same thought applies to any size machine. One way to circumvent the problem is shown in Fig. 6-6. You place the work on the table with an edge against the tool's arm. Then, using the arm as a pivot point, move the work about half its width into the saw blade. Repeat the procedure after you invert the work. This procedure does leave waste and a somewhat pointed shape, but the point is easy to remove by making a routine crosscut (Fig. 6-7). Actually, a single pivoting cut right across the board will work as well, but there

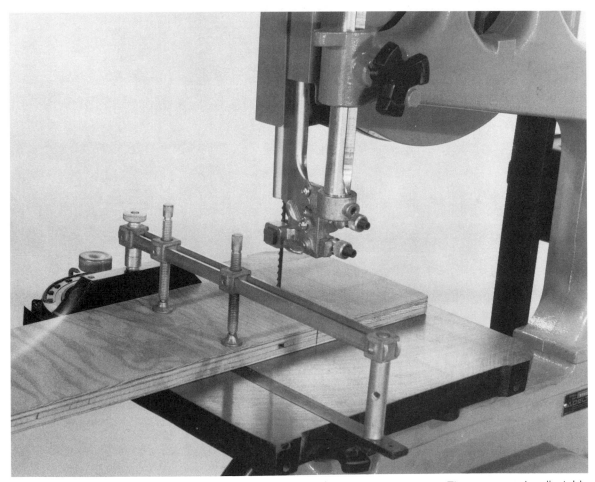

Fig. 6-2. A miter gauge hold-down clamp assembly keeps work secure during the cut. The accessory is adjustable for various stock widths and thicknesses. Pistol grip type hold-downs are available for many miter gauge designs.

will be more waste. The width of the workpiece affects the amount of waste with either method. You will waste about 1 inch of wood when you use the double-pivot system on an 8-inch board. The waste will increase to close to 3 inches if you accomplish the initial separation with a single pivot cut.

You can minimize waste even further if you make the separation cut with the stock on edge. This idea, of course, demands that the stock be narrower than the tool's maximum cut depth.

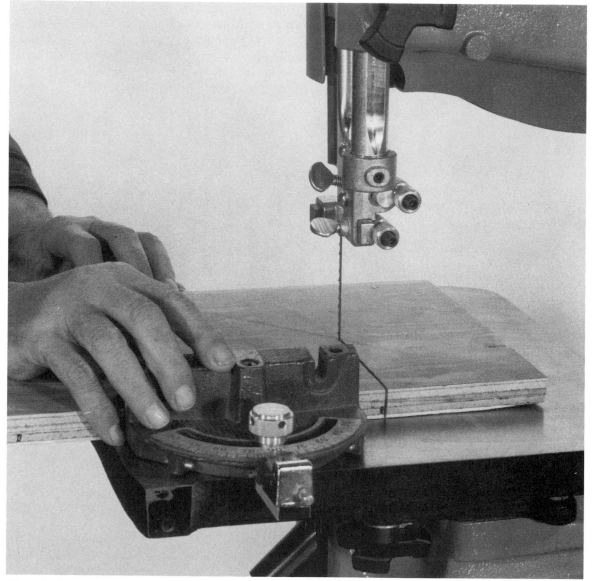

Fig. 6-3. One way to saw wide stock is to use the miter gauge backwards. Be sure that the gauge will be stable throughout the operation.

Fig. 6-4. A homemade accessory increases the distance between miter-gauge slot and saw blade. You can use the idea to provide a slot for a table that lacks one.

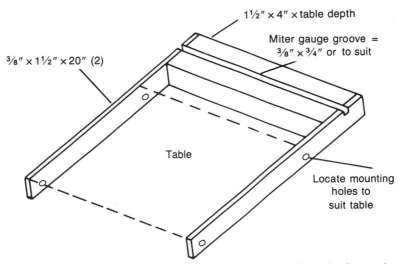

Fig. 6-5. These construction details for an extension table include a slot for a miter gauge. The extension also provides more work support.

Off-Angle Crosscutting

The normal position of a blade is with its teeth pointing directly forward, but if you twist the blade in its cutting area so it angles away from the arm, then you can feed work obliquely so you can crosscut long pieces, within width limits, without arm interference. A simple way to twist the blade is shown in Fig. 6-8. Run a platform, which can be plywood or solid lumber, about halfway into the blade. After you have backed top and bottom guides away from the blade, turn and clamp the platform so the blade will be twisted about 20 or 25 degrees. Keep the blade backups in correct position.

You now can crosscut as shown in Fig. 6-9, by feeding the work at an angle. Limit workpieces to a 4 or 5 inch width, but you can double by making a halfway cut, then backtracking, and making a second cut on the same line after you have turned the stock over.

Fig. 6-6. Using pivot cuts allows crosscutting of extra-long workpieces. Make the second cut after you have turned the stock over.

Blades that have been twisted with a wooden platform tend to return to standard position since they are constantly rubbing against the sides of the kerf, but the idea is good enough for occasional work. A more permanent technique is to modify the upper guides along the lines shown in Fig. 6-10. You can perform this technique by grinding or filing one end of each guide to an angle of 20 to 25 degrees. Thus, when you wish to use the off-angle cutting idea, you simply reverse the guides to twist the blade. Only the upper guides need the attention; the bottom guides are just backed away from the blade. Keep both blade backups as they should be normally. Blade tension and tracking do not require special attention. The gauge and width of a blade will bear on how it can be twisted. A ¼-inch or ⅜-inch blade cooperates nicely with the system.

Fig. 6-7. The pivoting technique for crosscutting long work leaves a small amount of waste that you remove with a routine cut. Don't view a high guard position in any illustration as a way to work. It's in that position for photo clarity only.

Crosscutting to Length

Many times you must cut a single or several similar components to a specific length. If you only need one piece, then it's unnecessary to establish a special procedure. You just mark the cutline and do the job freehandedly or with a miter gauge. When your project requires many parts, it's best to set up a mechanical means of establishing cut lengths. One of the easiest methods is shown in Fig. 6-11. Clamp a piece of wood to the tool's table so the distance from its bearing edge to the blade equals the length of needed parts. In this case, you are moving the work with a miter gauge. Cuts follow in sequence, with the work moved to abut the stop block for each of them.

Fig. 6-8. Working with a blade that is twisted away from the tool's arm allows crosscutting of long pieces. Here, the blade is twisted with an improvised platform that is then secured with a clamp.

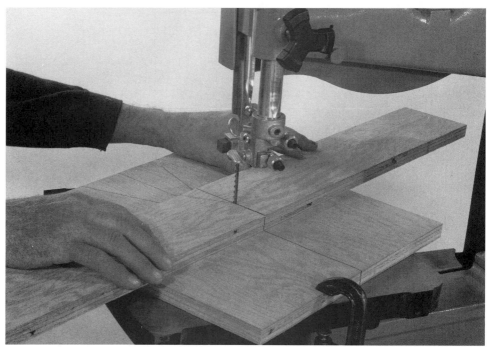

Fig. 6-9. A twisted blade allows an oblique-work feed direction to eliminate arm interference. It's not a cure-all since work width is still a limiting factor. The clamp must be back far enough so you can complete the cut.

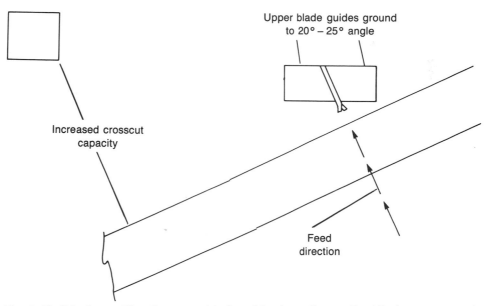

Increased crosscut capacity

Upper blade guides ground to 20° – 25° angle

Feed direction

Fig. 6-10. Grinding or filing the upper blade guides is another method that you can use to twist the blade. Guides are reversible so modifying them doesn't interfere with normal use. The guides on the Shopsmith band saw come preshaped for this application.

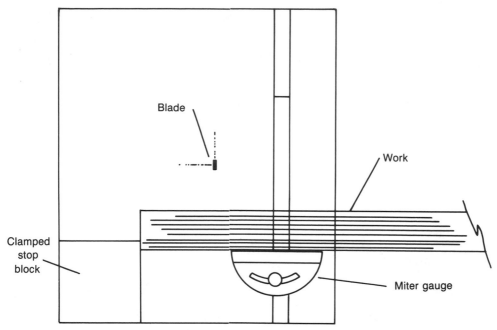

Blade

Work

Clamped
stop
block

Miter gauge

Fig. 6-11. It's always wise to use a mechanical means of judging the length of cutoffs when many similar ones are required. A stop block, clamped so the distance from its bearing edge to the saw blade equals the work length required, is a simple solution.

The procedure assumes that the cut length is within the blade-to-arm capacity of the machine. Consider that the cutoff is not the part that you need but is what you must remove from the base stock. For example, you need pieces 3½ feet long and are working with pieces 4 feet long. Establishing the position of the stop block so cuts will remove 6 inches of material will result in the component lengths you need.

You can use a fence that can be simply a straight piece of wood clamped to the table to gauge the length of cutoffs (Fig. 6-12). Never use this setup on a table saw because the work would bind between fence and blade and the blade's rotation would, among other things, cause kickback. It's feasible on a band saw since the blade moves vertically. Each part that you saw acts as a pusher to move the preceding piece out of the cut area.

You can accomplish a similar procedure without the use of a miter gauge if you use a suitable backing block (pusher) to move the work past the blade (Fig. 6-13). Return the backing block to a starting point after each cut so you can position the base material for the next sawing. It's important for the fence to be parallel to the side of the blade and for the two bearing edges of the backing block to relate in a 90-degree angle.

When a stop block is "stepped", you can use it as a gauge for cutoffs of various length (Fig. 6-14). Each step establishes a distance between its bearing edge and the saw blade.

RIPPING

Ripping, which is generally done with the grain—we say ''generally'' because some materials like particleboard and hardboard don't have a grain direction—is the operation that produces a part of a specific width. Like crosscutting, you can do it freehandedly, or you can establish cut control by working with a fence. Figure 6-15 displays an example of a ready-made fence. If one is not supplied with the tool, it probably will be available as an extra-cost accessory.

A guide that can serve very nicely for routine ripping operations can be simply a firm strip of wood with smooth, even edges, that you clamp to the table as in Fig. 6-16. A more sophisticated idea is the T-shaped project that is detailed in Fig. 6-17. It reduces mounting time since it needs clamping only at its free end and, if carefully made, will ensure parallelism between its bearing edge and the side of the saw blade. The only modification that might be required concerns the length of the arm. It can be longer or shorter depending on the size of the tool's table. Actually, if the arm is quite longer than the depth of the table, it will provide more support when ripping long pieces of stock.

Fig. 6-12. You also can use a fence, which in this case is just a straight strip of wood, to gauge the length of cutoffs. Working this way on a band saw is okay since the blade does not have the kickback potential of a circular saw. Note that a wood extension is secured to the miter gauge.

Fig. 6-13. It's also possible to saw pieces of similar length by using a backing block to move the work. Note the trick of using a large nail, driven at an angle into the backing block, as a handle. Move the block forward until the cutoff is past the blade.

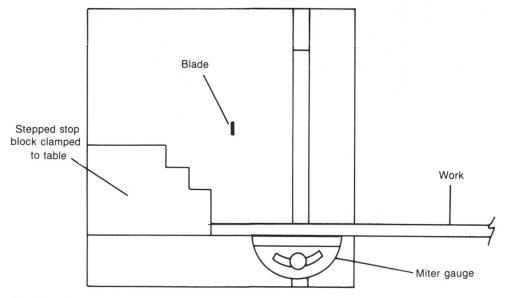

Fig. 6-14. You can use a stepped stop block to gauge cutoffs of different lengths. It can aid accuracy when a project requires multiple, similar pieces but in a variety of sizes.

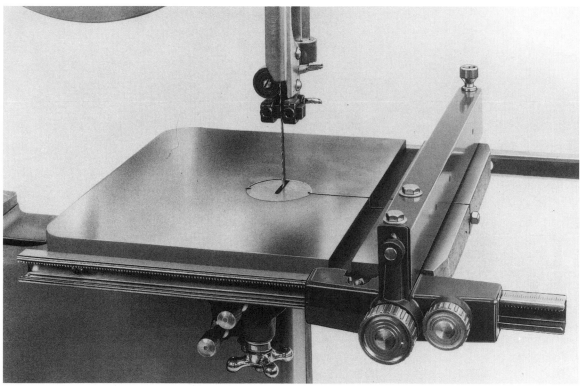

Fig. 6-15. You can equip most band saws with a rip fence. This sophisticated version is designed for Delta products. Like most concepts, you can situate the fence on either side of the saw blade.

Even more than when crosscutting, ripping against a fence demands a prime-condition blade. If you work with a very dull blade or one whose sharpness or tooth set favors one side, you will be frustrated when cutting and unhappy with the results.

Ripping is easier and results will be more uniform if you work with a wide blade (Fig. 6-18). Of course, the coarser the blade and the more pronounced its tooth set, the rougher the cut will be. If you work with a narrow, fine-tooth blade for the sake of cut smoothness, use a slower feed speed than you would when a heavy blade is mounted.

MAKE A KERF KEEPER

One of the problems that can occur when ripping, especially when the work is long, is the wood's tendency to pull together after the cut. When this pulling occurs, it can close the kerf and cause the blade to bind. A simple solution is to place a sliver of wood in the kerf to keep it open as cutting proceeds. A lifetime tool that is efficient for the purpose and will be on hand whenever you need it is shown mounted on a band-saw fence in Fig. 6-19. The accessory is designed so it is adjustable for various cut widths. As shown in Fig. 6-20, a C-clamp secures its distance from the blade; a wingnut holds the spacing between the keeper and the bearing side of the fence. Figure 6-21 offers construction details for the unit.

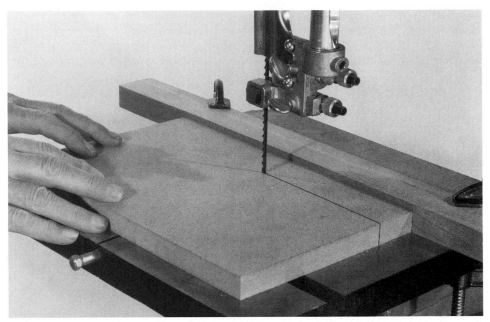

Fig. 6-16. A straight strip of wood will serve in good fashion for routine ripping operations. Guided rip cuts will be successful only if the blade is in prime condition and you don't force the cut.

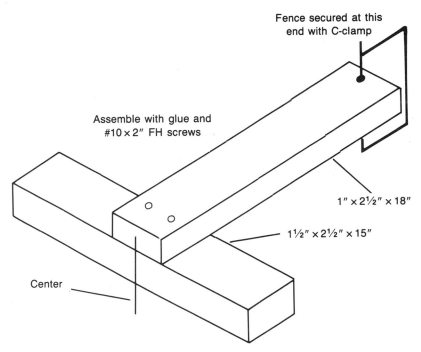

Fence secured at this end with C-clamp

Assemble with glue and #10 × 2″ FH screws

1″ × 2½″ × 18″

1½″ × 2½″ × 15″

Center

Fig. 6-17. T-shaped rip fence, that you can make, will serve nicely for any band saw. Hold it firmly against the front edge of the table as you secure the rear clamp.

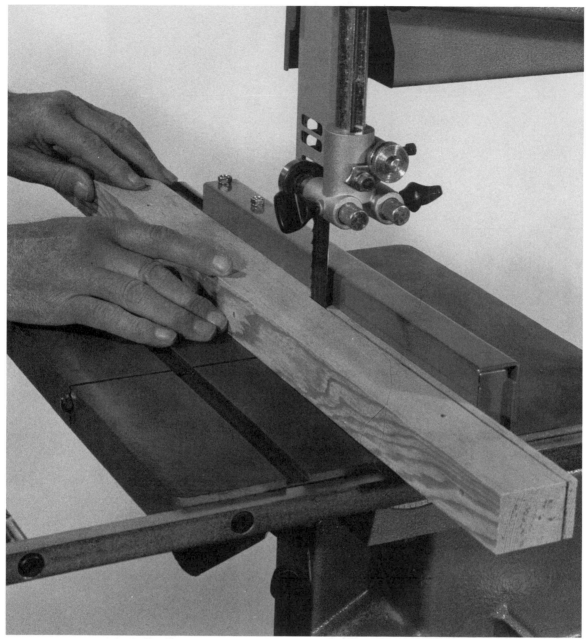

Fig. 6-18. Ripping, especially if the stock is tough and grainy, is easiest to do with a wide blade that has ample set. The penalty is a rough cut that requires sanding. You can use finer blades for smoother sawing, but a slow feed is necessary for acceptable results.

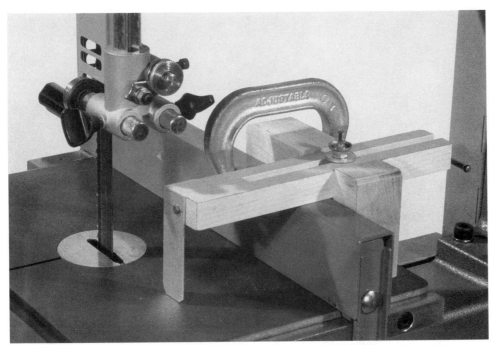

Fig. 6-19. Keeping the kerf open to avoid binding the blade when ripping will result in easier sawing and smoother cuts. This homemade accessory is designed for the purpose.

Fig. 6-20. The tool is adjustable for various cut widths and for distance from the blade.

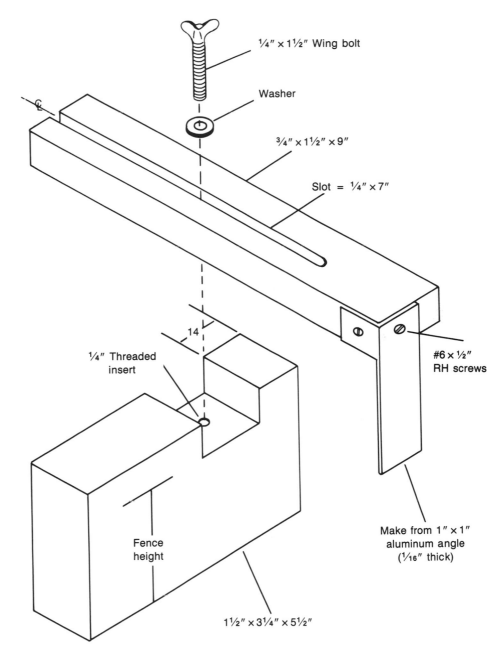

¼" × 1½" Wing bolt

Washer

¾" × 1½" × 9"

Slot = ¼" × 7"

14

¼" Threaded
insert

#6 × ½"
RH screws

Make from 1" × 1"
aluminum angle
(¹⁄₁₆" thick)

Fence
height

1½" × 3¼" × 5½"

Fig. 6-21. These construction details are for a kerf keeper. Round the front edge of the aluminum angle with a file and then smooth it with sandpaper.

Chapter 7

Resawing

RESAWING, WHICH IS USUALLY DONE PARALLEL TO THE GRAIN OF THE WOOD, IS ALSO straight sawing, but it differs from routine ripping since you cut with the stock resting on an edge (Fig. 7-1). The technique, which the band saw does better than any other sawing tool, is used most often to reduce the thickness of a board or to create thinner boards from a single piece of thicker material. That's why it's called "resawing"; the original material is sawed again. For example, you can change the thickness of a ¾-inch-thick board to ⅝ inch, or you can create two or more boards of equal or different thicknesses from a base material that is X-inches thick.

How wide a board you can resaw will depend on the depth-of-cut capacity of the machine. On the average, this capacity will be approximately 6 inches. Bench-top machines might limit the function to material that is about 4 inches wide, while others, like the Ryobi concepts, offer resaw capacities as high as 16 inches. Another factor is whether the manufacturer of a particular tool, like Delta, offers an accessory height attachment that you can use to double resaw capability.

TYPES OF SAW BLADES

Resawing is easier when the machine is fitted with a wide blade that has coarse teeth with significant set. The major reasons for the recommendation is that the kerf will provide ample room for the blade to move freely, the heavy teeth easily will remove waste to prevent clogging, and the blade's width will provide a stabilizing action so it will be easier to keep the blade cutting straight. Generally, the widest blade the machine can handle, (the average machine would range from ½ inch to ¾ inch with 4 or 5 teeth per inch) will provide respectable cutting action with minimum chance of clogging.

Clogging, or "jamming" as it's often named, is not a rare hindrance when resawing. Waste accumulates in the cutting area, and the kerf closes behind the blade so it's difficult to continue sawing or to backtrack. When, or if, you encounter the situation, switch off the machine and tap a sliver of wood into the kerf at a point away from the blade. With the sliver spreading the kerf, it might be possible to move the work to and fro enough to free the blade. If that doesn't work, hold the board at a point in front of the blade and jog it up and down as you pull it toward you. The use of a sliver to keep the kerf open is a good idea to accept as routine whenever you resaw any board, especially if the project material is a soft wood. It can often prevent the nuisance problem of clogging.

Fig. 7-1. Resawing is a band-saw technique that you use to reduce the thickness of stock or to produce several boards of equal or varying thickness from a single piece. The band saw ideally is suited for the procedure.

If your work schedule calls for an extended period of resawing, it will be wise to exchange the blade on the machine for a wide, skip-tooth design that has 3 or 4 teeth per inch. When there is a choice, use a blade with fewer teeth per inch for resawing soft woods.

All that has been said so far has to do with making resawing easier to accomplish, not with the smoothness of the sawed surfaces. The experienced band sawer will expect a degree of roughness and accepts that he will have to smooth the surfaces by passing them through a thickness planer or sander or by doing some work with belt and pad sanders. The beginner is not relieved from the additional chore.

Breaking from tradition is an option that is occasionally worth trying. In the case of resawing, and for the sake of smoothest cut results, you can try working with blades of width and tooth set that depart from conventional criteria—just so long as you are aware of possible negative endings. For example, if you work with a ¼-inch or ⅜-inch-wide blade that has slight tooth set, you will get smoother results, but there will be a distinct possibility that the blade, being flexible enough to be affected by internal grain lines, will bow in the cut. The result is kerf surfaces that are concave on one side and convex on the other.

It stands to reason that using blade widths that break with tradition will work better as the width of pieces being resawed diminishes. An idea to consider is shown in Fig. 7-2. First, you would kerf the stock to be resawed on a table saw so you re-

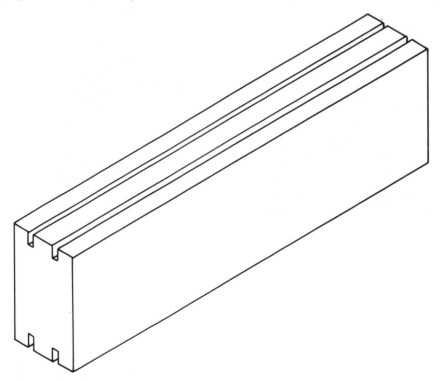

Fig. 7-2. Prekerfing, which you do on a table saw, reduces the amount of material the band-saw blade must saw through. It's an idea to use when a band saw is underpowered, and it aids accuracy since the kerfs provide a track for the blade to ride in.

duce considerably the amount of material the band-saw blade must work through. The prekerfing technique also can provide a solution for resawing maximum-width stock on a band saw that is underpowered for the job. Information from the Delta International people, who should know since they are band-saw experts from way back, reveals that resawing capacity for a band saw that is powered with a ⅓ hp motor is about 6 inches. If their 14-inch machine was equipped with the height attachment that makes it mechanically possible to resaw 12-inch-wide lumber, the ⅓ hp motor would not be adequate, unless the stock was prekerfed on each edge to a depth of 3 inches.

When the specifications for a band saw lists depth of cut as so many inches (resaw capacity), then we must assume that the motor supplied with the tool will offer adequate power.

GUIDES FOR RESAWING

You can do resawing freehandedly, especially if the cut is a short one, but most times it's best to employ a guide that helps to maintain the correct relationship between the blade and the work. A standard concept, called a pivot block, is demonstrated in Fig. 7-3 and detailed in Fig. 7-4. You clamp the guide to the table so its bearing

Fig. 7-3. A *pivot block* is a commonly used guide for resawing operations. It allows the operator to adjust work-feed direction when it is necessary because of blade lead. Clamp the guide so its bearing edge is in line with the saw blade.

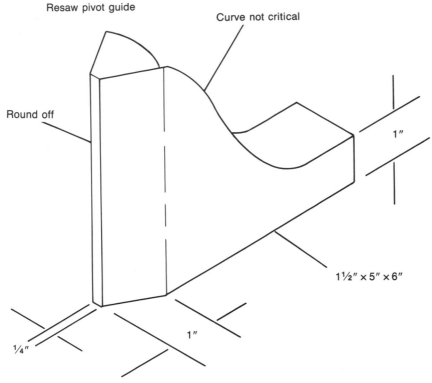

Resaw pivot guide

Curve not critical

Round off

1″

1½″ × 5″ × 6″

1″

¼″

Fig. 7-4. Typical design for a resaw pivot guide. You can modify its height and length to suit the depth of cut and the table size of the band saw.

edge is opposite the blade and at a distance that suits the cut thickness needed. Marking the cut line on the work is a good idea although experienced workers might find it unnecessary.

Use one hand on the back surface of the work to maintain contact with the guide while the other hand moves the work forward. The bearing edge of the guide is slight and rounded so that some feed-direction compensation is possible should the blade have a tendency to lead. Using a spring stick in the manner shown in Fig. 7-5 will allow the use of both hands to control the cut. Cut slowly until it's certain that the blade is on-line, then you can feed faster, but only to a point that the design of the blade allows. Forcing the cut is never a good idea. Keep a push stick handy and use it instead of fingers to complete the pass.

A point to remember for all resawing work is that the edge on which the work rides must be square to adjacent surfaces. If it isn't, the work will not bear against the guide as it should and you will have tapered cuts.

Another standard, but more sophisticated resawing guide, is shown in Figs. 7-6 and 7-7. The unit is actually a type of spring stick, but it incorporates a high fence that provides good work support. The fingers in the base of the accessory provide some flexibility so that a degree of compensation is possible should the blade have a slight lead. Many operators will have two of the special spring sticks so they can

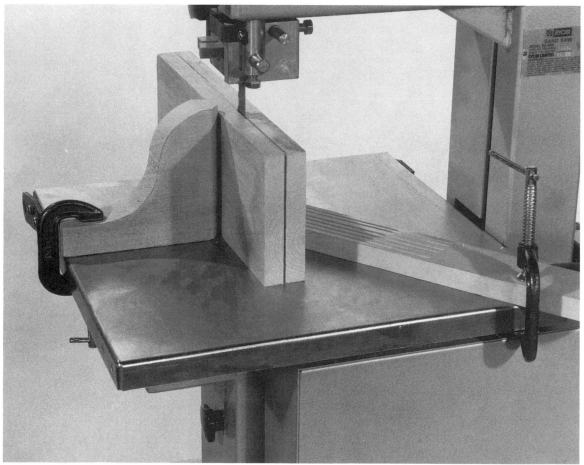

Fig. 7-5. You can use a spring stick to keep the work in contact with the guide as sawing progresses. This stick allows the operator to use both hands to control the cut. Use a pusher at the end of the cut so hands do not have to come close to the blade.

use one on each side of the work. Such a setup does much to ensure accuracy and will be especially helpful when you must resaw many similar pieces.

WORKING WITH A FENCE

It is not unusual for you to resaw by using the regular band-saw fence as a guide. Advantages are that the item is readily available and easy to position and secure for the job. A disadvantage is that the conventional fence is not high enough to provide the work support you might like to have. Compensation for this negative factor can be easy; just attach a wood facing to the fence to increase its height (Figs. 7-8 and 7-9). Another way to go is to make a special resaw fence like the example in Figs. 7-10 and 7-11.

A problem that you can encounter with a long fence, since the work must bear against its full length, is that it is not possible to make minor feed-direction adjustments

Fig. 7-6. A special type of spring-stick guide includes a tall fence that offers good work support. The slots in the base of the accessory allow enough flexibility so you can adjust feed direction for a slight blade lead.

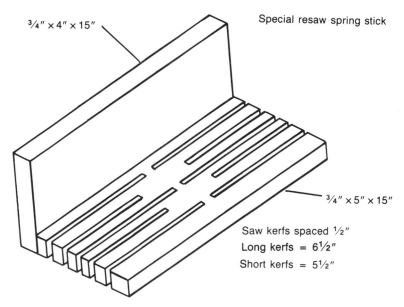

¾″ × 4″ × 15″

Special resaw spring stick

¾″ × 5″ × 15″

Saw kerfs spaced ½″
Long kerfs = 6½″
Short kerfs = 5½″

Fig. 7-7. These details are for a special resaw spring stick. Many operators make two of them so they can use one on each side of the work. It's a good way to go for production runs. The fingers will supply more spring action if the base is made of soft wood.

Fig. 7-8. A conventional rip fence is an acceptable resaw guide if the blade is in good condition. Attaching a wooden facing to the fence provides additional work support.

should the blade have a tendency to lead. It will be very helpful if you prekerf the work, but the ultimate solution is to be sure the blade is in good condition, sharp, and with uniform set.

RESAWING FOR DUPLICATES

Taking advantage of the resawing technique is a great way to go when you need many similar pieces. The base stock is preshaped and then sawed, each saw cut

Fig. 7-9. The Shopsmith miter gauge, when faced with an extension, also serves as a fence for the band-saw unit. The function is possible because the tool's table has two intersecting slots that are perpendicular to each other.

producing an identical part (Fig. 7-12). Now is the time to break the wide-blade resaw rule and use a fairly narrow blade with minimum set so sawed surfaces will be as smooth as possible and the slight kerf, one that results in very little waste, will allow you to produce a greater number of pieces (Fig. 7-13). A light, smooth-cutting blade also makes sense when resawing to produce quantities of, say, dentil-type molding (Fig. 7-14). A heavy blade with coarse teeth would raise havoc with the precut kerfs in the parent material.

Fig. 7-10. You can make a resaw fence that is exactly right for the tool you own. Be sure that its bottom edge and adjacent surfaces are square to each other.

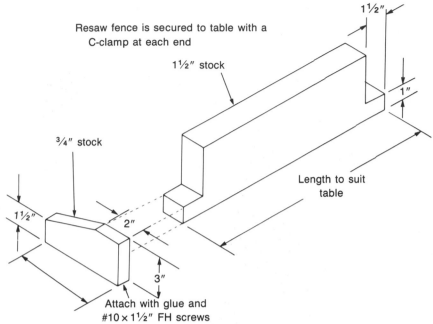

Resaw fence is secured to table with a
C-clamp at each end

1½" stock

3/4" stock

1½"

1½"

2"

3"

1"

Length to suit
table

Attach with glue and
#10 × 1½" FH screws

Fig. 7-11. These construction details are for a resaw fence. Homemade accessories of this nature are lifetime tools, so use a good hardwood for the project. Maple and birch are suitable selections.

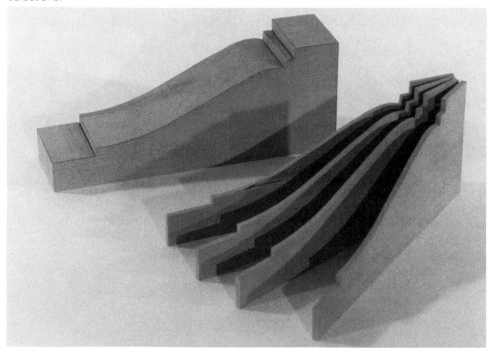

Fig. 7-12. You can resaw a block of wood that is shaped in a particular pattern to produce X-number of identical parts.

Fig. 7-13. Resawing the preshaped stock is one time when you can think about breaking the wide-blade rule. A narrow blade with minimum set results in smoother surfaces and less waste. You get more from the parent material because of the blade's narrow kerf.

Fig. 7-14. A slight blade with minimum set does a good job when resawing project material like dentil molding. A smooth-cutting blade plus a slow feed will not cause the excessive splintering and feathering around the kerf cuts like a coarse blade would.

Chapter 8

Angular Sawing

THREE BASIC ANGULAR CUTS WILL BE DISCUSSED IN THIS CHAPTER. THE *SIMPLE MITER* is cut across the width of the stock but at an angle other than 90 degrees; the *cross miter* also is cut across the stock width, but at an angle through its thickness; and *bevels* are cuts that are slanted through the stock's thickness, but parallel with the grain. The bevel, to identify its character, often is called a "rip bevel" or "rip miter." Some saw cuts combine a miter and a bevel; these are *compound-angle* cuts that will be discussed in chapter 9.

The term *miter* is a general one. It is derived from the words miter joint, which is the connection where you join miter-cut or bevel-cut components. The design of the project determines whether you do angular cutting across the stock or through its length. When the project is flat, for example a plain picture frame or a segmented assembly that is prepared for a particular use (Fig. 8-1), you can accomplish the sawing by moving the work with a miter gauge. You often would do cutting of this nature to provide base stock for circular and elliptical forms (Fig. 8-2).

When the project is deep, like the cylindrical shape shown in Fig. 8-3, then you saw with the tool's table tilted or, in the case of the Sears/Craftsman electronic machine with the blade tilted, and move the work along a fence.

ACCURACY IS CRUCIAL

Angular sawing is one of the more demanding woodworking chores. Miters and bevels usually are cut to prepare stock for joining. If two pieces must form a 90-degree corner when you assemble them, it's evident that there is no room for error in the angle of the cuts. Even if the error is minimal, just a fraction of a degree, if you multiply it eight times, which would be the case when making a square or rectangular frame, you can judge how frustrating the total error could be.

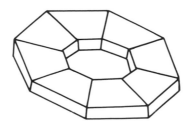

Fig. 8-1. Cut segments for polygons, when the work is flat, with a miter gauge. To determine the correct cut angle, divide 360 degrees by the number of segments, and then divide the result by two.

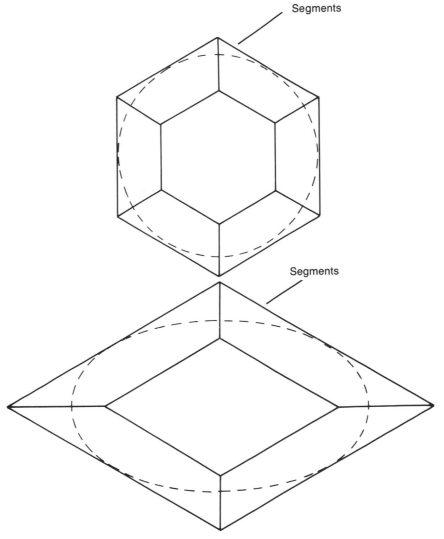

Segments

Segments

Fig. 8-2. Segments often are cut and assembled to provide base stock for circular and elliptical forms or when you need a particular interior shape. The dotted lines indicate the cut lines.

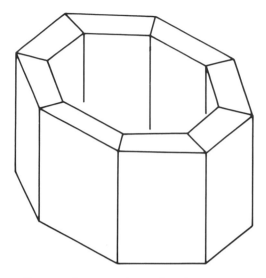

If segments are used on edge, they are cut
with tilted table or tilted blade

Fig. 8-3. Handle long, beveled segments for deep or wide projects like rip cuts but tilt the table or the blade to the necessary angle.

The answer to satisfactory work is not a secret; it is just a matter of being per-snickety when making miter-gauge settings or table settings and of making test cuts before cutting project components. Another factor for satisfactory work has to do with the band saw. Working with a blade in prime condition is critical. It's wise to use a blade with minimum set when sawing for joints since it will provide smoothest results. Even so, the sawed edges might not be ideal for assembly because of the washboarding characteristic of band-saw blades. When necessary, it's good practice to cut pieces a bit oversize so that some further attention, by hand with sandpaper wrapped around a block of wood or on a belt or disc sander, will bring the part to an acceptable condition.

This extra work isn't always necessary; much depends on the project. For example, a planter box, especially if it is to have a rustic appearance, doesn't require the attention a cabinet made of fancy hardwoods deserves.

Remember that when you do angular sawing for joinery, the cut angle is always one-half of the joint angle (Fig. 8-4).

MAKING CUTS

Since angular cuts that are required for joints must be precise, there is little point in thinking about doing them freehand. A partnership with a mechanical device is in order. When sawing simple miters, those needed for flat-frame structures, the helper is a miter gauge (Fig. 8-5). Pivot and lock the head of the accessory at the angle

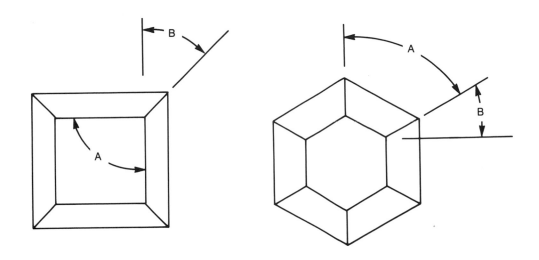

Polygon identification

# Sides	Name
3	Triangle
4	Square
5	Pentagon
6	Hexagon
7	Heptagon
8	Octagon
9	Monagon
10	Decagon
11	Undecagon
12	Dodecagon

Fig. 8-4. The cut angle for segments or for any mitered joint is always one-half of the joint angle.

required. Then, as in crosscutting, the work is held firmly in position against the gauge as you make the cut. It's good practice to mark the cutting line on the work with a protractor so you can judge accuracy as you make the cut. Move the work slowly, especially near the end of the cut to minimize the feathering that can occur when the blade breaks through.

When cut lengths are similar and the workpiece is flat, you can make subsequent cuts by flipping the stock for each one. Use the first piece as a pattern to mark the cutting line for the following one.

Work that you must cross-miter also is moved with a miter gauge. In this case, the head of the gauge is in zero position, but the tool's table is tilted to provide the required angle (Fig. 8-6). Here too, flipping the stock for each cut and using the first piece as a pattern allows consecutive cutting. Another way to gauge lengths when cuts are similar and cut length permits is to clamp a stop block to the table. After the first cut, you turn the stock over and abut it against the stop block to position it for the following cut.

If you can tilt the blade instead of the table of the machine, which is possible with the Sears/Craftsman concept, then you can make the pass with the workpiece resting on a horizontal table (Fig. 8-7). Working this way can provide convenience and aid accuracy since the operator doesn't have to worry, while cutting, about a workpiece's tendency to slide off a tilted table.

BEVELING

Bevel cutting also requires a tilted table but a fence guides the work. A fence guide can be a standard accessory or a homemade one like the T-model shown in Fig. 8-8. Whenever possible, and this relates to the width of the workpiece, position the

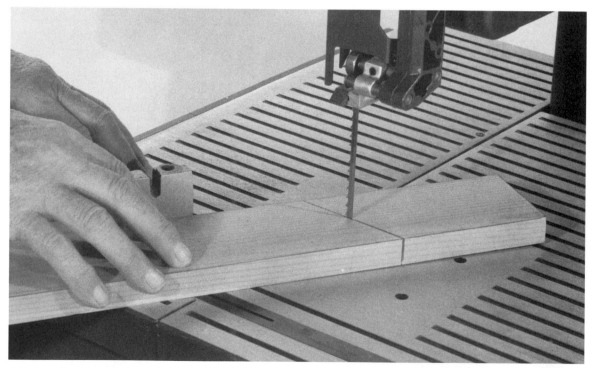

Fig. 8-5. Cut simple miters after you pivot the head of the miter gauge to the angle that is required. Keep the work firm against the gauge throughout the pass. Marking the cut line with a protractor will provide an ongoing accuracy check.

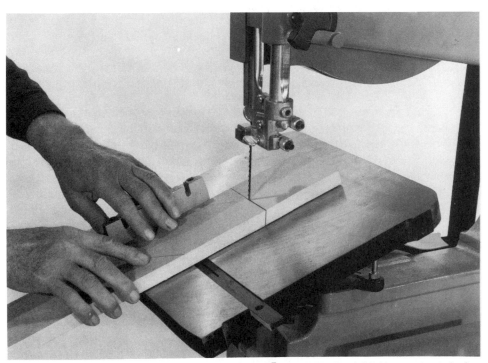

Fig. 8-6. Cross miters are done like crosscuts, but with the table tilted. Making test cuts before sawing project material is good practice.

Fig. 8-7. Being able to tilt the blade on a machine makes jobs like cross mitering more convenient to do. I point out again that illustrations with blade guards set too high are for photo clarity only!

fence on the "down" side of the table. This setup provides good support for the work so your primary concern is feeding the stock smoothly. It's often necessary, on wide work, to place the fence on the high side of the table. This position increases the attention you must apply to the procedure since, in addition to feeding the stock, you must be sure that it stays flat on the table and against the fence throughout the pass.

Figure 8-9 shows another type of homemade fence that you can use for beveling or, for that matter, simple ripping. The advantage of the U-shaped design is that its arms allow you to situate the fence farther away from the blade than is possible with a fence that you must mount on a table. This design allows you to use the more convenient "down" side of the table for wide stock. The U-shaped fence, as detailed in Fig. 8-10, is a simple project that you can secure to the machine's table with a few C-clamps.

Fig. 8-8. Perform bevel cutting as you would ripping, but angle the table as needed. Whenever possible, work with the fence, in this case the homemade T-design, on the "down" side of the table. This position guards against the work sliding away from the blade.

Fig. 8-9. A U-shaped fence, that you can make, is usable for routine ripping as well as bevel sawing.

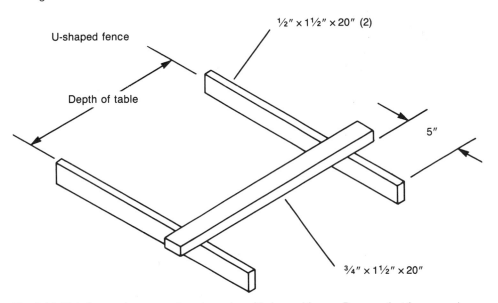

U-shaped fence

Depth of table

½″ × 1½″ × 20″ (2)

5″

¾″ × 1½″ × 20″

Fig. 8-10. This figure shows you how to make a U-shaped fence. Be sure that fence and arms are square to each other.

When the machine has a pivoting head so you can tilt the blade instead of the table, you minimize the problems that might be caused by work slippage (Fig. 8-11).

CHAMFERS

Chamfers are bevel cuts that remove only part of the work's edge. Tilt the table, or blade, to the angle required and move the work, which is guided by a fence, smoothly past the blade (Figs. 8-12 and 8-13). Whenever possible, do the cutting with a surface of the work on the table. When work width is more than the maximum distance you can situate the fence from the blade, it's okay to make the pass with the stock on edge. This position requires a little more attention to keep the work from rocking during the pass.

A V-BLOCK FOR MITERS OR BEVELS

The V-block shown mounted on the machine in Fig. 8-14, allows cutting bevels and cross miters while the tool table remains in normal position. In order for the jig to be accurate, you must assemble it so the blade will cut on the center of the "V".

Fig. 8-11. Here you see bevel cutting on a band saw that is designed for tilting the blade rather than the table. Since the work can't slide as it might on a tilted table, it's practical to use the fence on the left side of the blade.

Fig. 8-12. A *chamfer* is a bevel cut that removes only part of the work's edge. Follow the same cutting procedure that you would use for a full bevel.

Fig. 8-13. This figure shows cutting chamfers on tilting-head band saw. You can chamfer four edges without changing the setup. Make the final two cuts after you reverse the position of the stock. The procedure applies to any band saw.

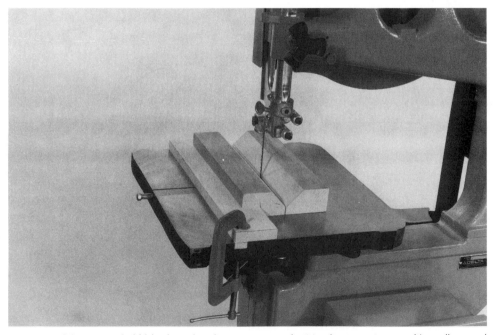

Fig. 8-14. A homemade V-block makes it more convenient to do many types of beveling and cross-mitering chores. Work will be accurate only if you are careful with construction. The blade must be on the center of the ''V.''

Position workpieces in the V-cut and then move them past the blade (Fig. 8-15). The jig is also useful for jobs like preparing stock for glue blocks. A square workpiece, after being halved in the jig, then is cut into individual pieces that will have a triangular cross section.

On the same order, you can accurately mark squares or even rounds that you are preparing to turn in a lathe for the lathe's centers. The idea is to move the work into the blade to make a cut only about 1/8 inch deep, then turn the work to make

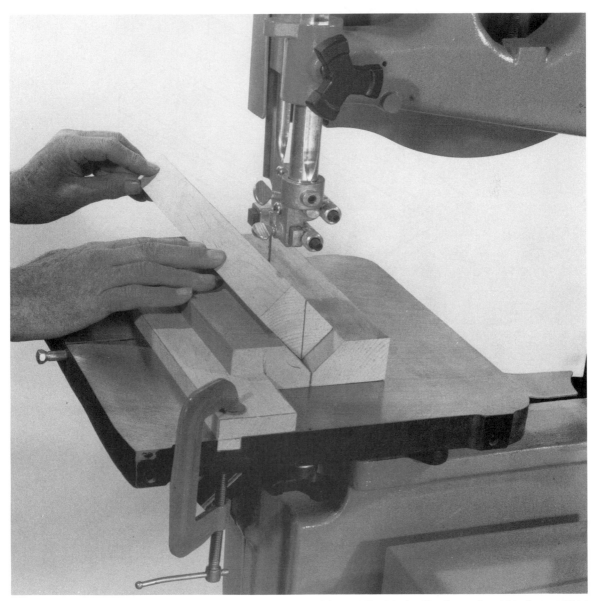

Fig. 8-15. Hold the work firmly in the V and move it smoothly past the blade. Cautions about blade condition also apply on operations like this.

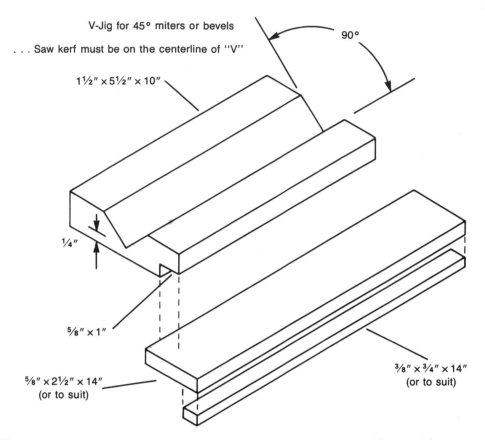

V-Jig for 45° miters or bevels

... Saw kerf must be on the centerline of "V"

90°

1½" × 5½" × 10"

¼"

⅝" × 1"

⅝" × 2½" × 14"
(or to suit)

⅜" × ¾" × 14"
(or to suit)

Fig. 8-16. Here you see how to make the V-block jig. You can form the V on a table saw or by making chamfer cuts on mating pieces that you then assemble edge to edge.

a second, similar cut. The center of the work will be where the two diagonal cuts intersect. The kerfs provide a means of easy entry for the lathe's spur center.

Construction details for a jig of this nature are offered in Fig. 8-16.

BEVELING ROUNDS

Circular components that must be cone shaped are cut freehand with the table tilted to the necessary angle (Fig. 8-17). Lathe enthusiasts find the procedure an especially useful band-saw feature since preparing stock this way before mounting it in the lathe reduces considerably the material that would otherwise have to be cut away with lathe chisels. The chore requires careful work handling for safety as well as accuracy. Work with an oversize block so the cut can be continuous and there will be enough excess material to keep hands away from the blade. Guard against work slippage— keep the guard where it should be!

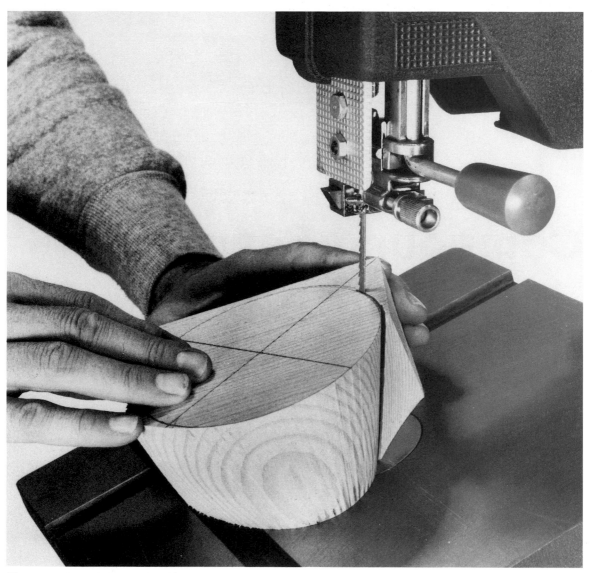

Fig. 8-17. You also can do beveling on rounds. Handle the work carefully to keep it from slipping away from the cut line. Start with oversize stock so there will be ample waste material for hands to hold on to and so you can cut in a continuous pass.

Chapter 9

Compound Sawing

THE TERM *COMPOUND SAWING* COVERS TWO ESSENTIAL SAWING ACTIVITIES. ONE OF THE sawing activities involves combining straight cuts—a miter cut and a bevel cut—for the type of joint shown in Fig. 9-1, which is required on projects that have sloping sides. Picture frames that slope toward or away from the wall, boxes with inclining sides, truncated pyramid shapes, peaked figures, require compound-angle joints.

The second area of compound sawing has to do with curve cutting on adjacent sides of the base stock. The technique is a band saw exclusive that makes possible the production of furniture components like the cabriole leg (Fig. 9-2). The cabriole leg is established as the standard form to demonstrate compound-curve sawing since it blankets the entire procedure, but you will recognize that you can use cuts of this type for many other woodworking chores.

COMPOUND-ANGLE JOINTS

A simple miter requires a miter-gauge setting, while you can accomplish a cross miter or bevel with a tilted table. The compound-angle cut calls for you to use both settings simultaneously, each at a specific angle (Fig. 9-3). If simple miters and bevels, as emphasized in chapter 8, require precise settings and super careful work handling, you can accept that such attention is even more crucial for compound cuts.

This kind of work usually is considered a job for a table saw, where there is better control over cut smoothness, and you saw with a rigid blade as opposed to a flexible one. However, results can be successful if you work carefully to avoid possible hazards.

It's a good idea to view projects that require compound-angle joints as box-type structures that might have four or more sides, each side with the same degree of tilt. To produce uniform tilt and to ensure that joints will mate as they should, you must use specific miter and bevel angles. Table 9-1 supplies the correct settings for projects with various numbers of sides and different slope angles. If words alone aren't convincing enough for the need of accurate sawing, the table should convince you. Notice that for the miter or bevel, or for both, the setting required is to a fraction of a degree.

Because of the size or shape of the workpiece, sometimes it is impractical to work with a miter gauge. It's possible then to mark the shape of the part on the wood and to work freehandedly. The tilt of the table will supply the bevel angle while hands, instead of a miter gauge, will guide for the miter cut.

A similar situation occurs when project components are overly long. The solution is to use a tapering jig to move the stock (Fig. 9-4). The sawing of simple tapers is another phase of band-saw work, but chapter 10 will cover it.

COMPOUND-CURVE SAWING

Compound-curve sawing is a technique that allows you to produce similar or dissimilar profiles on adjacent sides of the stock. While the shape of a cabriole leg provides an excellent way to demonstrate the technique of sawing, you should not overlook the procedure for the production of ornamental forms that you might use as finials on posts or for preshaping blocks to prepare them for turning in a lathe.

The first step in the production of a cabriole leg is to ensure that the base stock is square. If adjacent sides form an angle of more or less than 90 degrees, the band-saw cuts will not be true. Next, using a carefully made cardboard pattern, mark the profile of the project on adjacent sides of the wood as shown in Fig. 9-5.

Fig. 9-1. The compound angle joint, which is accomplished by cutting a bevel and a miter simultaneously, is required for projects that have sloping sides.

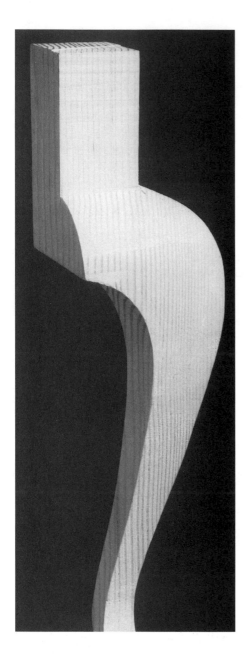

Fig. 9-2. The cabriole leg is a typical project that you can produce by compound-curve sawing. The band saw is the only woodworking tool that allows the technique.

Sawing starts by following the profile on one side of the stock (Fig. 9-6). Make the short cut first, and then backtrack out of it so you can complete the cut by starting a new cut from the opposite end. Plan sawing so there will be a minimum number of waste pieces since you will have to return them to original positions to prepare the wood for the second step.

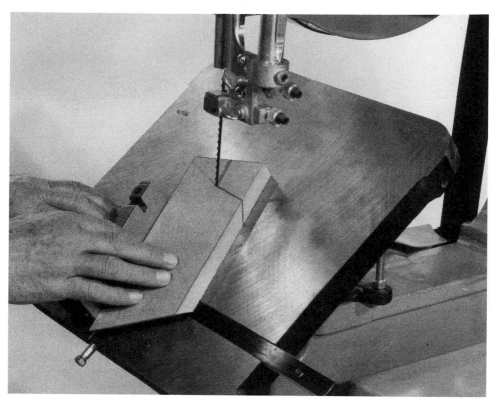

Fig. 9-3. Compound-angle cuts require a miter-gauge setting and a table tilt. Exercise great care when making the setting and feeding the stock. Test cuts are in order to prove the adjustments before cutting good stock.

Table 9-1. Degree Settings Required for Compound Miter Cuts (for Projects with Sloping Sides).

SLOPE ANGLE	4 SIDES		6 SIDES		8 SIDES	
	Bevel	Miter	Bevel	Miter	Bevel	Miter
10°	44¼	80¼	29½	84½	22	86
20°	41¾	71¼	28¼	79	21	82
30°	37¾	63½	26	74	19½	78¼
40°	32½	57¼	22¾	69¾	17	75
50°	27	52½	19	66¼	14½	72½
60°	21	49	14½	63½	11	70¼

The second step is to saw the profile on the adjacent side of the stock, but you can do this only after you have returned waste pieces so the wood resembles its original, solid shape. This assembly is necessary so the block will have a firm base to rest on for final sawing and so you can restore pattern markings (Fig. 9-7). Reattach waste pieces by tack nailing or by using a sufficient amount of tape. If you use nails, be sure to place them so they won't be on a cut line or in a position that will mar the leg. After the second sawing phase, all waste pieces fall away to reveal the shape of the leg (Fig. 9-8). You are something like the sculptor who envisions the form that the block of marble contains.

Fig. 9-4. Cut compound angles on long stock by working with a taper jig. How to make and use a taper jig will be explained in chapter 10.

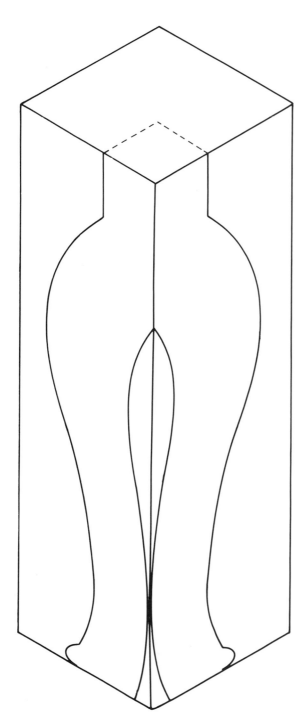

Fig. 9-5. The first step in the production of a cabriole leg is to mark the pattern on adjacent sides of the stock. A cardboard pattern is okay, but if you plan extensive use, it's best to make it from a material like hardboard.

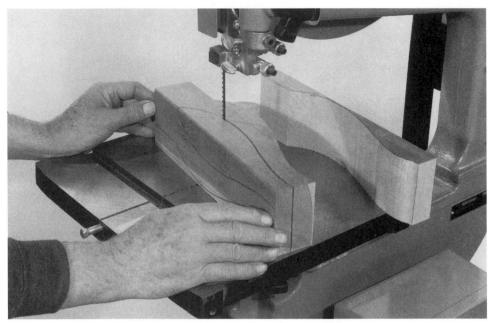

Fig. 9-6. The first step in sawing is to follow the pattern on one side of the stock. Make any necessary short cuts first. Work so that you will remove waste in full pieces.

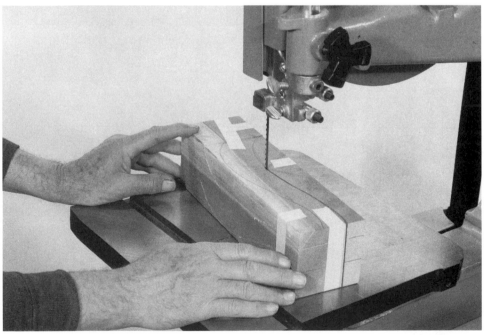

Fig. 9-7. You can accomplish the second sawing step after you return the waste pieces to their original positions by taping or tack nailing. This procedure provides a solid base for the project to ride on and restores any part of the pattern that you might have removed during the first cuts.

The form that emerges after band sawing is not always the finished product. For one thing, even if you plan to use the sawed unit as it is, you must sand all of its planes. Usually, you can accomplish this sanding by working with hand-held sandpaper and with drum sanders that are chucked in a portable electric drill or in a drill press.

Fig. 9-8. When sawing is complete, waste pieces fall away to reveal the shape that was concealed in the wood. What further use might you have for the discards?

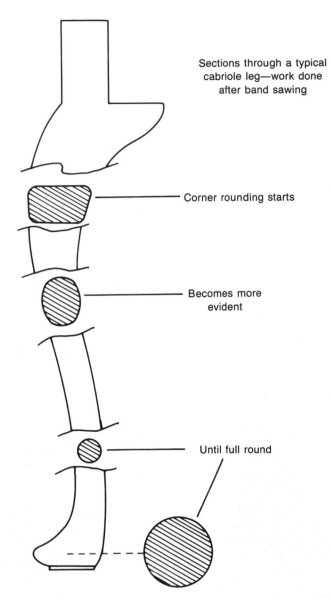

Sections through a typical
cabriole leg—work done
after band sawing

Corner rounding starts

Becomes more
evident

Until full round

Fig. 9-9. Cabriole legs usually get further treatment after band sawing. The cross sections shown here are typical of the additional attention. In a small shop, you can do the work with sandpaper and tools like rasps and spokeshaves.

You can add further embellishments, like the details in Fig. 9-9, to achieve the project's final appearance. In a professional shop, where any number of similar components must be produced, the added touches usually are accomplished by special setups and procedures on a stationary shaper. The experienced turner can do the job on a lathe. In a small shop with limited equipment, you can accomplish perfectly acceptable results by working with sandpaper, rasps, spokeshaves, and so on.

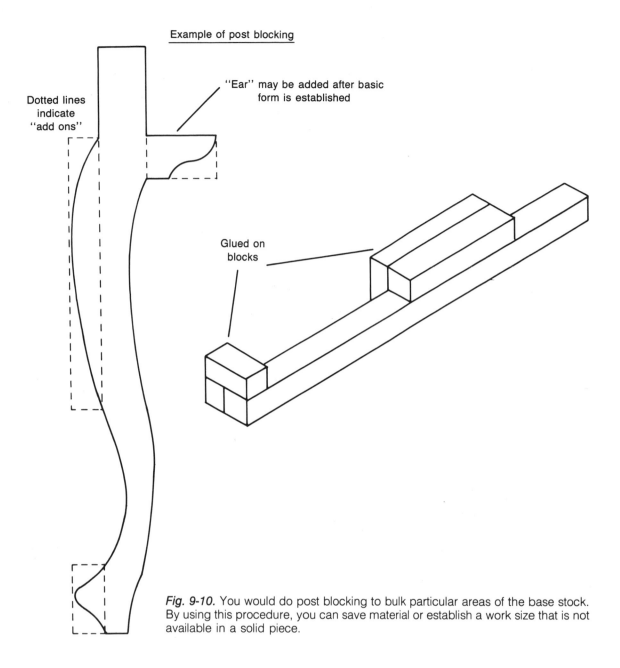

Example of post blocking

"Ear" may be added after basic form is established

Dotted lines indicate "add ons"

Glued on blocks

Fig. 9-10. You would do post blocking to bulk particular areas of the base stock. By using this procedure, you can save material or establish a work size that is not available in a solid piece.

A method called *post blocking* often is used when preparing base stock since it isn't always possible to obtain a piece of wood that is large enough for the full shape of various cabriole-leg designs and styles. This method requires you to add blocks, where needed, to the starting block (Fig. 9-10). Projections, *ears* as they are called, often are added to each side of the leg. You can add the extra pieces initially and cut them along with the leg shape, or you can glue them on later after you have cut them individually to correct profile. Then you can treat them to conform with the general appearance of the leg.

In any event, you should carefully select added parts to match the color and grain of the main part. A post-blocked project should appear as if it was cut from a solid block; careful craftsmanship will achieve that goal.

Except for its general motif, there is no prescribed shape or size for the cabriole leg, not unless you are duplicating an existing piece of furniture. Legs can be short and shaped like the example shown in Fig. 9-11. This design often is seen on low chests and cabinets. Profiles also can be fairly basic on leg lengths that are okay for tables (Fig. 9-12). The long one is suitable for dining tables while the shorter ones are suitable for coffee and end tables.

It's often the case that the cabriole shape is confined to the lower portion of a furniture component that serves as both *stile* (vertical-frame piece) and leg (Fig. 9-13). In such cases, you should use post blocking so you will need a minimum amount of material for the part. It's also a good idea for you to cut the stem of the piece to size and sand it smooth before you do post blocking.

FLARED LEGS

Compound sawing is the band-saw technique that you use to produce furniture legs that have curved profiles or that flare in the foot area in one or two directions (Fig. 9-14). When curves are compound, the sawing procedure to follow duplicates the steps for the cabriole leg. You saw on one side of the stock and again on the adjacent side after you have returned the waste pieces.

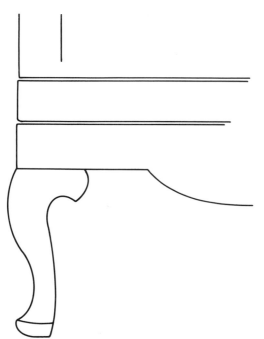

Fig. 9-11. Short cabriole legs often are used on chests and similar furniture. You can be original with the design while still maintaining the basic motif.

Example of cabriole legs

Pattern is used on two adjacent sides of the stock

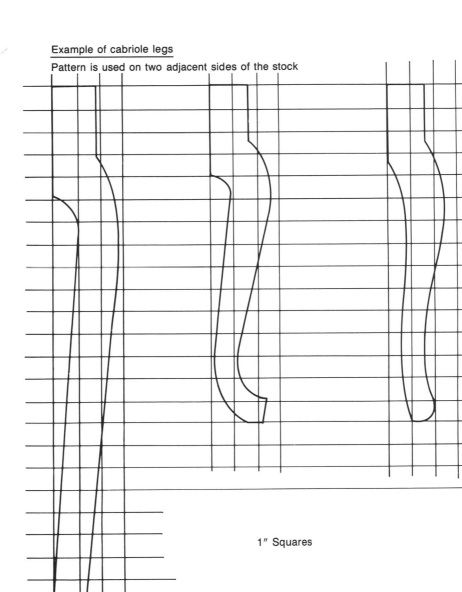

1″ Squares

Fig. 9-12. Here are some examples of cabriole legs. The long one is suitable for a dining table and the short ones are for coffee or end tables.

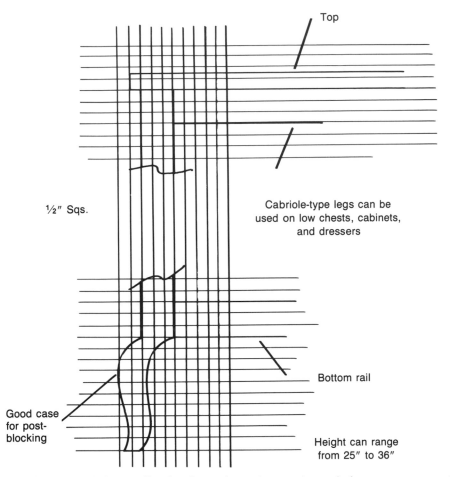

Top

½″ Sqs.

Cabriole-type legs can be used on low chests, cabinets, and dressers

Good case for post-blocking

Bottom rail

Height can range from 25″ to 36″

Fig. 9-13. The cabriole-leg profile often is used as a foot on the end of corner components. Here is a typical situation where you should consider post blocking.

If the leg flares in only one direction in the foot area, then you need only to saw on one side. Legs of this style are often straight and square, with the flare confined to the foot area. In such cases, you should use the post-blocking idea to block the area that you will saw. This technique will save material, and you can saw and sand the main part of the leg before you glue on the extra blocks. You must choose the added pieces very carefully for color and grain so that when you complete the job, it will look like you cut the leg from a solid block of wood.

PRESHAPING STOCK FOR TURNING

Most turning blocks that you mount in a lathe without prior attention require a considerable amount of work with lathe chisels before they even begin to approach the final profile. Taking advantage of the band saw's compound-sawing feature can reduce that phase of turning to a minimum. Sawing proceeds in standard fashion after you mark the material as it would for a cabriole leg (Fig. 9-15).

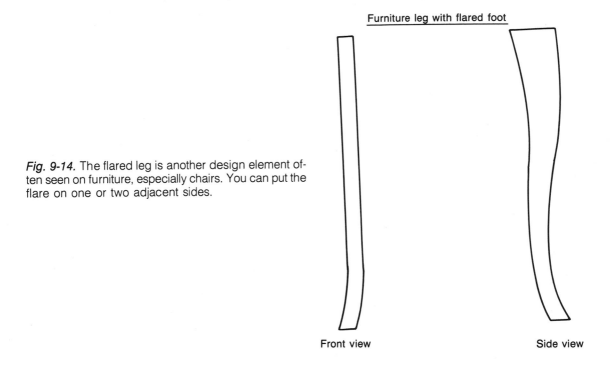

Furniture leg with flared foot

Fig. 9-14. The flared leg is another design element often seen on furniture, especially chairs. You can put the flare on one or two adjacent sides.

Front view

Side view

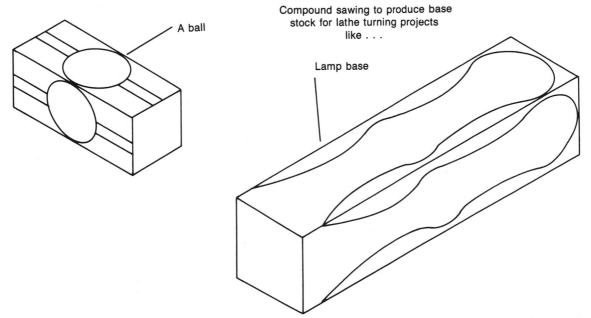

A ball

Compound sawing to produce base stock for lathe turning projects like . . .

Lamp base

Fig. 9-15. Craftsmen who enjoy lathe work will find that the band saw is an ideal tool for reducing stock to rough form before they mount it between centers.

Turning a ball shape is certainly a case in point. All that will remain of the turning block after you have sawed it are projections for the lathe centers and the bulked-center area for shaping the ball.

FUN WITH COMPOUND SAWING

Compound sawing can result in arbitrarily sculptured forms like the example shown in Fig. 9-16. You might not be impressed with results the first time you try the idea, but if you experiment a bit with scrap wood, you will be in a better position to judge the shape that will emerge from the procedure. You can display projects of this nature, after you sand them smooth and finish them, as a type of woodworking art, or they can serve more practically as, say, lamp bases. Sawing is done freehand; no patterns are used.

The first step, after selecting a suitable block of wood, is to saw an arbitrary curve through its length. Repeat the procedure on an adjacent side after you tape the sawed pieces together. Again, the curve is freehand, following any line that suits your fancy. The two saw cuts will result in four pieces of wood (Fig. 9-17) that you assemble in the special way that is demonstrated in Fig. 9-18. After you locate or relocate the parts, as shown, you glue them together to form a single, unique shape.

Designing your own unique shape is a "fun" phase of band-saw operations that will have interesting results. The single example that was shown in Fig. 9-16 doesn't begin to show the intriguing shapes that are possible.

Fig. 9-16. This simple example shows you what results when you pursue the fun-with-compound-sawing idea. The project can have contours that are more complex.

Fig, 9-17. The initial, arbitrary curve cutting on adjacent sides of the stock will produce four pieces with different profiles.

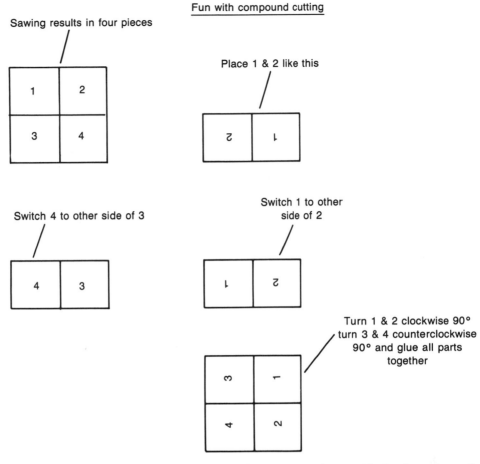

Fun with compound cutting

Sawing results in four pieces

Place 1 & 2 like this

Switch 4 to other side of 3

Switch 1 to other side of 2

Turn 1 & 2 clockwise 90° turn 3 & 4 counterclockwise 90° and glue all parts together

Fig. 9-18. To achieve the final result, you must arrange and assemble the four pieces like this figure shows. The drawing shows a view from the end of the parts.

Chapter 10

Special Applications

WHEN YOU CONSIDER THAT ANY RUDIMENTARY OPERATION ON ANY POWER TOOL IS EXtraordinary if you only think of it in terms of savings in time and effort, why should a special chapter be devoted to special applications? Times exist when substituting a mechanical means of controlling the cutting can make it easier to work accurately, and other times an innovative jig will allow faster production of duplicate pieces. Also, several particular band-saw functions don't fit into day-to-day woodworking. You might never want to spiral a dowel or shape fence pickets or do a particular kind of bevel sawing that lets you create, for example, a deep bowl from a flat board. The ideas, however, will be on hand should you need them. Often, being exposed to tool-wise thinking leads to original thoughts that solve unique problems.

JIGS FOR CIRCULAR WORK

Cutting circular components on a band saw is a common procedure that requires no particular finesse other than careful sawing so that you will have to do only minimum sanding to smooth the perimeter. Still, you can work more accurately and be better equipped for producing multiple, similar pieces if you work with a pivot jig like the one shown in Fig. 10-1. You must impale workpieces on the pivot point and rotate them in a clockwise direction (Fig. 10-2).

You should consider several important factors in order to get true circles and to saw smoothly. The line between the pivot point and the saw blade must be perpendicular, and the pivot must be on-line with the cutting points of the blade's teeth. You will know quickly if you do not adhere to these basic requirements. If, as described in Fig. 10-3, the pivot point is aft of the teeth, the blade will tend to lead to the outside of the circle. The blade will try to cut inside the circle if the pivot is forward of the ideal location.

Fig. 10-1. A pivot jig provides a central point on which you can impale work and then rotate it to provide perfect circular components. The distance from the pivot point to the blade is adjustable so you can cut discs of various diameters.

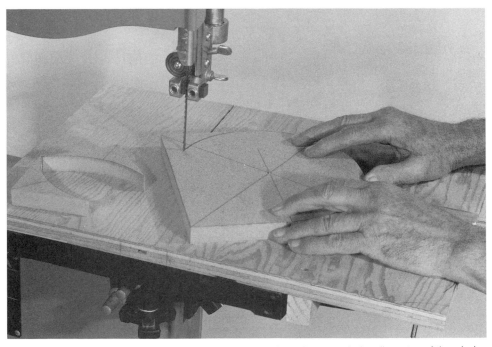

Fig. 10-2. The stock can be square with edge dimensions that match the diameter of the circle. In this case, you would press the work against the saw blade before you press it down on the pivot. Feed direction is clockwise.

177

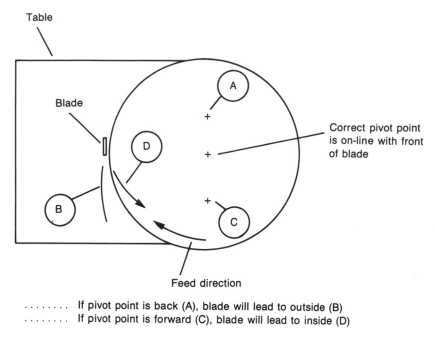

Table

Blade

A

+

D

+

Correct pivot point
is on-line with front
of blade

B

+

C

Feed direction

. . . . If pivot point is back (A), blade will lead to outside (B)
. . . . If pivot point is forward (C), blade will lead to inside (D)

Fig. 10-3. Here are some factors to be aware of when establishing the pivot point. It is also important for the blade to be sharp and have uniform set.

Another factor to consider is the condition of the blade. You can make some feed-direction adjustments when a blade has lead and you are cutting freehand, but not when you are using a jig for cut control. If a blade is troublesome on straight cuts, it will be equally harassing with jig work. The blade must be sharp and have a uniform set.

You can begin sawing in two ways. The stock can be square with sides that match the diameter of the circle. In this case, you would press it firmly against the blade and then move down to engage the pivot. If the stock is oversize, make a freehand cut to the circle's perimeter, and then it is seated. The latter system wastes some wood but can be more convenient since cutting will be continuous. When the stock is of minimum size, the blade will have to make an entry four times. Chances are that there will be rough spots at each of those points.

You do not have to confine pivot sawing to individual pieces. When you need multiples, you can make a pad of separate pieces, and then saw as you would for a solid block. The pad that is being pivot cut in Fig. 10-4 is composed of eight pieces of ¼-inch plywood. A 2-inch-thick pad is hardly a chore for a band saw.

You can be somewhat innovative with pivot cutting as long as uniform curves are involved. For example, by working with offset centers, you can nicely round the ends of a rectangular workpiece or a square one as shown in Fig. 10-5. Establish the pivot points on a centerline; spacing of the points from a true center determines the radius of the arcs.

Figure 10-6 supplies information that will enable you to duplicate the jig that has been shown in the photos. You can make pivot pins from $^{10}\!/_{32}$ machine screws. They

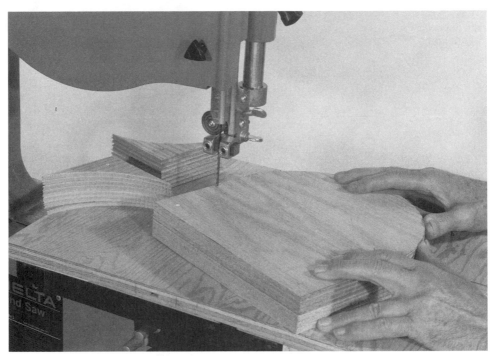

Fig. 10-4. You also can use the pivot-sawing technique to produce multiple, similar pieces. Here, a number of ¼-inch-thick blanks are being sawed simultaneously.

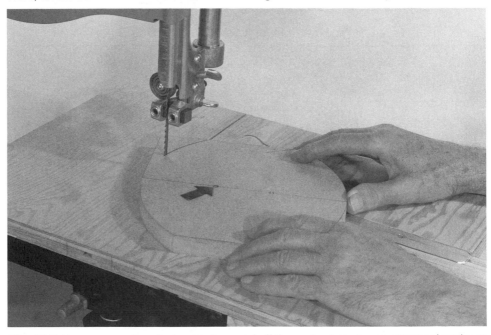

Fig. 10-5. You can use the pivot guide to round off the ends of square or rectangular pieces if you drill the work for a pair of offset centers. The position of the pin remains the same for each cut.

179

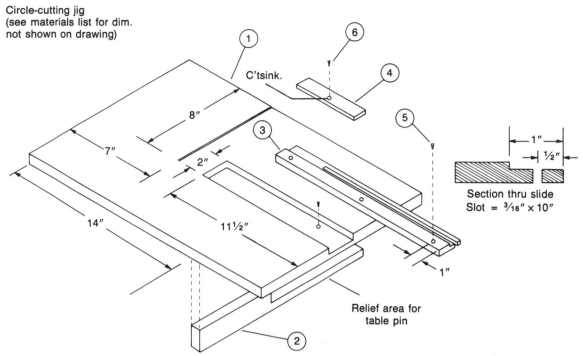

Circle-cutting jig
(see materials list for dim.
not shown on drawing)

C'tsink.

8"

7"

2"

14"

11½"

Section thru slide
Slot = ³⁄₁₆" × 10"

1"

½"

1"

Relief area for
table pin

Fig. 10-6. Here are construction details for a versatile circle-cutting jig. The clamp ledge allows you to secure the jig to the tool's table with C-clamps. The pivot points are made from $^{10}\!/_{32}$ machine screws.

Table 10-1. Materials List for Circle-cutting Jig.

Key	Part	No. of Pieces	Size (in Inches)				Material
1	Platform	1	¾	×	14	×	20	Plywood
2	Clamp ledge	1	¾	×	1½	×	14	Hardwood
3	Pivot slide	1	⅜	×	2	×	14	Hardwood
4	Hold-down	1	⅛	×	1	×	5	Aluminum
5	Threaded inserts	4	$^{10}\!/_{32}$				
6	FH screw	1	$^{10}\!/_{32}$ × ¾				

can be short if the work is just impaled or long if it's okay for the work to have a center hole. To make them, first remove heads by hacksawing and then chuck them in an electric drill so you can use a file to shape one end to a point.

AN OVERHEAD PIVOT JIG

The overhead pivot jig that is on display in Fig. 10-7 has several advantages. You can adjust the pivot, since it is on the topside, for correct location after the work is in position. Being able to swing the slotted arm to left or right can provide some compensation should the blade have lead. Bolt the arm to a length of bar stock that substitutes for the right-hand blade guide. Be sure the bar stock is square and smooth at the end that will bear against the blade.

The sawing procedure is standard. The square you are sawing can have side dimensions that match the diameter of the circle, or it can be oversized so a lead-in cut before setting the pivot will allow you to make a continuous pass (Fig. 10-8). Figures 10-9 and 10-10 demonstrate how you can use the jig to saw arcs of similar shape. Figure 10-11 suggests still another function—creating elliptical forms. Figure 10-12 supplies construction details for the jig.

LARGE CIRCLES

The pivot jigs are fine for most work, but when you need an extra-large circle, you must think of establishing an independent pivot point. Figure 10-13 depicts one idea.

Fig. 10-7. Situate the overhead pivot by means of a length of bar stock that replaces the regular right-hand blade guide. You can control its height by the position of the blade guard.

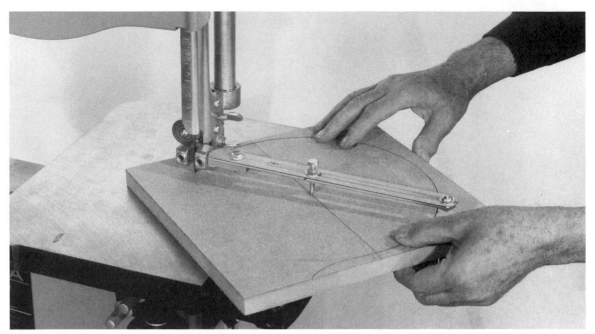

Fig. 10-8. The advantage of the overhead design is that you can situate the pivot after you place the work. Here, the circular cut was started with a lead-in cut to the project's perimeter.

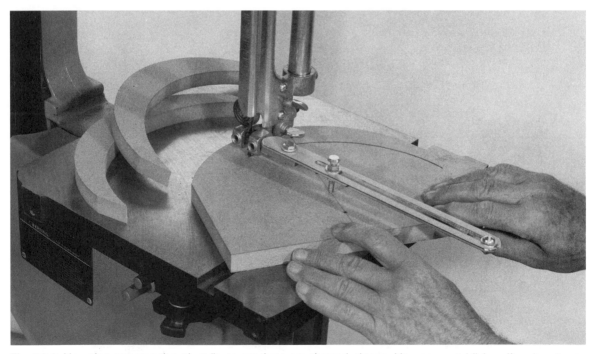

Fig. 10-9. You also can use the pivot jig to produce arc-shaped pieces. You can establish uniformity of cuts by accurately spacing pivot points.

Fig. 10-10. These examples are of shapes that you can produce by using the arc-cutting technique.

Fig. 10-11. You also can use pivot jigs to shape elliptical forms. Establish center points on a common centerline. Two cuts are required; make each one using a different pivot location. The arrow indicates the point that was used for the first cut.

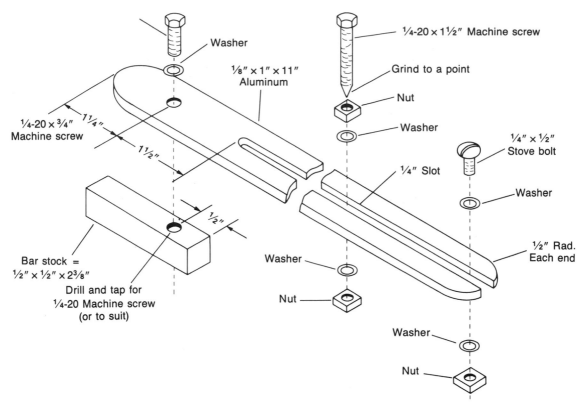

Fig. 10-12. This figure shows you how to make an overhead pivot guide. One end of the bar stock on which the arm is mounted will bear against the saw blade. It substitutes for the regular blade guide so be sure it is square and smooth.

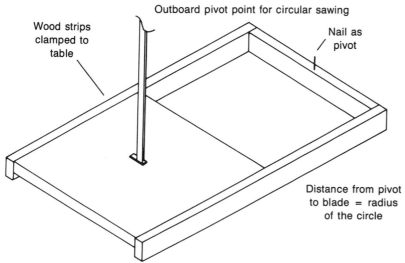

Fig. 10-13. Here is one way to establish a pivot point for controlled sawing of circular components that are too large for the pivot jigs.

Actually, any system will do that will provide a pivot point that is far enough from the blade for the radius you require. For example a 2 x 4 that you have adequately braced, a sawhorse with a length of wood clamped vertically, even a long board that you clamp to the underside of the tool's table will work. The important factor, always, is that you must locate the pivot correctly in relation to the saw blade.

BENDING WOOD WITHOUT STEAMING

Bending wood without the special equipment that is available to commercial establishments is within the scope of small shops because of two special techniques. One technique is called *kerfing*; the other technique is called *thinning out*.

Kerfing involves making a series of equally-spaced cuts into the back surface of the material. The kerfs are deep enough so the solid material that remains becomes flexible enough, somewhat like a veneer, so you can bend the wood sufficiently to conform to a curve or even a full circle. The depth and the spacing of the kerfs, even their width, which you can control by the gauge of the blade and its amount of set, are critical factors that should relate to the species and thickness of the wood. The deeper the kerfs and the closer they are, the more flexible the wood becomes.

Some experimental work might lead you in the right direction, but it also might be wasteful of time and material. It's better practice to follow a particular test procedure that will offer an approximation of what you need to do. The test subject must be the same species and thickness as the material you plan to bend. Make a kerf in the test piece deep enough so it leaves about $\frac{1}{16}$ to $\frac{1}{8}$ inch of surface material, and then organize it on a flat surface as suggested in Fig. 10-14. Lift the free end

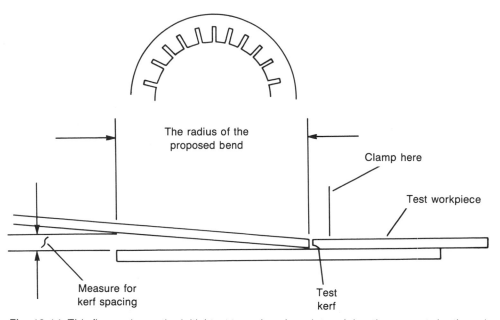

Fig. 10-14. This figure shows the initial test to make when determining the correct depth and spacing of the kerfs needed to bend a component. It isn't foolproof, but it's better than being arbitrary.

of the wood until the open end of the kerf comes together, and then take the measurement indicated in the drawing. This measurement is the kerf spacing with which to start.

When cutting, it's best to set up a control so that kerfs will be equal in depth and spacing. One way to accomplish this control on the band saw is to work along the lines shown in Figs. 10-15 and 10-16. Place each cut that you make over the guide pin so you will position the work for the cut that follows. The stop block ensures cuts of equal depth. A second method is demonstrated in Fig. 10-17. Mark the extension, attached to the miter gauge, for correct spacing. Line up the last cut made with the mark and consequently, you have positioned the work for ensuing cuts.

When workpieces are long enough for the tool's arm to create interference, it's a simple matter to pivot the head of the miter gauge a few degrees so the workpiece

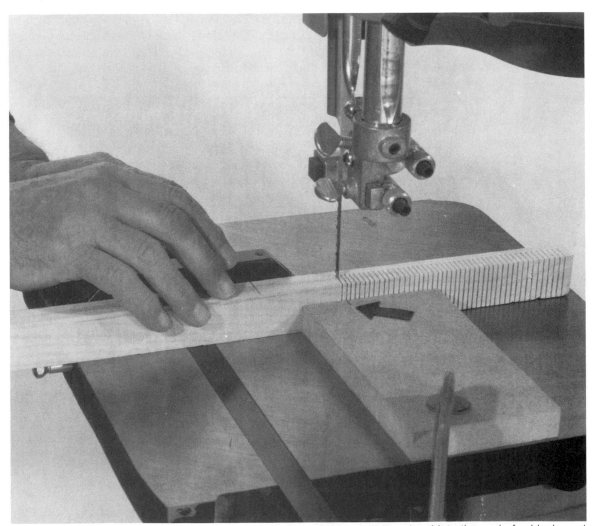

Fig. 10-15. Here is one way to control kerf spacing. Drive a slim, headless brad into the end of a block, and then clamp the block so the distance between brad and blade will equal the spacing.

Fig. 10-16. Place each cut that you make over the brad to position the work for the following cut. The block also acts as a stop to control the depth of the cuts.

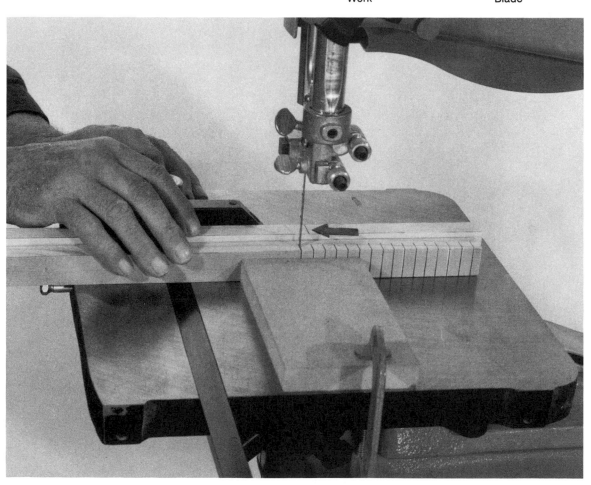

Clamped block acts as stop to control kerf depth

Nail in block is kerf-spacing pin

Kerfs

Work

Blade

Fig. 10-17. Here is an alternate method of gauging kerf spacing. Mark an extension, secured to the miter gauge, for the distance between kerfs. Aligning the last cut with the mark will place the work correctly for the following kerf.

Fig. 10-18. Thinning out simply means reducing the thickness of the stock to leave a veneer-like surface that will be flexible enough to bend.

can clear the arm. This pivot results in kerfs that are at a slight angle, but that will not affect how the wood will bend.

Don't force the kerfed piece into the bend you need too quickly unless the curve is slight. Bending in stages, and even applying hot water to the area you are bending, will get the job done with little chance of splintering. You can use wood dough to fill the kerfs if the edges of the bent pieces will be exposed.

THINNING OUT

Thinning out is another system that you can use for bending wood. Often it is done to supply a facing strip for a curved area on a project. The process is simple; it merely involves sawing to reduce the thickness of the stock in the area you are bending to leave a veneer-thick surface. The thickness of what is left will depend on the degree of bend. It can be ⅛ inch or more or ¹⁄₁₆ inch and less. Saw on the band saw as shown in Fig. 10-18. Make the straight end cuts first. Then make an entry so you can proceed to cut to one of the initial cuts. You have finished the job after you have flipped the work over and turned it end-for-end.

Generally you support thinned sections with backing blocks (Fig. 10-19). When the bend is in a confined area, it's best to saw the thinned area a bit longer than

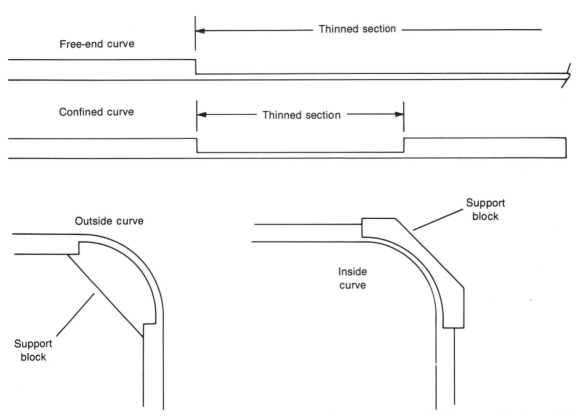

Fig. 10-19. Use the thinning-out method to supply a facing strip for curved areas of cabinets and furniture. Use support blocks to bulk what would otherwise be a weak area of the structure.

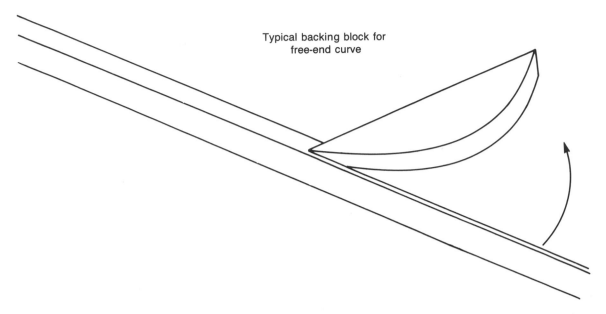

Typical backing block for
free-end curve

Fig. 10-20. If the thinned area will abut another component of the project, it's best to produce an extra long piece, and then trim it to size after checking it on the assembly.

necessary so fitting will be easier. Thinning longer than necessary is also wise when the work is free at one end (Fig. 10-20). Trim the part to fit after you have attached it.

SAWING TAPERS

Tapers are saw cuts that you make at an oblique angle across the stock. The same concept is true of simple miters, but since tapers are usually quite long, it's best to think of the cutting procedure as similar to ripping. A regular rip cut, guided by a fence, produces pieces with parallel sides, but since the taper is an angular cut, it's necessary to cut them freehand or use a positioning device together with a fence so the work will be at the correct angle for the cut.

Often, the device (jig) is a board that has been shaped especially for the work so you can saw in the manner shown in Fig. 10-21. The jig is straight on one side to ride against the fence, slanted on the opposite side to gauge the amount of taper. You must move the jig and the work as a unit until you complete the cut. The product can be the part that you remove or the section that you cradle in the jig.

You can make a similar device—a multi-step jig—to guide work that requires equal tapers on two or four edges (Fig. 10-22). Following is a typical procedure used to produce square, tapered legs for tables and chairs. Situate the fence so the distance from it to the blade equals the width of the body of the jig, plus that of the workpiece.

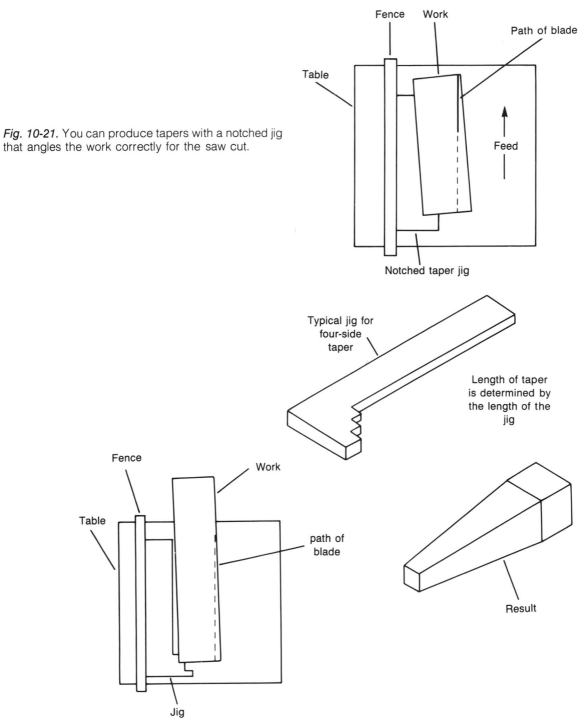

Fig. 10-21. You can produce tapers with a notched jig that angles the work correctly for the saw cut.

Fence   Work

Path of blade

Table

Feed

Notched taper jig

Typical jig for four-side taper

Length of taper is determined by the length of the jig

Fence

Work

Table

path of blade

Jig

Result

Fig. 10-22. You use stepped jigs for components that require equal tapers on two or four edges. This method is a good way to produce square, tapered legs for tables and chairs.

Make the first cut with the work positioned as indicated in the first step. Then flip the stock and, using the same step, make a second cut. You have finished the job if the taper is required on two edges. For a four-sided taper, repeat the procedure, but position the work according to the second step. Determine the degree of taper by the dimensions of the steps.

Jigs of this nature are designed for producing a specific component. To be prepared for general tapering operations, it's necessary to have a jig that you can adjust for various angles. These jigs are available commercially, usually as accessories for a table saw, but they are just as practical for a band saw (Fig. 10-23), or you can make one like the example used in Fig. 10-24. The homemade version consists of two, straight pieces of hardwood that are hinged at one end and connected at the opposite end by a slotted adjustment arm that you can make from hardwood

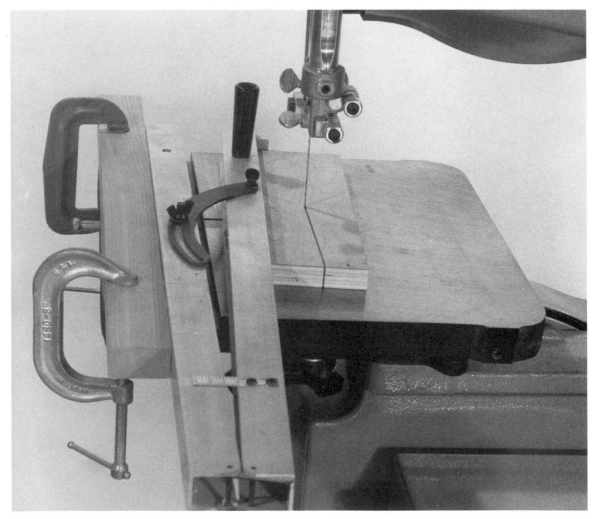

Fig. 10-23. Here you see a commercial taper jig in use. The jig is adjustable, so it is available for various tapered angles.

or by using a length of ⅛-inch-thick- **x** -1-inch-wide aluminum (Fig. 10-25).

It's best to attach the hinge while the two arms of the jig are clamped together. At the same time, scribe a line across both pieces, 12 inches away from the hinged end. By measuring between the marks, you can set the jig for the amount of taper per foot that is required. If, for example, a 12-inch-long component requires a ½-inch taper, you just lock the adjustment arm so the distance between the marks is ½ inch. If the taper is required on both edges of the stock, open the jig an additional ½ inch and make a second cut after you have flipped the stock. The same jig produces compound-angle cuts if you use it with the table tilted (Fig. 10-26).

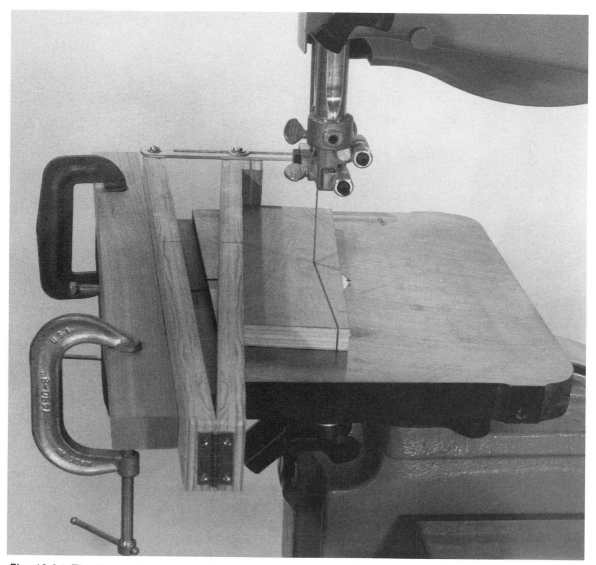

Fig. 10-24. This figure shows a variable taper jig that you can make. Stop cutting as soon as the blade has moved through the work, otherwise you might cut into the adjustment arm.

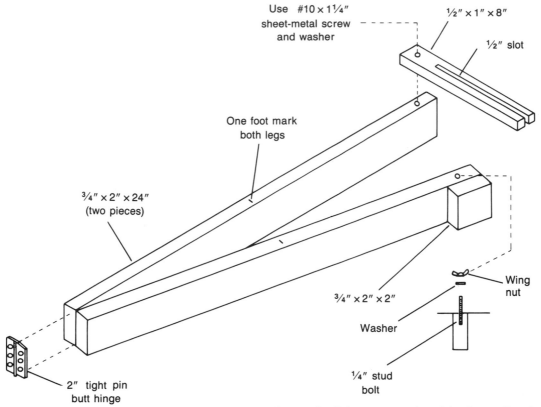

Use #10 × 1¼"
sheet-metal screw
and washer

½" × 1" × 8"

½" slot

One foot mark
both legs

¾" × 2" × 24"
(two pieces)

¾" × 2" × 2"

Wing
nut

Washer

2" tight pin
butt hinge

¼" stud
bolt

Fig. 10-25. This figure shows you how to make an adjustable taper jig. Select two, good, straight pieces of hardwood for the legs.

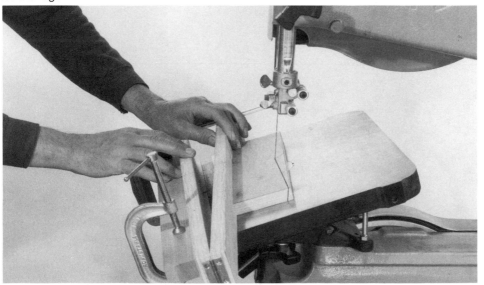

Fig. 10-26. You also can use taper jigs for long, compound-angle cuts. The only difference from normal procedure is that you tilt the table.

It's pretty rare in woodworking when the degree of taper can be arbitrary. To work precisely, check the math that is offered in Fig. 10-27.

SAWING ROUND STOCK

Sawing round stock or cylindrical work of any type, whether the cut is across a diameter or longitudinal, always presents problems of some degree regardless of the tool you use. The band saw, because its blade cuts consistently downward, is less troublesome than, say, a table saw, whose circular blade is more likely to jog work about and cause kickback.

Sawing dowels to length on a band saw can be as simple as the procedure shown in Fig. 10-28. Clamp the fence to provide the correct cutoff length; hold your

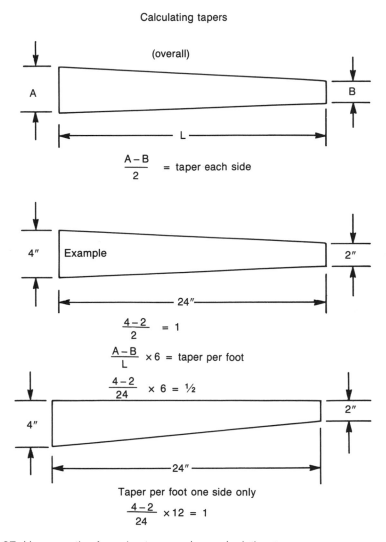

Calculating tapers

$$\frac{A-B}{2} = \text{taper each side}$$

$$\frac{4-2}{2} = 1$$

$$\frac{A-B}{L} \times 6 = \text{taper per foot}$$

$$\frac{4-2}{24} \times 6 = \frac{1}{2}$$

Taper per foot one side only

$$\frac{4-2}{24} \times 12 = 1$$

Fig. 10-27. Here are the formulas to use when calculating tapers.

work firmly against the miter gauge as you make the pass. The negative action to guard against is the blade's tendency to spin the dowel. A V-block jig, like the one shown in Fig. 10-29, should be on hand for operations of this nature. You have more assurance that the work will stay put when you cradle it nicely in the "V." The V-shape is easy to produce on a table saw, but if you do not have one, make the body of the jig by band sawing generous 45-degree chamfers on separate pieces of wood and then gluing them together. Construction details for the basic jig are shown in Fig. 10-30. In use, you move the jig forward only to the point where you cut through the work. Then you return it to a starting position clear of the blade.

A more sophisticated concept is demonstrated in Fig. 10-31. The body of the jig is similar to the basic design, but has a wider rear area to accommodate an adjustable stop. Thus, you can organize the jig for the production of any number of similar-length pieces. When making the jig (Fig. 10-32), establish the position of the V-shaped stop after you have constructed the adjustable arm and correctly positioned it.

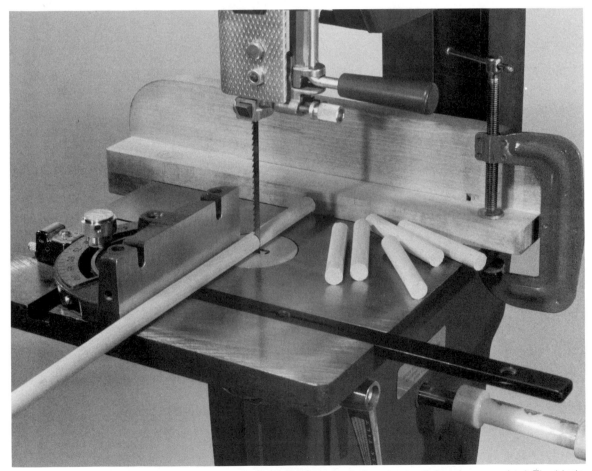

Fig. 10-28. Simple setup will gauge length accurately when many similar pieces of dowel are required. The blade will tend to spin the work, so be sure to hold it firmly against the miter gauge.

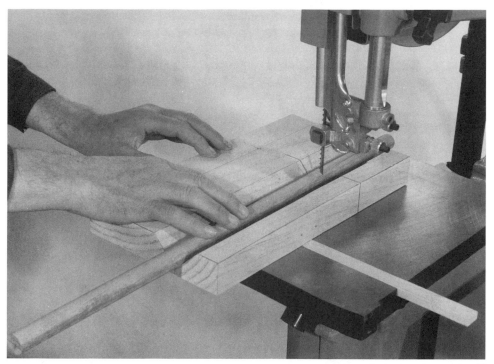

Fig. 10-29. A V-block makes it easy to crosscut round stock. It's less likely that the work will spin when it is cradled in the V.

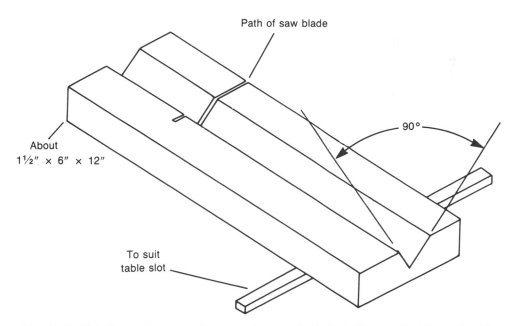

Fig. 10-30. This figure shows you how to make a basic V-block. Be sure that the path of the kerf will be at right angles to the ''V''.

An accessory for the jig is shown in place in Fig. 10-33. The item is a hold-down that will keep the work in position throughout the cut. You might not view it as a critical addition since the work already is cradled in the "V," but anything that adds convenience and makes it easier to work accurately is worth considering. Also, you can use the jig, as will be shown in chapter 11, for sawing metal cylinders and thick-walled steel tubing, both of which require a lot of sawing time. In such cases, you surely will appreciate the hold-down. You can make the accessory by following the details in Fig. 10-34.

Longitudinal sawing of cylinders is another story. The process is essentially ripping, but not one to attempt freehand or by using a fence as a guide. It is highly doubtful that the cut will remain on a true longitudinal axis. The answer, again, is a V-block jig, but one that you position parallel to the blade so the blade will be on the centerline of the "V" (Fig. 10-35). The alignment guide that you see is added so the work will not rotate while you saw it (Fig. 10-36). Longitudinal sawing is a great way to split ready-made or custom-made spindles so they become identical pieces of half-round molding (Fig. 10-37).

The jig for this work can be a length of 2 x 4 or 2 x 6 with a centered V cut that you just clamp to the table, or you can make it in a more efficient fashion by following the suggestions in Fig. 10-38.

Fig. 10-31. A more sophisticated V-block includes an adjustable stop that you use to gauge the length of multiple, similar pieces.

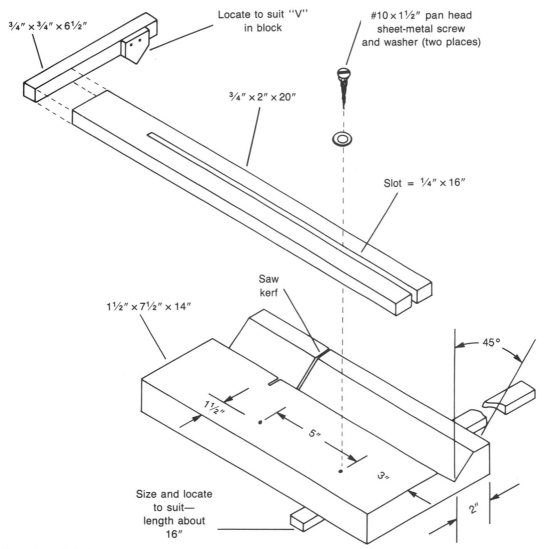

¾" × ¾" × 6½"

Locate to suit "V" in block

#10 × 1½" pan head sheet-metal screw and washer (two places)

¾" × 2" × 20"

Slot = ¼" × 16"

Saw kerf

1½" × 7½" × 14"

45°

1½"

5"

3"

2"

Size and locate to suit— length about 16"

Fig. 10-32. This figure shows you how to make the advanced V-block. You need the V-shaped stop block so you can handle even small diameter dowels in the jig.

SPIRALING ROUNDS

As any woodworker knows, dowels that are used in wood connections will hold more strongly and will provide for excess glue to escape if they are spiral cut. True, ready-made units of various lengths and diameters are available, but situations that require custom-making attention do arise. In such cases, you can do the work very nicely on a band saw (Fig. 10-39).

You can control the pitch of the spiral by the tilt of the table which can be anywhere between 10 and 15 degrees. Position the miter gauge, which is secured with a clamp, so the blade will cut into the work about ¹⁄₁₆ inch. Hold the work very firmly against the face of the miter gauge as you make contact with the blade. You will find that the *pitch*—the distance between spirals—will be controlled automatically, but you must guard against allowing the work to rotate faster than the blade needs, to do the cutting. Use one hand to hold the work in position and the other to rotate it. You will learn soon enough how to synchronize work rotation with blade action.

Figure 10-40 demonstrates that you can use the same technique to lay out the spiral path on larger rounds that will receive additional shaping attention by hand or on another machine.

SAWING PARALLEL CURVES

When a single component with uniform, similar curves on opposite edges is required, it's best to simply cut the part freehand and then follow with whatever sanding is required. You are justified in adopting a special procedure when the project calls for multiple pieces. A simple setup that utilizes a fence is suggested in Fig. 10-41. The first step is to saw the beginning curve freehand. Make subsequent cuts by passing the work between the fence and the blade. The arc being cut must be tangent to the fence throughout the pass, and the point of contact with the fence must be

Fig. 10-33. The hold-down is an accessory for the advanced V-block jig. You will appreciate it when you use the jig to saw metal materials like thick-walled steel tubing and jobs that require a lot of sawing time.

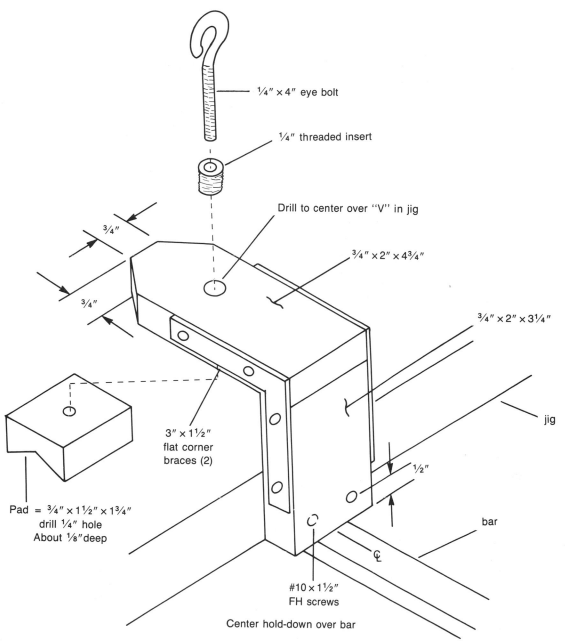

¼" × 4" eye bolt

¼" threaded insert

Drill to center over "V" in jig

¾"

¾" × 2" × 4¾"

¾"

¾" × 2" × 3¼"

jig

3" × 1½" flat corner braces (2)

Pad = ¾" × 1½" × 1¾"
drill ¼" hole
About ⅛" deep

½"

bar

₵

#10 × 1½" FH screws

Center hold-down over bar

Fig. 10-34. This figure shows you how to make the hold-down. The metal corner braces supply necessary reinforcement.

in line with the blade's teeth. You will be in a better position to control these factors if you start by making a mark on the fence to indicate the point that is on-line with the blade.

A second method calls for the guide that is shown in Fig. 10-42. As shown in Fig. 10-43, you would clamp the guide to the table so its point is in line with the blade's teeth. While the fence idea allows cutting of uniform curves, you can use the guide method, since the area on each side of it is not restricted and allows room for manipulating the work, to duplicate irregular and reverse curves. It's a good idea, after a cut, to smoothly sand the next edge that will bear against the guide before proceeding with the following cut. The work will move more easily since the sanding chore will eliminate any washboarding.

PATTERN SAWING

Pattern sawing is a practical system that allows sawing any number of duplicate pieces. The guide jig that is required is detailed in Fig. 10-44. Figure 10-45 shows how you should organize it on the band saw. The end of the guide arm, which can be concave or convex depending on the work you are doing, must be smooth and suitably notched for the blade you are using. Be sure that the center of the curve on the guide arm is on-line with the blade's teeth.

Fig. 10-35. You should use V-blocks so you can make longitudinal cuts through cylinders safely and accurately. Position the jig parallel to the blade and so the blade is on the center of the "V".

Fig. 10-36. The alignment guide, which can be a piece of thin sheet metal, is a necessary part of the jig. It rides in the kerf to keep the project from turning as you saw it.

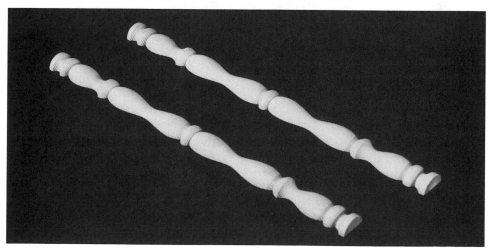

Fig. 10-37. Splitting shaped spindles to produce half-round molding is an easy chore for the longitudinal V-block.

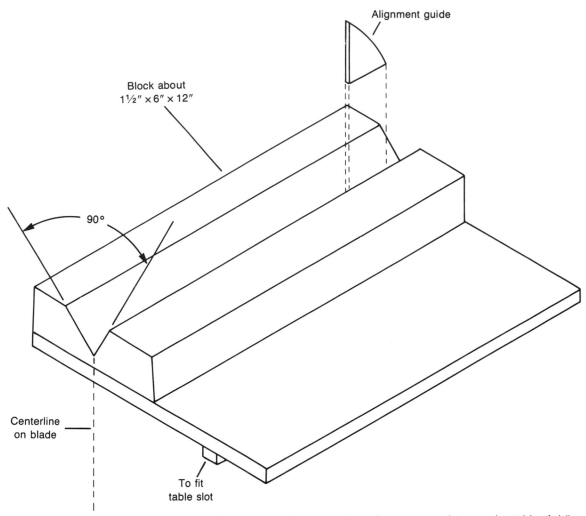

Alignment guide

Block about
1½″ × 6″ × 12″

90°

Centerline
on blade

To fit
table slot

Fig. 10-38. The jig will be easier to use if you mount it on a platform that you can clamp to the table. Adding a "miter-gauge bar" provides for quick positioning.

The first step is to make a pattern for the desired shape of your work. It must be accurate and have very smooth edges so there will be minimum friction when it rides against the guide. Next, drive a few screws or nails through the pattern so they protrude on the underside ⅛ inch or so. The projecting points allow you to press the pattern down on rough-cut workpieces so you can move the two of them as a unit.

Sawing, as shown in Fig. 10-46, is a matter of keeping the pattern in constant contact with the guide. This technique is a kind of blind sawing since you can't actually see the blade moving through the workpiece. Work slowly until you get the feel of manipulating the workpiece correctly. If the blade tends to cut into the pattern, stop the operation and make the notch in the guide arm a bit deeper. Actually, there should be a very slight clearance between the blade and the edge of the pattern.

JIG FOR UNIFORM ARCS

You can use a type of pattern sawing to cut duplicate curves, but the curves must be uniform; that is, they must be the arc of a circle. The setup is shown in Fig. 10-47. Cut the guide and the pattern to the same radius you must have for the work. The sawed edges, which will be in contact throughout the pass, must be very smooth. The blocks on which you have secured the guide serve two purposes. They elevate the guide so work can slip under it, and they provide for clamping the guide in correct position. Provide a notch in the guide to house the blade. As with all sawing of this

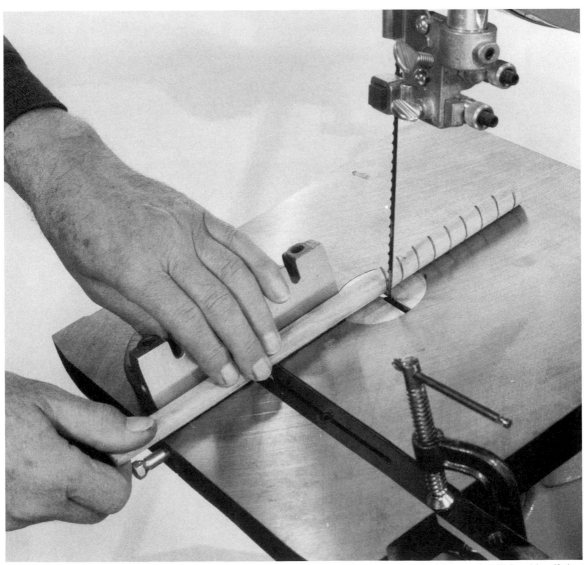

Fig. 10-39. You can control the pitch, when cutting spirals, by the tilt of the table. The work will feed itself, but you must guard against it turning faster than the blade requires.

type, the pattern has nails or screws passing through it so you can force it down to secure the work. As you move the pattern in contact with the guide, the blade will saw the same shape in the workpiece.

HOW TO BEVEL A CURVE

An interesting system for beveling curves is shown in Fig. 10-48. Cut the bearing edges of the pattern and guide to the same radius. Form the groove in the pattern for the bevel angle required, and size it so the workpiece will fit tightly. If you err with the size of the slot, nail a small block across it so the work will stay put when you move the pattern.

You can use standard pattern-sawing procedures, to some degree, for beveling curves. Tilt the band-saw table to the angle required and bevel the guide and pattern

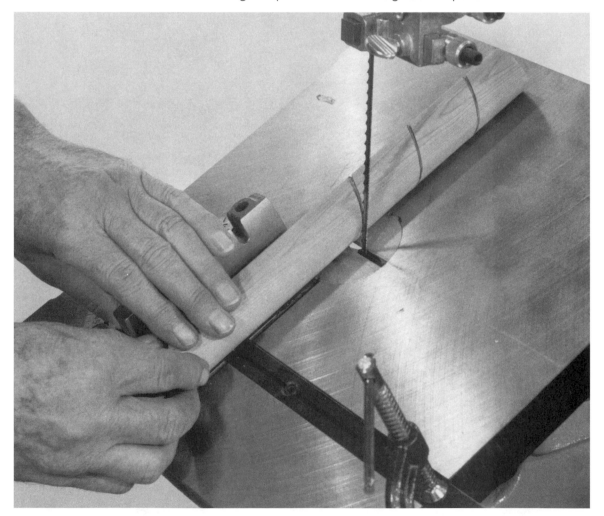

Fig. 10-40. The spiraling technique can mark the path for true spiral shapes that will be produced by hand or on another machine.

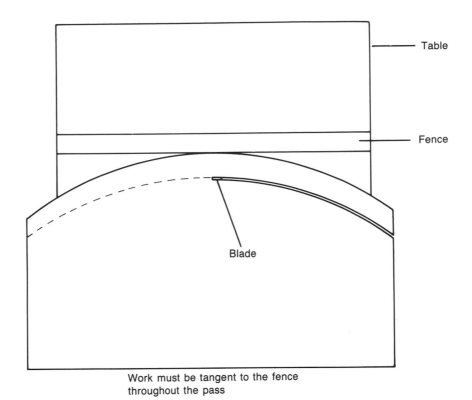

Table

Fence

Blade

Work must be tangent to the fence
throughout the pass

Fig. 10-41. You can do parallel curve cutting by using a fence as a guide. The first curve is cut freehand, then you pass the work between the fence and the blade. Keep the arc tangent to the fence throughout the pass.

accordingly. Cut in routine fashion except for allowing for the bevel angle. Results will be more satisfactory if you limit the idea to beveling uniform curves.

NOTCHED JIGS

Generally, you use notched jigs to expedite sawing of odd-shaped pieces or to ensure accuracy when you require many similar pieces. Example applications include producing small wedges that you might need for some woodworking joints, removing corners from a square to form an octagon, or simply to facilitate making an angular cut that would be difficult to guide with a miter gauge.

The jigs are simple affairs but must be designed specifically for the job on hand. The example shown in Fig. 10-49 demonstrates the technique. The shape of the part that you need or the area that you must remove from the base stock is cut into a board that has parallel sides. One edge of the board rides the fence, the opposite edge is in line with the saw blade. Move the jig and the work past the blade as a unit. Most times it's necessary to use one hand to move the jig and the other hand to keep the work in position, so it's wise to choose a board for the jig that is wide enough for safe handling. If you don't observe the rule, use a push stick to move the jig.

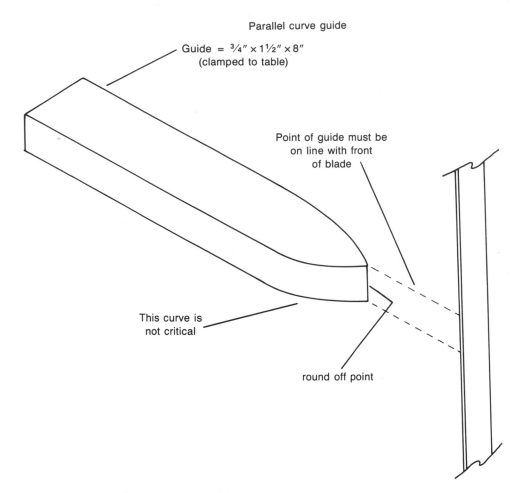

Parallel curve guide

Guide = ¾″ × 1½″ × 8″
(clamped to table)

Point of guide must be
on line with front
of blade

This curve is
not critical

round off point

Fig. 10-42. A special guide for parallel curve cutting is simple to make.

END-SHAPING JIG

The shaping of the top end of fence pickets is a common example of how you assemble and use a jig of this type. Construction details for a typical jig design are offered in Fig. 10-50. A plywood platform that you can clamp to the saw's table supports a work table that you can pivot because of the dowel pin that passes through it into the platform. The jig's table has a fence that is parallel to the saw blade and that is situated to accommodate the width of the parts that you will cut. The position of the pin from the blade equals the radius of the arc and, like all jigs of this nature, you must locate it for alignment with the blade's teeth.

Place workpieces against the fence and abut them against the nail stop. When you rotate the work table in a clockwise direction, the blade saws an arc through the project. Two cuts are required; the second one being made after you invert the stock (Fig. 10-51). You can change the distance between blade and pin simply by relocating the jig's platform. Thus, it's possible to do the same type of cutting on project pieces of various widths. You are not limited to cutting arcs that meet at a central point—the *Gothic arch*. You can position the jig so you will only round off the corners of the project.

UNIQUE BEVEL-SAWING APPLICATION

You might be of an age to remember the collapsible drinking cup, the ingenious design of metal rings that stored flat, but that wedged together when you pulled one end and so formed a deeper cone. Bevel sawing of the type we will discuss imitates this concept. Actually, since internal cutting is involved, a jigsaw is the ideal tool for the technique. With some changes in procedure, you can accomplish very acceptable results on the band saw.

Figure 10-52 tells the story of how you can get a deep shape from a flat board. If you cut an internal circle with the table in normal position, the core piece will fall through the base stock. If you tilt the saw table about 5 degrees, both the disc and the opening will have beveled edges and the disc will fall only part way through the opening. If you cut a series of concentric-beveled rings, each one will jam in the opening it was cut from and a cone shape develops. The more rings that are cut, the deeper the cone.

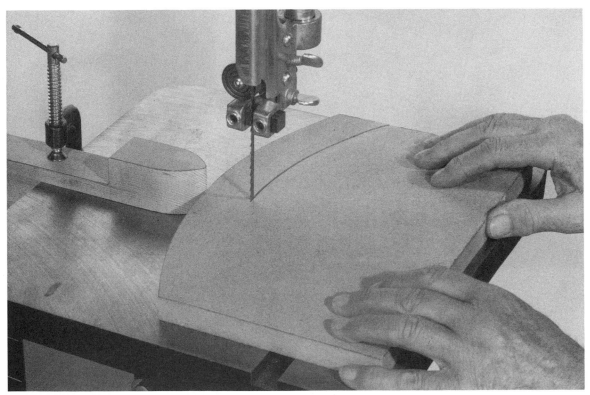

Fig. 10-43. Clamp the guide to the table so its point is on-line with the blade's teeth. It's critical to keep the work in constant contact with the guide. Also, the blade must be in prime condition.

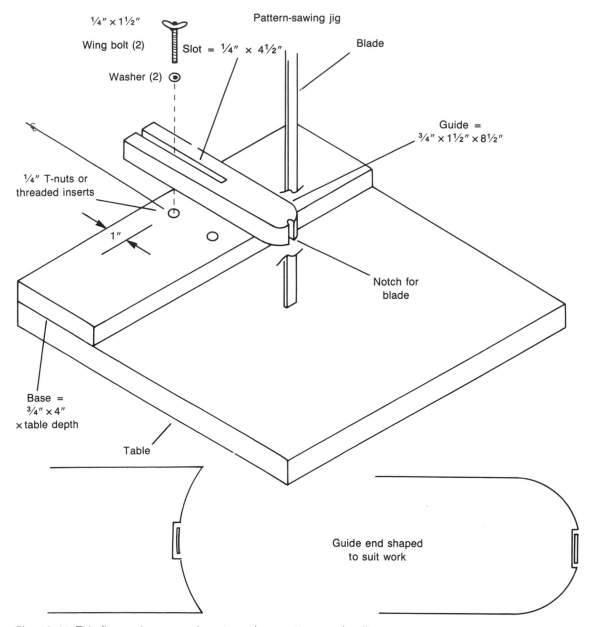

¼" × 1½"

Wing bolt (2)

Washer (2)

Pattern-sawing jig

Slot = ¼" × 4½"

Blade

Guide =
¾" × 1½" × 8½"

¼" T-nuts or
threaded inserts

1"

Notch for
blade

Base =
¾" × 4"
× table depth

Table

Guide end shaped
to suit work

Fig. 10-44. This figure shows you how to make a pattern-sawing jig.

On a jigsaw, since it works with short, straight blades, you can saw concentric rings without a lead-in cut since you can drill blade-insertion holes for each required cut. You can't work that way on a band saw, but a solution is shown in Fig. 10-53. You would cut parts as semicircles and then glue them back together as full rings (Fig. 10-54). When the components are ready, coat the mating edges with glue and jam the pieces together to form a bowl shape like the example in Fig. 10-55.

Fig. 10-45. This figure shows you how to mount the pattern-sawing jig on the table. You can elevate the guide arm on small blocks when you use the jig to saw material that is thicker than ¾ inch.

Fig. 10-46. The pattern, cut to the shape that is needed for the components, rides against the guide arm. Saw the work, moving along with the pattern, to the same profile. Take it easy until you get the feel of moving the pattern correctly.

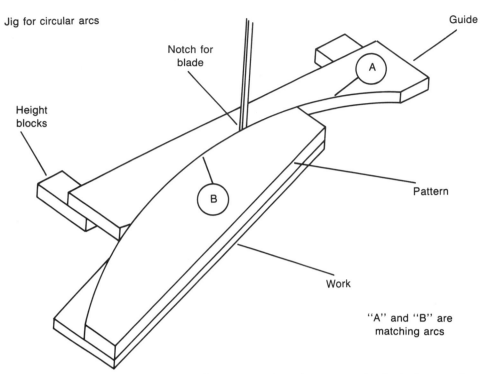

Jig for circular arcs

Notch for blade

Guide

Height blocks

A

B

Pattern

Work

"A" and "B" are matching arcs

Fig. 10-47. You can saw duplicate, uniform curves by using a setup that is similar to pattern sawing. The curve in the guide must match the one in the pattern.

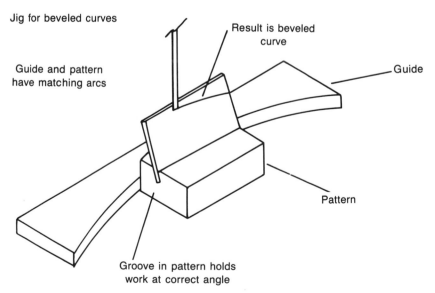

Jig for beveled curves

Result is beveled curve

Guide and pattern have matching arcs

Guide

Pattern

Groove in pattern holds work at correct angle

Fig. 10-48. Beveled curves are not day-by-day requirements, but you can form them this way should you ever need them. The matching, bearing edges of pattern and guide control the curve in the work.

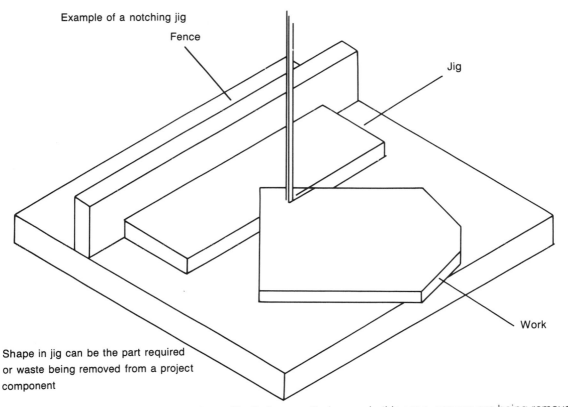

Example of a notching jig

Fence

Jig

Work

Shape in jig can be the part required
or waste being removed from a project
component

Fig. 10-49. Notching jigs are designed specifically for a particular use. In this case, corners are being removed from the base stock.

The technique isn't limited to circular forms. You can cut along the lines suggested in Fig. 10-56. Assemble the pieces by using the staggered joints shown in the drawing, or put them together as half-assemblies (Fig. 10-57), which you then join to complete the project.

A variation that allows a continuous cut on the band saw is to mark the cut line as a spiral (Figs. 10-58 through 10-60). The spiral cut will result in the same kind of projection you get with concentric rings. Creating the bowl shape will be a bit more difficult, but using slim brads to hold the projected shape until the glue sets will work okay.

Bevel sawing can have very practical applications. For example, as demonstrated in Figs. 10-61 through 10-63, you can use this method to create storage pockets for tools and other items.

You should follow some general rules regardless of the project you have in mind. Total projection will depend on factors like the thickness of the stock, the amount of table tilt, and the width of the kerf. The less tilt you use, the greater the projection of individual pieces. The more pieces you cut, the greater the project's depth. However, minimum tilt, combined with many pieces that have a narrow cross section, will result in a shape with very thin wall thickness. The project will be weak, and it will be difficult to do a good job of gluing.

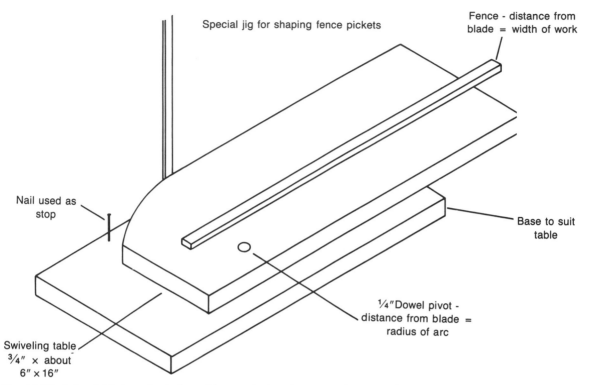

Fig. 10-50. A jig of this type is designed for producing the same shape on the end of components. Producing a Gothic arch on the end of fence pickets is a typical application.

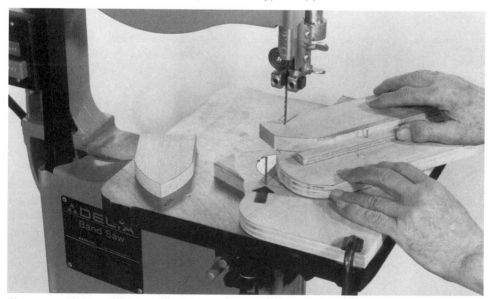

Fig. 10-51. Hold workpieces against the fence and abut them against the nail (arrow) that serves as a stop. Rotate the swiveling table clockwise to make the cut. A second cut, after you have turned the stock over, completes the job.

Factors that affect the bevel cutting technique

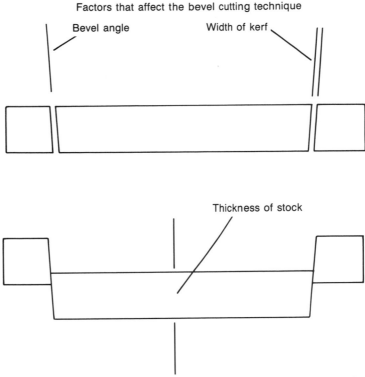

Bevel angle   Width of kerf

Thickness of stock

Fig. 10-52. When you cut an internal piece at a slight bevel, the disc will jam into the part you cut it from. That's the secret of the special bevel-sawing technique.

Semicircles bevel-cut

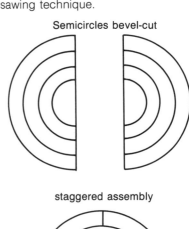

Fig. 10-53. Unlike the jigsaw, you can't pass band-saw blades through an entry hole, so you must do bevel sawing in half steps. Saw very carefully with a sharp blade that has minimum, uniform set.

staggered assembly

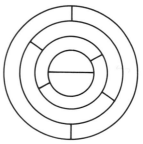

Fig. 10-54. Join the half cuts to form full circles. Staples, which you can remove later, provide an easy means of holding the parts together until the glue sets.

Fig. 10-55. Each ring will fit tightly into the next one like a barrel's bung in its tapered hole. The more concentric rings that you cut, the deeper the project will be. However, rings with a very narrow cross section will result in a weak project. You can mount an assembly like this in a lathe and turn it to a true bowl shape.

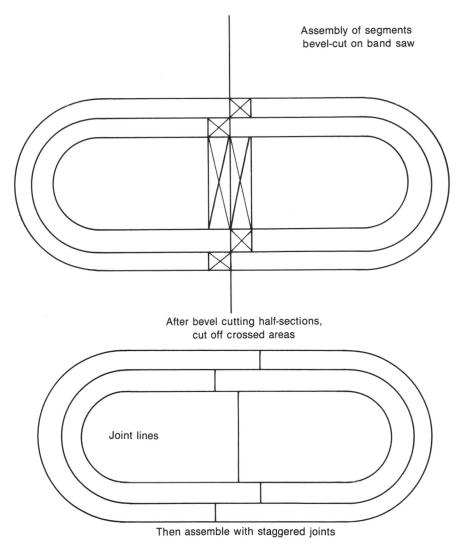

Assembly of segments
bevel-cut on band saw

After bevel cutting half-sections,
cut off crossed areas

Joint lines

Then assemble with staggered joints

Fig. 10-56. Bevel sawing is not limited to circular projects. The only reason for cutting the ends of the pieces after you have bevel-cut them is so you can assemble the project with staggered joints.

Using a table tilt of two to five degrees will work well in materials from ¼ inch to ¾ inch thick providing you don't work with a blade that cuts a very wide kerf. You'll find that a ⅛-inch or ¼-inch blade with slight set will work fine on the band saw. When in doubt about blade size or table tilt, make a single test cut in a piece of the material you plan to use.

One very critical point to remember when sawing is that the inside piece—the part that will project—must always be on the same side of the blade. Placing it otherwise will change the direction of the bevel, and that's trouble. The pieces will not go together as they should.

Fig. 10-57. You can glue bevel-sawed pieces together as half assemblies that you then join to complete the project. The idea works okay, but a single joint line will not have the strength that results from staggered joints.

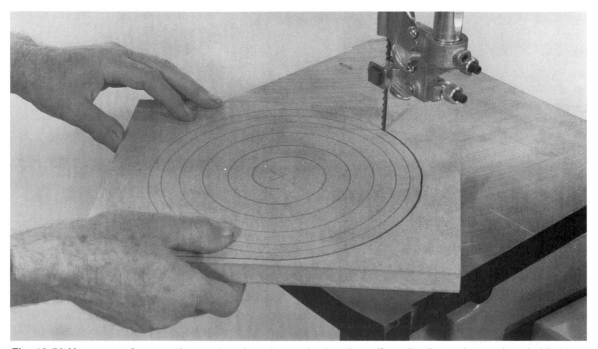

Fig. 10-58. You can perform continuous bevel-sawing on the band saw if you lay the project out in spiral fashion. To form a spiral, use a string between a center post and a pencil. Then, with the string taut, rotate the pencil about the center post.

Fig. 10-59. Spiral bevel sawing is an acceptable technique, but, obviously, requires considerable backtracking. It's best to turn off the machine and very carefully ease the blade back to its starting point.

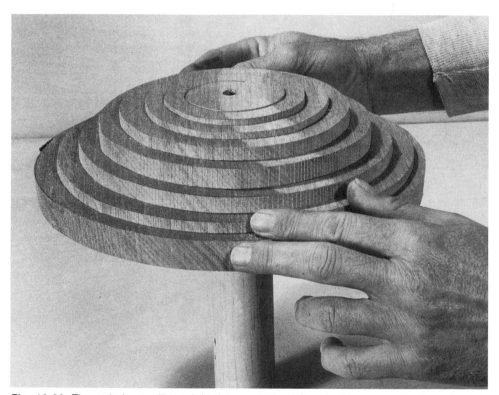

Fig. 10-60. The spiral cut will result in the same kind of projection you get with concentric rings. Gluing will be a bit more difficult but you can use brads to hold the layers in position. A band clamp will also help.

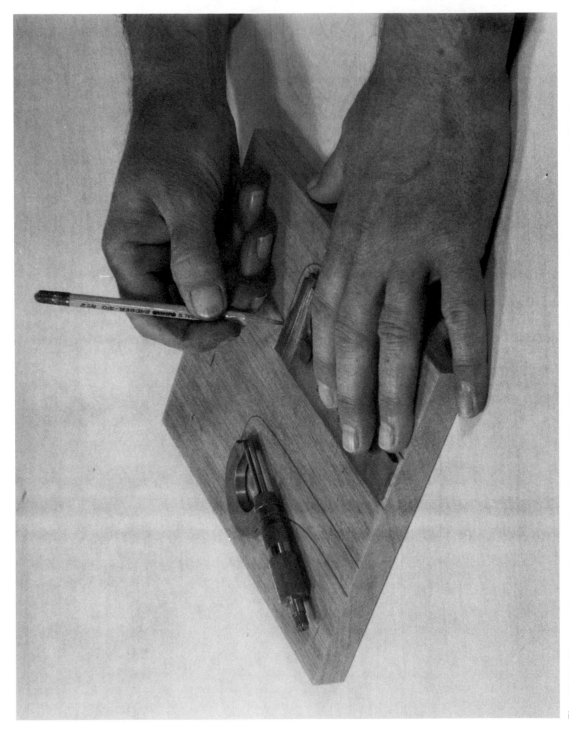

Fig. 10-61. You can do bevel sawing to create pockets in which you can safely store tools and other materials. The first step is to use the item as a pattern for marking the wood.

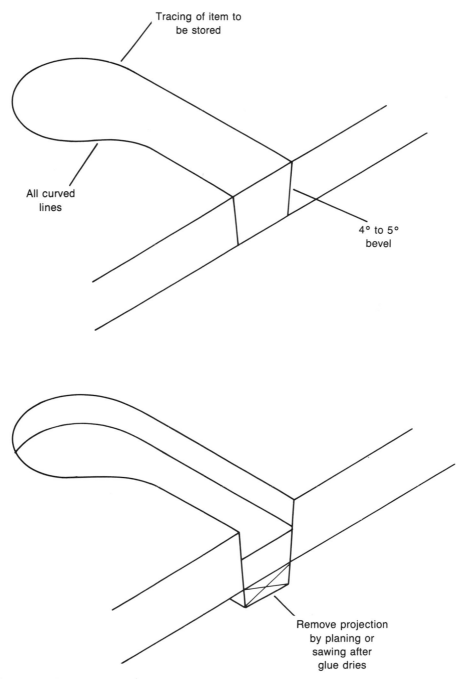

Tracing of item to
be stored

All curved
lines

4° to 5°
bevel

Remove projection
by planing or
sawing after
glue dries

Fig. 10-62. The second step is to glue the internal piece into the part from which it was cut. You can remove the projection after the glue dries, but it might be easier to first resaw it to approximate thickness before gluing it. You then can sand the sawed surface smooth.

Fig. 10-63. Creating pockets is a way to produce sliding shelves that require less space than drawers. If the project is a cabinet, the shelves can slide in grooves that you form in side members. Pockets can provide a safe way to store precision tools.

Chapter 11

Sawing Metals

THE BAND SAW IS SUITABLE FOR SAWING ALL KINDS OF METAL AS WELL AS WOOD. Actually, the original concept was intended pretty much for wood sawing only. Thanks, however, to improvements in the tool such as speed changers (either built in or available as accessories), improved techniques for metal-sawing situations, and, especially, advances in blades and blade-metal technology, the tool is now used extensively in industry and, to some extent, in small shops for general metal-sawing.

Of course, you don't work with metals as you do with wood. It's okay, as we mentioned in chapter 2, to use a conventional wood-cutting blade at regular wood-sawing speeds when confronted with a job that calls for sawing soft metals. But being equipped for general metal work that involves thick pieces of ferrous metals, heavy steel tubes, and so on, is another story. While it's possible to find a suitable metal-cutting blade for almost any band saw, synchronizing the blade with a speed that is efficient for the job calls for speed-changing capability.

USING THE CORRECT BLADE

In general, blades that are designed specifically for sawing metals have finer teeth and usually work better with more teeth to the inch than those that are efficient for wood. Tpi (teeth per inch) can run from a low of six to as high as 32. The thinner the material you are cutting, the more tpi the blade should have. Soft metals like aluminum, brass, or copper cut best with coarser-toothed blades. Having a set of metal-cutting blades that include those with 24, 18, and 14 tpi is a good idea for routinely working in a small shop, but they will not cover all contingencies.

Bimetal band-saw blades are specially produced for maximum cutting speed and resistance to abrasion. The back of the blade is carbon-alloy steel that is resilient and lasts a long time due to a heat-treatment process. The cutting teeth, which are welded in place with an electron beam, are made of high-speed steel, which is also specially heat treated. The result is a more efficient metal-cutting blade. It's a good blade for anyone who does a lot of band sawing, especially in thick stock. The blades are expensive—a ½-inch unit can cost close to thirty dollars—but faster cutting, and a long life might justify the investment.

Metal-cutting blades must withstand a lot of stress so even "normal" ones are usually specially tempered and hardened. Sharpening them, even if you chose to take on such a chore, requires special equipment that you aren't likely to consider for a small shop. Used correctly, the blades have an excellent survival rate, so discarding them when they dull is not wasteful.

TOOTH STYLES

You will find, with the exception of a wave-set blade, that tooth styles recommended for metal sawing don't differ too much from those on wood-cutting blades (Fig. 11-1). Blades that have every tooth set in alternate directions should be very familiar since they don't differ at all from the type of blade that usually is supplied as standard equipment with a machine. If it's the only blade you have, it isn't untoward to use it at woodworking speeds for sawing soft metals.

The regular design, with its unset (raker) tooth between pairs of set teeth, is recommended for clean cutting of tougher materials like steel and cast iron. The wave set concept is literally so; groups of teeth curve gently, alternating to left and right just as you find in the common hacksaw blade. If you have ever cut by hand with a hacksaw, you will have a good idea of how a wave-set band-saw blade works. The design is especially fine for sawing thin materials and metal tubing and pipe. Blades of this type usually have a maximum number of teeth per inch and minimum set, so they leave an edge that is reasonably smooth.

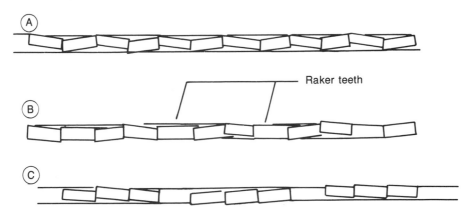

A . . . . All teeth set alternating left and right
B . . . . Regular (reg) or "raker" set has unset tooth between pairs of set teeth
C . . . . Wave set has groups of teeth "waving" to left and right

Fig. 11-1. These drawings are of tooth designs that are found on metal-cutting blades. Except for the wave set, they don't differ too much from wood-sawing blades.

The tpi of a blade is as important as tooth configuration. Clogging can result if you use a blade with many fine teeth to saw thick material. Conversely, you can damage a blade that doesn't have enough tpi in relation to the thickness of the project material or you can strip its teeth (Fig. 11-2). Probably the best rule to try to abide by is that a minimum of three teeth should be in contact with the work throughout the pass.

The minimum-turning radii of blades that was discussed in chapter 2 applies to metal-sawing blades as well as wood cutters. However, the fact that you are sawing in material much harder than wood results in a more confining kerf. It's possible that a blade of a particular width won't make as tight a turn when sawing metal as it could when sawing wood. It's not likely that the kind of metal sawing you do will be as intricate as wood-sawing chores, so the radii business might be a moot point. Good practice says never to try to force a blade around a turn it can't negotiate with reasonable ease.

I have found, through experience, that a good choice of metal-cutting blade in a shop that primarily is involved with woodworking is one with regular set, ½ inch wide, and with about 18 tpi.

BLADE SPEEDS

In order for a band saw to provide the most efficient speed for every metal-sawing contingency, it must be equipped with a speed-changing mechanism. There's no way to escape this fact. You can purchase some machines, like Delta's 14-inch unit, with or without the special equipment that is shown attached to the machine in Fig. 11-3. A combination of reduction gear box and sets of matching step pulleys allows speeds that range from 40 to 3000 fpm (Fig. 11-4). Other companies, like Sears Roebuck (Craftsman tools), offer as accessories speed-reduction units that you can add to the machine. Even so, it isn't likely that the most efficient speed for every operation and blade, as suggested in Table 11-1, will be available. The only out is to come as close as possible to the ideal speed.

It wouldn't make sense, here, to describe the steps to take to achieve speed changes on various machines. The book would just repeat information that is provided with the tool or the accessory. However, it does make sense for owners to accept as bible the instructions that the manufacturers offer.

Fig. 11-2. To avoid blade damage and stripping, two or three teeth must be in contact with the work's edge.

Fig. 11-3. Delta's 14-inch band saw is available with or without a speed-changing mechanism. The system consists of a gear-reduction box and matched step pulleys. Without an addition of this type, a band saw can't be considered a complete metal-sawing machine as well as a wood cutter.

A FEW GENERAL THOUGHTS

You perform metal sawing at speeds slower than are required for wood. You should cut tough materials like steel, and any thick materials, at speeds that are slower than those best used for soft materials and thin stock. When a blade speed is too high, the teeth will do more rubbing than cutting. They will just slide across the metal with little effect, and they will dull more quickly than they should. Feed pressure should be just enough to keep the blade working. If you feed too fast, you will be forcing the blade. On the other hand, being too cautious won't accomplish as much as the blade is capable of performing.

WORK HANDLING

The standard table insert does not supply maximum support close to the blade, which is why thin materials, especially soft sheet metals that are not supported in a special way, will have a considerable amount of burring on the underside of the cut (Fig. 11-5). You can minimize this negative factor by using a fine-toothed blade, but it will occur. One way to solve the problem satisfactorily is to make a substitute insert with a kerf that allows no clearance around the blade (Fig. 11-6). The homemade insert, which you can make of aluminum or even a material like hardboard, will provide

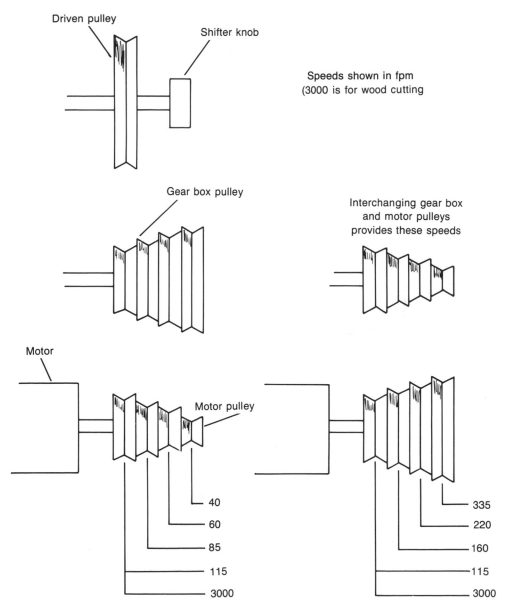

Speeds shown in fpm
(3000 is for wood cutting

Fig. 11-4. These speeds are available on the Delta machine. The owner's manual supplies the information that you need to make changes.

support at the exact point of cutting and, consequently, will minimize the burring if not eliminate it entirely.

Another method is to clamp a backup board to the table after you have kerfed it by the blade in use. Like the special insert, it provides zero room between the blade and the work support (Fig. 11-7). The idea is especially useful when you make straight, fence-guided cuts.

Table 11-1. Suggested Blades and Speeds for Metal Sawing.

MATERIAL	THICKNESS OF WORK							
	UP TO 1/16″		1/16″–1/4″		1/4″–1″		OVER 1″	
	Teeth*	Speed**	Teeth*	Speed**	Teeth*	Speed**	Teeth*	Speed**
Aluminum	18	2200	14	2200	6	340	6	340
Brass	18	2200	14	340	14	340	8	250
Soft Bronze	18	340	14	340	10	250	8	175
Hard Bronze	18	340	14	250	14	175	10	125
Copper	18	340	14	340	10	250	8	175
Cast Iron	18	250	14	175	14	125	10	125
Pipe	18	340	18	340	18	175	14	125
Carbon Steel	24	175	18	175	14	175	10	125
Steel Alloy	18	175	14	125	14	125	14	125
Thinwall Tubing	32	250	18	125	--	---	--	---

*Teeth per inch
**Surface feet per minute

The same thought applies when a curved cut is required. In this case, you must tape the work or otherwise hold it to the backup board and saw the pieces simultaneously (Fig. 11-8). To carry this idea a bit further to the point of guaranteed results, think about sandwiching the work between two sheets.

Toothless blades, those that cut with tungsten-carbide particles and that were described in chapter 2, have an abrasive cutting action, so it is likely that they will provide relatively fault-free cuts without the use of special inserts or backup boards (Fig. 11-9).

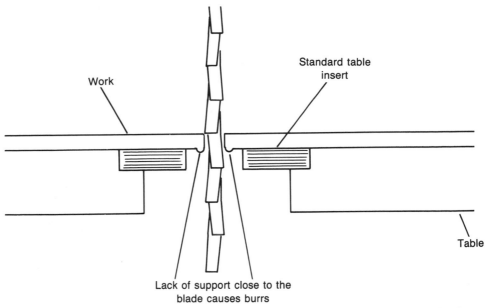

Work

Standard table insert

Table

Lack of support close to the
blade causes burrs

Fig. 11-5. Burring on the underside of the work is not avoidable when sawing thin sheets because the work is not supported close enough to the cutting area. You will need special setups to eliminate the burring.

Special insert
for sawing
sheet metal

Fig. 11-6. One way to guard against excessive burring is to make a special insert that leaves zero room around the blade. Use the standard insert as a pattern for the auxiliary item, but kerf it with the blade in use.

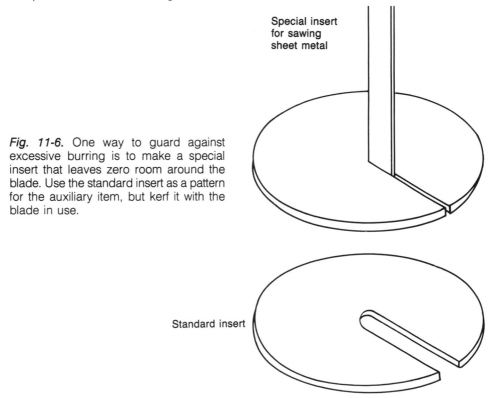

Standard insert

Fig. 11-7. A backing board, which you should make from a material like hardboard or dense plywood, will also minimize burring. This design is a good setup for straight cuts.

Fig. 11-8. When curved cuts are involved, you can tape the work material or otherwise secure it to the backing board. Another system calls for sandwiching the work between sheets.

TYPICAL WORK HOLDERS

Sawing hard materials calls for the use of a holding device to keep workpieces firmly in correct alignment and to reduce operator fatigue. Jobs like cutting through metal bar stock or thick-walled steel tubing take a lot of time, during which the operator must constantly hold the work tightly to maintain the feed direction and to avoid chattering. This fact is especially true of round stock, whether solid or tubular, since the blade's tendency to rotate the workpiece is part of the nature of the job.

A simple V-block is a quick solution, but a jig that is composed of matching blocks that you can pull together with screws or bolts that pass through them offers a more practical way to work (Fig. 11-10). Operating this way reduces problems to merely feeding the work correctly, and even this chore is easier since it's just a question of keeping the side of the work holder in line with the blade. V-blocks are not limited to securing tubular material. They also are suitable for solid rounds and for square stock, whether solid or of channel configuration (Fig. 11-11).

If you wish, you can add a wooden bar to the underside of the jig to fit the table's miter-gauge slot. The added piece will make it even easier to feed the work correctly. Be sure to attach the bar so that the V-blocks will run parallel to the blade.

Fig. 11-9. Grit-Edge, toothless blades cut with hundreds of particles of tungsten carbide. Cut edges will be acceptably smooth even without the use of a backing board.

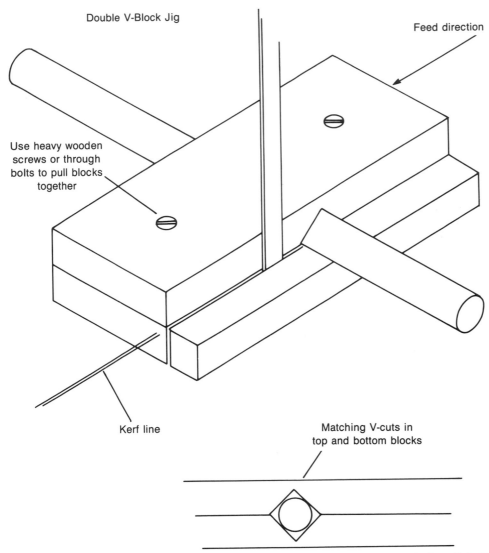

Double V-Block Jig

Feed direction

Use heavy wooden
screws or through
bolts to pull blocks
together

Kerf line

Matching V-cuts in
top and bottom blocks

Fig. 11-10. Matching V-blocks that you can pull together with screws or bolts will hold workpieces securely. They will help you work more accurately and will eliminate the chore of having to keep the work from rotating because of the blade's drag.

You also can use the V-blocks that were demonstrated in various chapters for wood sawing for metal work. Figure 11-12 illustrates how you can use the basic V-block, combined with a miter-gauge hold-down, to grip work. Figure 11-13 proves that the more sophisticated V-block project, with hold-down, is equally suitable.

IMPROVISE AN AUTO FEED
Many metal-sawing jobs require a lot of time. Keeping a heavy piece of work in contact with the blade throughout the sawing process can try your patience and stress your

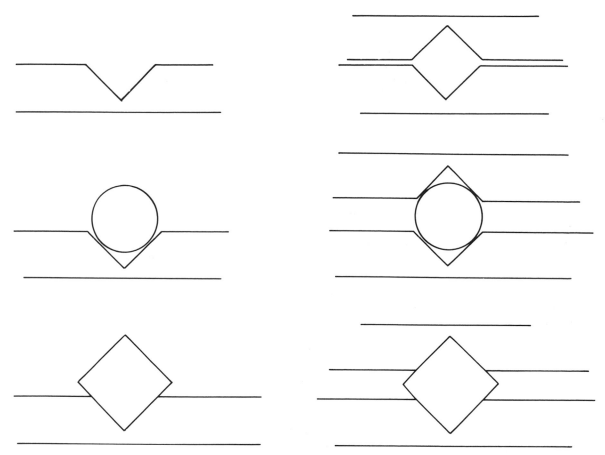

V-Blocks—single or double—can be used to secure square as well as round stock

Fig. 11-11. V-blocks are suitable holders for square as well as round stock. You also can use jigs of this type to grip plastic tubes or cylinders.

fingers. Other ways exist to get around this tiresome procedure. Some of them involve extra-cost accessories like a screw feed, but you can get by quite nicely by duplicating the arrangement that is shown in Fig. 11-14. A miter-gauge hold-down, together with a V-block, grips the work; a weight that connects to the gauge with a strong line that passes over a pulley supplies the feed pressure. An important component that is not shown in the photograph is a stop block that you clamp to the table so feed pressure will halt as soon as the blade has passed through the work.

The weight to use depends on the job. The use of the drill vise is just an example of what you can do. A more flexible arrangement would be to attach a small container to the line. Then add weights until the blade is cutting consistently and without being forced.

A way to provide for mounting a pulley when you are unable to copy the hold-down arrangement is shown in Fig. 11-15. The project can do double duty—its base can be long enough to act as a stop for the work.

Fig. 11-12. A basic V-block, together with a miter-gauge hold-down, provides excellent work security. One clamp of the hold-down bears on the V-block, the other one bears on the work.

Fig. 11-13. The more advanced V-block jig serves nicely for metal as well as wood cutting. You will appreciate the hold-down since metal sawing usually requires a lot of time.

Fig. 11-14. Here is one way to improvise an automatic feed. A strong line that travels over a pulley connects the weight to the miter gauge. In this case, it was possible to attach the pulley to the rear post of the hold-down. It isn't shown here, but the arrangement should include a stop block that will halt the feed action as soon as the blade is through the work.

SAWING OTHER NONWOOD MATERIALS

Handling plastics doesn't differ too much from wood sawing. A general rule is to feed as fast as the blade allows. This rule helps to avoid problems like clogged kerfs and overheated material. Wood-sawing speeds with blades that have 10 or 14 tpi generally will provide good results. Some plastics chip rather easily so you should avoid coarse-cutting blades. It's okay to work with a narrow, fine-toothed blade if you are striving for smoothest cuts, but be aware that you can soften some plastics by cutting friction, and this can cause waste material to "weld" in the kerf.

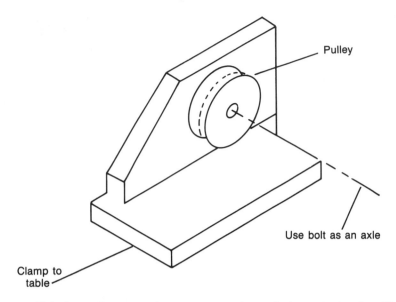

Pulley

Use bolt as an axle

Clamp to table

Fig. 11-15. This figure shows you how to arrange for an independent pulley. The base can be long enough to act as a stop. Position it on the table so it won't interfere with how the miter gauge must move.

Materials like plasterboard and fiberglass, even cardboard and thin hardboards, will have smoother edges when you use a blade with about 14 or 15 tpi. You can obtain acceptable results when sawing materials like veneers and plastic laminates when the blade has generous tpi—24 or more. Always remember when sawing thin material, that the blade must have 2 or 3 teeth in contact with the work's edge. When you are unable to follow the rule, which might be the case when sawing a veneer-type material, it's best to saw with the material on a backing board or to sandwich it between sheets, which is the same system that was suggested for sawing thin, metal sheets.

Chapter 12

The Band Saw
As a Sander

YOU CAN TRANSFORM A BAND SAW INTO A TYPE OF BELT SANDER BY SUBSTITUTING abrasive loops for saw blades. Since the machine is limited to sanding belts that are ½ inch or 1 inch wide, the extra function is not intended as a replacement for conventional belt sanders that work with belts as wide as 6 inches, but for many routine sanding chores and especially when intricate shapes are involved, the tool doesn't have to apologize to anyone. The standard tool to which the band saw as a sander might be compared is the sander/grinder, like the example shown in Fig. 12-1.

The sander/grinder routinely is used to smooth metals. While you also can use the band saw to smooth metals, the practice is not recommended. The major reason is that sanding or grinding of ferrous metals will produce sparks that can travel to the interior of the machine where they might nestle into accumulations of wood dust. The situation can be tricky; sparks can furtively smolder for a time before graduating to fire.

BACKUPS FOR SANDING BELTS

Special guides or *platens* are available for band saws that offer the sanding option. They will be available as extra-cost accessories if they are not supplied with the machine. The sanding kit might include a single, flat platen, or it might include two units. The second unit would have a shaped bearing surface that makes it more usable for smoothing curved work (Fig. 12-2).

You would install backups between upper and lower blade guides in some manner that is peculiar to the machine in use. Whether the accessory comes with the machine or is added, instructions for correct assembly will be provided.

Fig. 12-1. The band saw, when fitted with a sanding belt instead of a saw blade, works something like a sander/grinder. The advantage of this tool is that you can use it to smooth internal cutouts by passing the belt through the work before you install it over the wheels.

Fig. 12-2. The main parts of an accessory kit that allows band-saw sanding are platens that are situated between upper and lower blade guides to support the belt when pressure is applied against it. Platens might be flat, or they might have a shaped bearing surface.

You can use most any band saw for sanding even if special equipment is not available, simply by making your own belt supports. Actually, customizing backups is a good idea even when ready-made ones are available since it affords the opportunity to shape support edges that are exactly right for the job on hand. The ideas that are offered in Fig. 12-3 are just starters to lead you in the right direction. You can face backups with thin or thick pieces of felt or a similar material; this facing is a nice idea when you need a soft backing for the sanding belt. Be sure to adjust the normal roller support so it is free of the belt, and to back off or remove the guides that normally are used on the right-hand side of a saw blade. When you are working without a belt, support is also an acceptable method of working. It is one that is quite useful when, for example, you are smoothing compound curves.

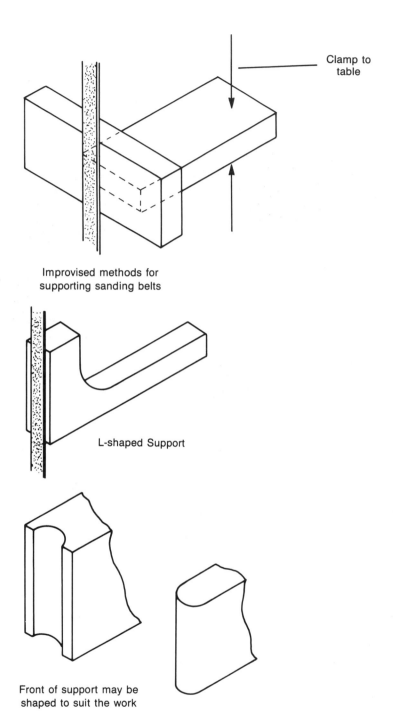

Clamp to
table

Improvised methods for
supporting sanding belts

L-shaped Support

Front of support may be
shaped to suit the work

Fig. 12-3. Sanding belts can be supported by custom-designed backups. Even when standard platens are available, making your own often can solve or facilitate a particular sanding requirement.

SANDING BELTS

Ready-to-mount sanding belts in various grits and, sometimes, with a choice of abrasive like aluminum oxide or garnet, will be available for your machine (Fig. 12-4). Garnet is a good choice for general wood sanding and aluminum oxide, also usable on wood, is the accepted choice for metal. The *grit* to choose—grit being the size of the abrasive particles—depends on the job. Use coarse grits to remove a lot of material fast; use finer grits when the work is in reasonably good shape from the beginning. You do not always have to follow the procedure that calls for starting with a coarse grit and working down through finer ones. Roughing up an edge with coarse sandpaper is unnecessary if all it needs is a light touch.

Belting in various widths, grits, and abrasive material is available in bulk form, usually in rolls of fifty yards. This bulk form requires that the worker assemble his own belt loops, but you have the advantage of economy and of being able to produce a belt that is not available ready-made for the machine you own. Assemble homemade belts as follows.

The length of the belt must equal that of the saw blades the machine uses, plus allowance for a lap that you will need to make a joint (Fig. 12-5). Make matching cuts at about a 45-degree angle, and then remove the particles in the lap areas by working with an abrasive stone. It's not a difficult chore, but you will find it easier to accomplish if you first use a brush to wet the area with water. It's possible, with the area wet, that you can remove abrasive particles by scraping with something like a putty knife. Whatever the system, work toward the cut end of the belt.

Fig. 12-4. Ready-to-mount sanding belts in various grits and abrasive materials are available. You can make your own when the manufacturer of the tool does not make them available or when you need a special abrasive material or grit size.

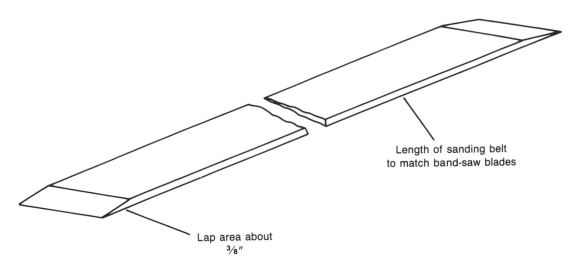

Length of sanding belt
to match band-saw blades

Lap area about
3/8"

Fig. 12-5. Cut bulk belting to match the length of the saw blades plus the area needed to connect the strip as a loop. Make cuts at about a 45-degree angle and then remove the abrasive particles in the joint area.

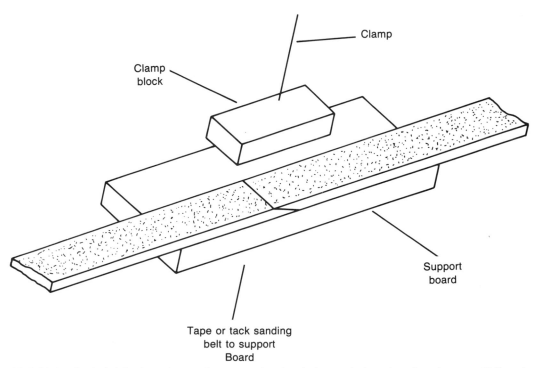

Clamp

Clamp
block

Support
board

Tape or tack sanding
belt to support
Board

Fig. 12-6. Make the belt joint by using ordinary ready-mixed glue and clamping the pieces until the glue has set. Use wax paper between the belt and the support board and under the clamp block so excess glue won't cause adhesion where you don't need it.

You can finalize the connection by improvising a clamping system like the one shown in Fig. 12-6. Use ordinary, ready-mixed glue, but if it is too viscous, it can leave a bump that will interfere with smooth sanding. You can judge results by making a test joint in some scrap belting. If necessary, thin the glue with a small amount of water. When clamping, place pieces of wax paper under the belt and between the belt and topside clamp block. If the support board and the clamp block are wide enough, you will be able to prepare several belts at the same time.

Install sanding belts as if they were saw blades, using tracking and tensioning adjustments to seat them correctly. Supply only as much tension as you need to keep the belt taut.

SANDING PROCEDURES

You perform belt sanding at regular wood-sawing speeds. Your first attempt immediately will make you aware of how rapidly the belt can cut. If you were to move a piece of soft wood directly into the belt, you would form a notch in no time. Therefore, feed pressure must be very light and you must move the work steadily, to the right or the left (Fig. 12-7). Hesitating at any time during the pass while the work is in contact with the belt will result in mars that you can remove only by additional sanding.

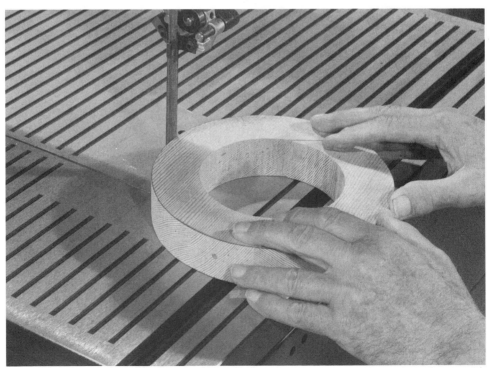

Fig. 12-7. The secret of acceptable sanding on the band saw is a light touch and a steady, uniform rate of feed. Keeping the work in one position, or pausing during the pass, will cause imperfections that you only can remove by additional sanding. This additional sanding can be critical if you are sanding to a precise dimension.

You will do most sanding freehandedly, but when straight edges are involved, it's okay to work with a guide. For example, you can move mitered edges across the belt with a miter gauge (Fig. 12-8). A gentle touch is essential to keep the work from pushing the belt off the wheels. It is better to make a few light passes than a single, heavy one. Maintain a uniform, steady rate of feed. When bevels are involved, it's okay to work with a tilted table just as you would when sawing.

Fig. 12-8. You can sand straight cuts freehand, but you will work more accurately if you employ a mechanical device to guide the feed direction. Here, the miter gauge is set to the same angle that you used for the saw cut. Be sure that there is light contact between the work and the abrasive surface.

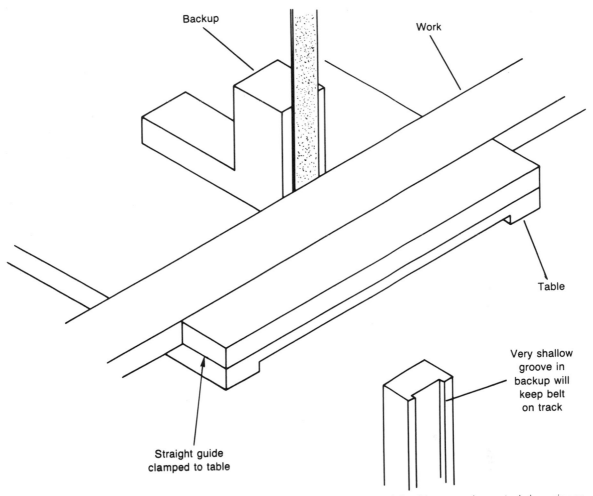

Labels in figure:

Backup

Work

Table

Very shallow groove in backup will keep belt on track

Straight guide clamped to table

Fig. 12-9. A setup like this will ensure that you will sand long edges straight. It's a good way to bring pieces to uniform width or to "joint" edges of boards that you will assemble edge to edge. On all jobs like this, you must be careful to work so you don't push the belt off the wheels.

Figure 12-9 suggests a system that you can use for smoothing long edges—a kind of jointing operation. Clamp the guide parallel to the belt and position it to accommodate the width of the work. You can get by without the special belt support, but making one will help ensure that you will not move the belt off the wheels. The work will be successful only if you move it steadily past the belt. Hesitate at any point and the belt will dig into the edge. This technique will prove especially useful when you need many parts of equal width or when you need to prepare edges of workpieces that will join edge to edge.

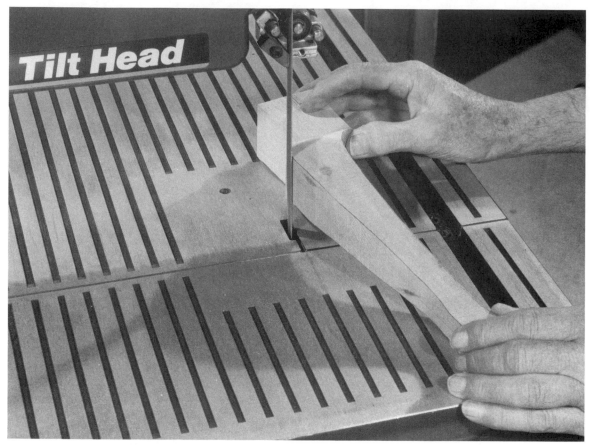

Fig. 12-10. You can smooth compound curves, round off edges, and do similar jobs best by eliminating the backup for the belt. This setup allows the belt more flexibility to follow contours. In situations like this, loosening belt tension can be helpful, but don't overdo it!

For some jobs, like contour sanding or when you wish to round off sharp corners, it's best to work without a belt backup (Fig. 12-10). As you can imagine, you must take special care when manipulating the work to keep the belt tracking correctly. On some jobs of this nature, it might help to loosen tension, but just a bit—only enough to supply some belt flexibility.

You can sand plastics as well as wood, but be careful with thermosetting types or any material that can become soft due to the friction heat created by sanding. Make contact with the belt in brief periods so you can allow the material to cool between applications.

Remember that sanding belts are cutting tools. Each abrasive particle removes its own share of wood. Allow the belts to cut at their own speed. Forcing won't accomplish anything more than blemished work and damaged, broken, or clogged belts.

Also remember that safety goggles and a dust mask are important factors of good practice.

Chapter 13

A Sampling of Projects

THERE IS A LOT OF ENJOYMENT IN BECOMING PROFICIENT WITH POWER TOOLS AND IN learning some of the "secrets" that are routine with professionals. But the whole purpose of the exercise, the real fun, lies in putting your knowledge to use, whether for maintenance chores or remodeling or making household accessories that are practical or just decorative.

Except for some necessary chores like drilling holes, which is a job that you can do with a portable electric drill or on a drill press, you can accomplish all of the projects that follow on the band saw. Of course, as a woodworker, you might have other tools in the shop and, if you choose, there is no reason why you can't use them cooperatively with the band saw. If you wish to make a long, straight cut on a table saw, or use an individual belt/disc sander or a drum sander in a portable drill to smooth edges—why not?

You must follow some basic ground rules. The most important one, obviously, is working carefully so project components will come together as they should. Even the basic butt joint won't be as strong as it can be unless mating surfaces or edges are flat and square.

Use a ready-mixed woodworker's glue in all connections but don't, as many of us do, feel that more is better than just enough. It's a nuisance to have to clean away excess glue that is squeezed out under clamp pressure, and it's wasteful. Spread glue with a small brush after you have pressed a bead of it from the container. On porous surfaces, like an edge on plywood, allow a first, light application to soak in, and then apply a second one. Most times, glue is required on both surfaces of the joint; but, instructions that you should read on the container might suggest otherwise.

Use finishing nails or wood screws as reinforcement. A general rule for selecting nail sizes is that they should penetrate into the part being joined by about two-thirds of their length. It's a rule that you often must ignore because of component thicknesses, but stay as close to it as possible. Drive finishing nails below the surface of the wood with a suitable nail set, and then fill the cavity with wood dough. It's wise when working with hardwoods and when nailing is required near an edge, to first drill a pilot hole that is smaller in diameter than the fastener. It will be easier to drive the nail and will avoid splitting.

The nail-length theory also applies to wood screws and also is subject to change. Screws always require a pilot hole. You can get by by punching a starting hole with an awl if the screw is small and the wood is soft, but drilling is usually required. Correct installation calls for a pilot hole, a shank hole, and a countersink or a counterbore. You can accomplish this installation with individual tools, but it's much better to work with screw-hole bits that form everything at once. Purchase the special bits in sets since a single unit won't do for all sizes of screws.

Drive flathead screws flush with the surface of the wood and, in hidden areas, leave them exposed. If you don't want them to appear, drive them into counterbored holes, and then fill the cavity with a wooden plug that you can sand flush, or with a *wooden button*, an item that has a convex head that shows above the surface of the wood as a decorative detail.

Use wooden pads when clamping to avoid marring surfaces. Keep work clamped as long as necessary. With some glues, you can remove clamps after as little as thirty minutes. This procedure reduces waiting time, but remember that the joint won't have full strength until a considerably longer period of time. Get the facts by reading the instructions on the container.

Sand all components as you complete them. It's much better to work this way since only a minimum of attention will be required after final assembly.

BAND-SAWED BOXES

You can cut band-sawed boxes from one piece of base stock that can be a glued assembly or a solid piece (Figs. 13-1 through 13-7). A glued assembly offers the opportunity to use contrasting woods so the project will be even more interesting. Sizes are usually small so you can handle them more easily on the machine. The shape of the box is where you can be imaginative. Boxes can be square or rectangular or have curved profiles; they even can be made in shapes that resemble animals.

A suitable blade for work of this nature will be ¼ inch wide with 14 tpi. When radii are too tight for the ¼-inch blade, switch to a ⅛-inch blade. Both blades will be slight, which is good, since a minimum-width kerf is desirable. Use a guide when making straight cuts and be very cautious when sawing curves. You must return parts that are cut to original positions, so the closer they "jive" the more successful the project will be. Thickness of pieces that are cut off—parts that become components—can vary, but they should not be more than about ³⁄₁₆ or ¼ inch.

The technique is actually a reverse procedure. Normally, when making a box with a drawer, you would prepare individual pieces and then assemble them. When band sawing boxes, you create components by "breaking down" a solid block and then reassembling the parts to form the project.

Basic Procedure for Band-Sawed Boxes

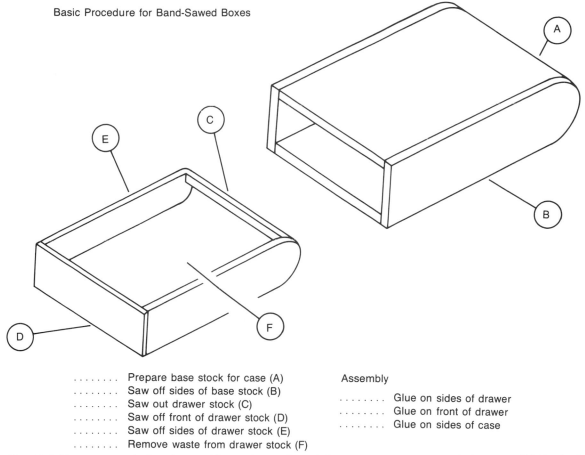

```
. . . . . . . .  Prepare base stock for case (A)        Assembly
. . . . . . . .  Saw off sides of base stock (B)
. . . . . . . .  Saw out drawer stock (C)               . . . . . . . .  Glue on sides of drawer
. . . . . . . .  Saw off front of drawer stock (D)      . . . . . . . .  Glue on front of drawer
. . . . . . . .  Saw off sides of drawer stock (E)      . . . . . . . .  Glue on sides of case
. . . . . . . .  Remove waste from drawer stock (F)
```

Fig. 13-1. You can create band-sawed boxes by sawing all the necessary components from a solid block of wood. Do the sawing with a ¼-inch or ⅛-inch blade that has about 14 tpi.

CLOWN PLAQUES

Projects of the type shown in Figs. 13-8 through 13-11 usually are considered jobs for a jigsaw but you can produce them successfully on a band saw if you work with a slight blade, say, one that is ⅛ inch wide and has about 14 tpi. Even so, you probably will have to do some backtracking, so examine the project carefully before starting to saw, so you can determine where to make relief cuts. It's also feasible to drill holes where it would be a bit rough even for a small blade to get to.

Use the standard enlarging-by-squares method to transfer patterns to the wood or to a sheet of paper that you can use with carbon paper to mark the workpiece. The system consists of drawing suitably-sized squares and then marking intersections at points that coincide with where the pattern outline crosses them in the illustration. Connect the points freehandedly or, if necessary, by using something like a French curve.

If you are interested in producing many projects, don't forget about the pad-sawing technique that you can use.

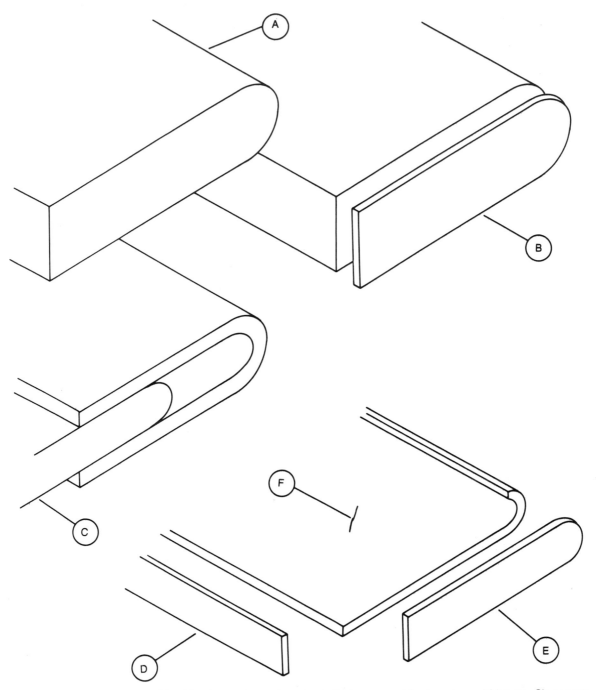

Fig. 13-2. Here you see the identification of the various parts that you need for band-sawed boxes. Since you must return the parts that you cut away to the original positions, it's essential that you saw very carefully and that you make kerfs as narrow as possible. Check these letter identifications with those in Fig. 13-1.

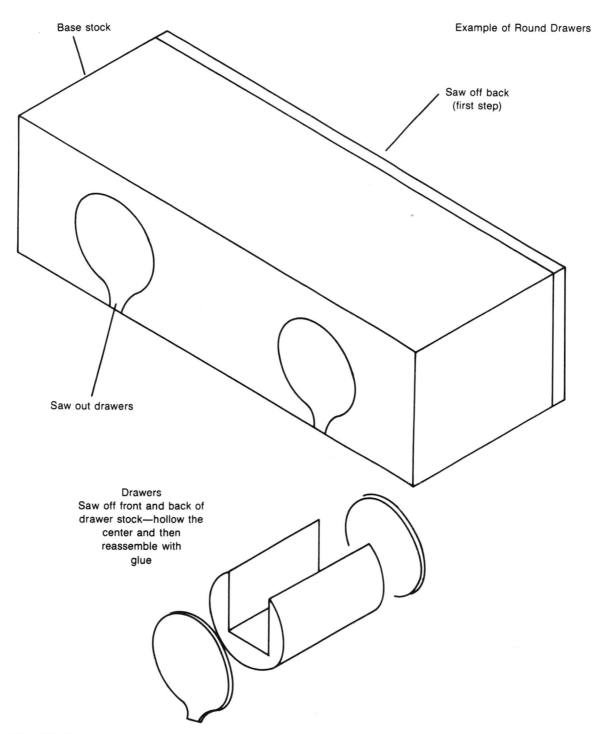

Base stock

Example of Round Drawers

Saw off back
(first step)

Saw out drawers

Drawers
Saw off front and back of
drawer stock—hollow the
center and then
reassemble with
glue

Fig. 13-3. You can produce round drawers by a continuous cut. The base stock does not have to be rectangular, and you can size it to hold as many drawers as you would like to include.

Pedestal Box With Round Drawer

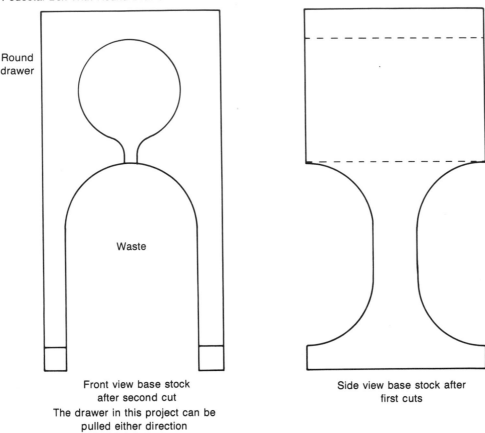

Round drawer

Waste

Front view base stock
after second cut

The drawer in this project can be
pulled either direction

Side view base stock after
first cuts

(See Fig. 13-3 for construction of round drawer)

Fig. 13-4. You are limited on the design of the project only by your imagination. When you do not close the project on one side, you can open the drawer from either direction.

A TRIO OF BIRD FEEDERS

Bird feeders are fun projects, and the enjoyment continues when, to use a cliche, our "feathered friends" discover them (Figs. 13-12 through 13-16). Make the bases first, then it will be easier to size and to locate the correct position for other components. It's also a good idea, at this time, to drill the holes for the perches, especially if you can form them on a drill press.

Since these projects are outdoor projects, use a waterproof glue and aluminum or galvanized fasteners. Don't forget the pad-sawing technique for producing the two, identical sides.

END TABLE

Begin construction of the end table (Figs. 13-17 and 13-18), by making a pad of the four pieces that are required for the legs. If you choose to reinforce the joint for

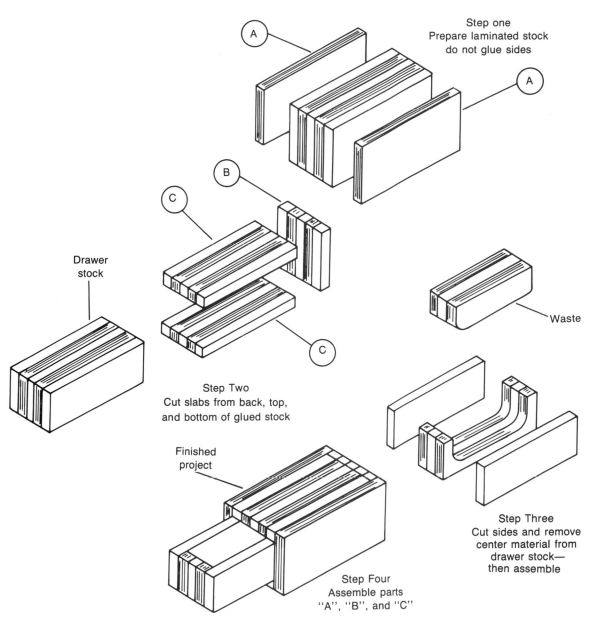

Fig. 13-5. Preparing the base stock by laminating layers of contrasting wood can make the project even more interesting. Note that you do not have to glue on the side pieces at the start, since you would have to saw them off anyway. A good glue job when doing the laminating is very important.

the half-leg shapes with dowels, drill the holes that are needed while the pieces still have straight sides. Saw the pad to the shape that is required and sand edges before you separate the pieces. Save the outside waste pieces since you will use these to present parallel sides for the clamps that you use to hold the leg components together until the glue sets.

Fig. 13-6. The only sawing required for this band-sawed box, other than shaping the base block, is cutting out the shape of the drawer.

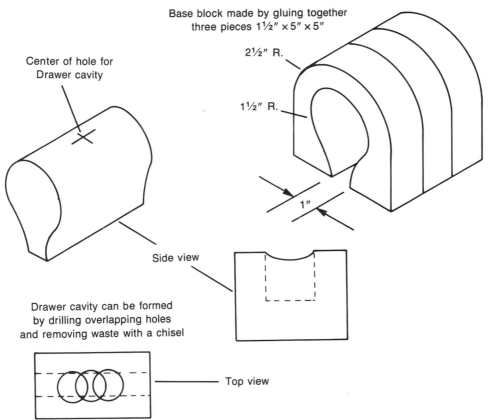

Base block made by gluing together three pieces 1½″ × 5″ × 5″

2½″ R.

1½″ R.

1″

Center of hole for Drawer cavity

Side view

Drawer cavity can be formed by drilling overlapping holes and removing waste with a chisel

Top view

Fig. 13-7. Hollow out the drawer by boring overlapping holes and then cleaning away the waste with a chisel. Make handles for the drawer by gluing short pieces of ¼-inch dowel into shallow holes.

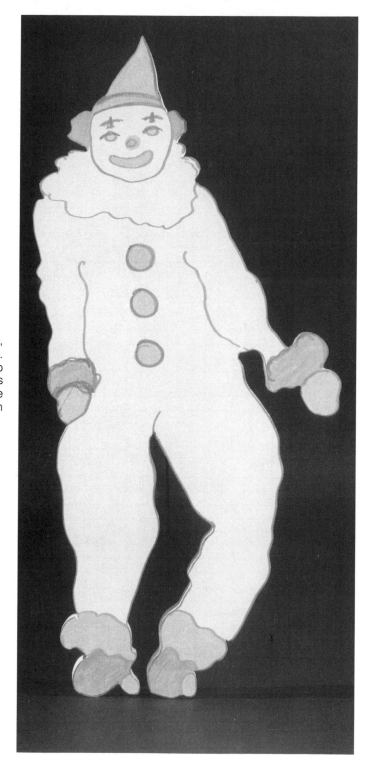

Fig. 13-8. Clown plaques, or similar figures, are perfectly feasible to do on a band saw. You can mount them on wooden bases to stand independently or place them on walls with double-faced tape. You choose the material—¼-inch plywood or ¾-inch lumber—it doesn't matter.

Fig. 13-9. Here is a diagram of clown plaque #1. Coat the project with white paint; add details with reds and greens.

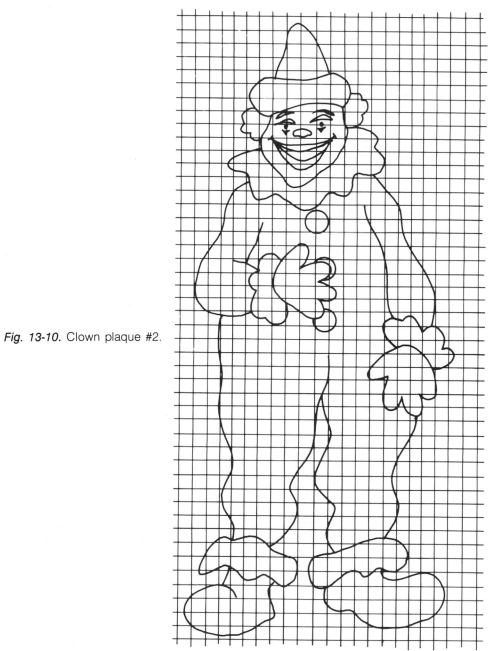

Fig. 13-10. Clown plaque #2.

The top is composed of three 1-inch- x -6-inch boards that are glued edge to edge, with or without dowel reinforcement. The slab is reduced to its final dimensions after the glue has set. You can begin final assembly by attaching the top and then including the rails and the shelf or by first connecting the legs with rail and shelf components and then adding the top.

Fig. 13-11. Clown plaque #3.

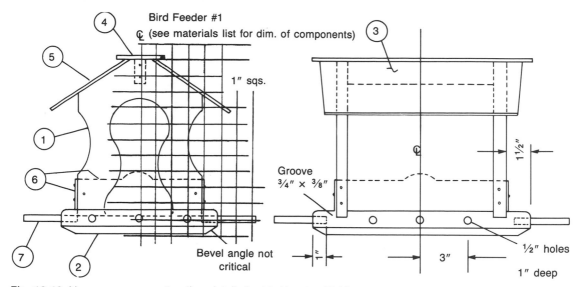

Fig. 13-12. Here you see construction details for bird feeder #1. You can produce both sides for this and similar projects in one operation by using the pad-sawing technique.

Table 13-1. Materials List for Bird Feeder #1.

Key	Part	No. of Pieces	Size (in Inches)				Material
1	Sides	2	¾	×	8 ×	10	Pine
2	Base	1	1½	×	10 ×	14	Pine
3	Brace	1	¾	×	1½ ×	9½	Pine
4	Ridge	1	¼	×	3 ×	14	Exterior plywood
5	Roof bds.	2	¼	×	6 ×	13	Exterior plywood
6	Sides	2	⅛	×	2½ ×	11	Plastic
	Ends	2	⅛	×	2½ ×	8	Plastic
7	Perch	12	½D.	×	4		Dowel

A DUET OF FIVE-BOARD STOOLS

Five-board stools are popular projects that hark back to Early American design (Figs. 13-19 through 13-22). They can serve as footstools or as stands for, among other things, potted plants. You can begin both projects by tack nailing similar pieces together so you can saw the legs simultaneously. Sawing will be easier if you first bore holes to provide for the top, arced areas of the design.

Projects like this often are *distressed*; that is, made to appear as if they have been in use for a long time. Round off corners as if by wear, and add abuse signs by whacking surface areas with a length of light chain. You should perform this treatment only to the point when blemishes appear to have been accidental.

Fig. 13-13. This project is for bird feeder #2. Posts are 1-inch dowels set in shallow holes in base and top components.

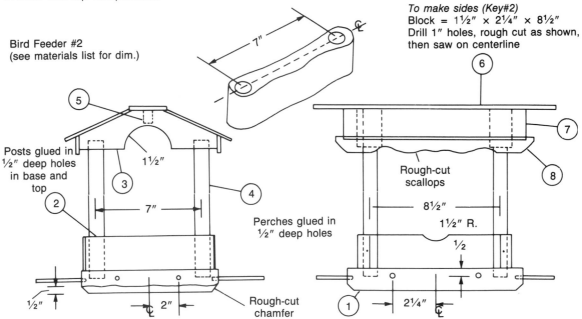

Bird Feeder #2
(see materials list for dim.)

7"

To make sides (Key#2)
Block = 1½" × 2¼" × 8½"
Drill 1" holes, rough cut as shown, then saw on centerline

6

7

8

5

Posts glued in ½" deep holes in base and top

3

2

1½"

7"

4

Perches glued in ½" deep holes

Rough-cut scallops

8½"

1½" R.

½

½"

2"

Rough-cut chamfer

1

2¼"

Fig. 13-14. Here you see construction details for bird feeder #2. Note that you make the sides by drilling holes in one piece of stock and then sawing it in half to get duplicates.

Table 13-2. Materials List for Bird Feeder #2.

Key	Part	No. of Pieces	Size (in Inches)			Material
1	Base	1	1½ × 9 × 11½			Pine
2	Side	2	¾ × 2¼ × 8½			Pine
3	Top	2	1½ × 2½ × 9			Pine
4	Posts	4	1″D. × 7½			Dowel
5	Brace	1	1 × 1¼ × 7			Pine
6	Ridge	1	⅜ × 2½ × 16			Redwood
7	Roof	2	⅜ × 5½ × 12			Redwood
8	Trim	2	⅜ × 1½ × 13			Redwood
9	Perch	8	⅜ D. × 3			Dowel

Fig. 13-15. This photo shows you bird feeder #3. The projects are popular, as you can see by the evidence left by visitors.

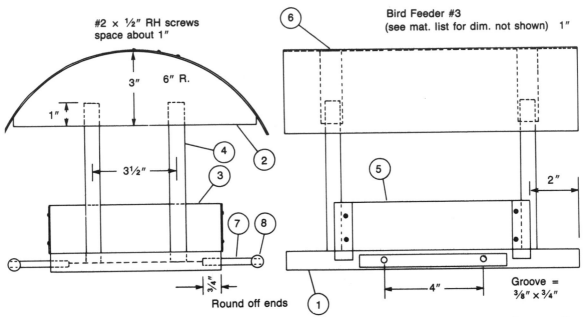

Fig. 13-16. Here is the diagram to make bird feeder #3. Start attaching the plastic laminate roof at the centerline. Bend and secure as you work toward the eaves. Drill holes for the screws.

Table 13-3. Materials List for Bird Feeder #3.

Key	Part	No. of Pieces	Size (in Inches)				Material
1	Base	1	¾	×	7	×	12	Pine
2	Top	2	¾	×	3	×	10	Pine
3	Bottom	2	¾	×	2⅜	×	7	Pine
4	Posts	4	⅝D.	×	6			Dowel
5	Sides	2	⅛	×	2	×	8	Plastic
6	Roof	1	1⁄16	×	12	×	18	Plastic laminate
7	Perch support	4	¼D.	×	4½			Dowel
8	Perch	2	½D.	×	6			Dowel

Assemble either project by first connecting the legs with the rails and then adding the top piece.

PLANT STAND

This project combines traditional lines with a modern finish (Figs. 13-23 and 13-24). It's a purely decorative piece that will serve well as a support for a good-size plant container. Cut all parts to the shapes that are shown before doing any assembly. Drill for and install the dowels after you have glued the rear leg in place.

Fig. 13-17. This end table has traditional lines. Knotty pine is a good material for this type of project.

End table
(see materials list for dim. not shown on drawing)

. . . . top = three edge-glued pieces
. . . . legs = two edge-glued pieces

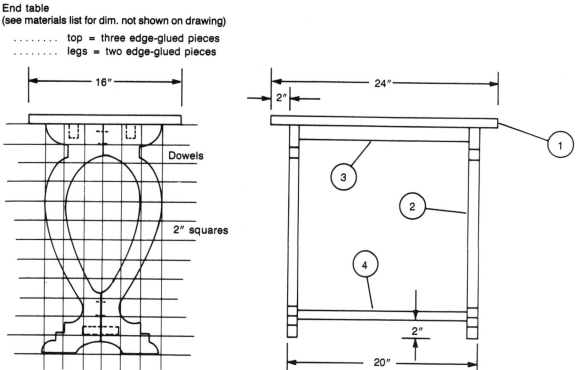

Fig. 13-18. This figure shows you how to make the end table. The legs are two-piece affairs that you glue together after you shape profiles. You can join the leg parts and even the pieces for the top with or without dowel reinforcement. In either case, mating edges must be flat and square.

Finishing calls for a very smooth sanding job, followed by an application of pigmented sealer. Then, finish the job with several applications of lacquer with a light sanding between applications and after the final one. You can use paste wax to restore the sheen that you remove by sanding.

Table 13-4. Materials List for End Table.

Key	Part	No. of Pieces	Size (in Inches)					Material
1	Top	3	1	×	6	×	24	Pine
2	Legs	4	1	×	8	×	24	Pine
3	Rails	2	1	×	1½	×	18	Pine
4	Shelf	1	1	×	4	×	18	Pine

Fig. 13-19. Here you see five-board stool #1. Projects might differ in size and design and construction methods, but they always consist of legs, rails, and a top. Here, the rails are inset in notches cut into the legs.

Fig. 13-20. Five-board stool #2, shown here, is made with heavy materials, rounded edges, and some distressing done with a light chain, which give the project a hand-hewn look. The top is attached to legs with screws driven through counterbored holes that are then plugged with wooden buttons.

SERVING TRAY

Make the sides first, producing twins by utilizing the pad-sawing technique (Figs. 13-25 and 13-26). Drill the holes for the dowels that serve as handles before you take the pad apart. Alignment, when assembling, will be easy if you install the dowels as you clamp the sides to the base.

TRAY WITH RAISED EDGE

This project is offered to provide an opportunity to try the special bevel-sawing technique (Figs. 13-27 and 13-28). Shape the stock to the form suggested in the drawing and then use a compass to mark the central form. Tilt the band-saw table to 5 degrees and, after making an entry cut, saw out the circular section. Close the entry kerf by using a slim piece of wood to coat mating surfaces with glue, and then clamp it. The final step is to force the circular cutout into place after you have treated appropriate areas with glue.

Remember that successful bevel sawing depends on using a slight blade with many teeth that have uniform set—not to mention a very careful work-feed direction.

Table 13-5. Materials List for Five-Board Footstool #1.

Key	Part	No. of Pieces	Size (in Inches)	Material
1	Legs	2	¾ x 8 x 8	Pine
2	Rails	2	¾ x 2 x 16	Pine
3	Top	1	1½ x 9 x 18	Pine

Five-Board Stool #1 (see materials list for dim. not shown on drawing)

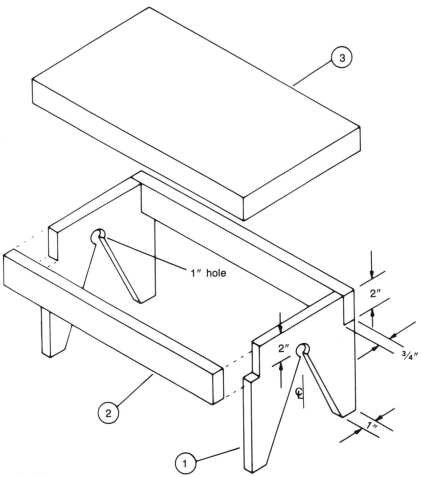

Fig. 13-21. Use the pad-sawing method to cut legs simultaneously. Drill the 1-inch hole before making the angular cuts.

Five-Board Foot Stool #2
(see materials list for dim. not shown on drawing)

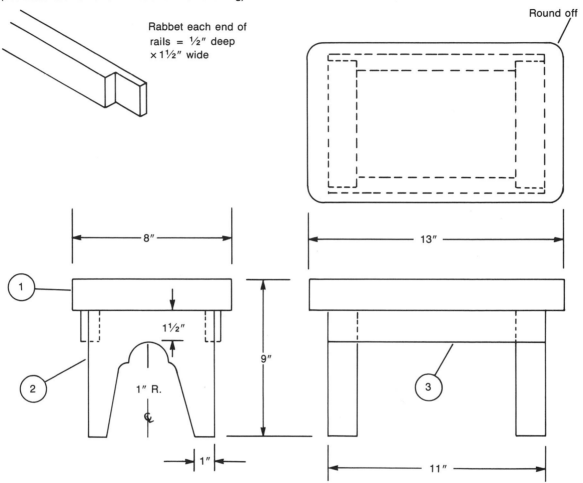

Rabbet each end of
rails = ½" deep
× 1½" wide

Round off

8"

13"

1

1½"

9"

2

1" R.

¢

1"

3

11"

Fig. 13-22. Details are shown for five-board stool #2. The rabbet cuts are simply notches that are cut into each end of the rails.

Table 13-6. Materials List for Five-Board Footstool #2.

Key	Part	No. of Pieces	Size (in Inches)					Material
1	Top	1	1½	×	8	×	13	Pine or Maple
2	Legs	2	1½	×	6½	×	7½	Pine or Maple
3	Rails	2	¾	×	1½	×	11	Pine or Maple

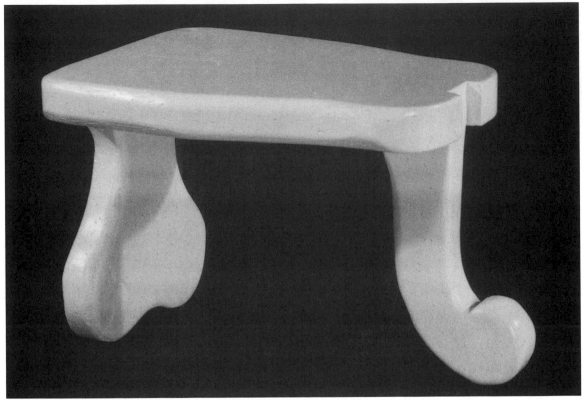

Fig. 13-23. The plant stand was finished with several coats of white lacquer. Its tripod design makes it suitable for its intended purpose, but not for sitting. Although components appear rough, you must sand them very smooth before you apply lacquer.

SPANISH-STYLE TABLE

You can achieve the motif of the Spanish-style table through the use of heavy materials and details that appear to be hand carved but that you actually can do with a portable router (Figs. 13-29 through 13-32). Legs are quite wide, so you must prepare the base stock by edge gluing two pieces of stock with real dimensions of 2 inches thick × 10 inches wide. Do the joining step after you have assembled pairs of pieces as a pad for sawing bottom and side profile shapes. Making two pads for sawing is suggested since four pieces, each 2 inches thick, would be too much for the average band-saw's depth of cut. Follow the same procedure when producing the brackets.

The top, like the legs, requires two pieces of material that you join edge to edge and then saw to final dimensions after the glue has set.

Attach the top to the legs by using glue and drilling for, and then installing, 4-inch-long wood screws. Counterbore holes for the screws so you can hide them with wooden plugs. Attach the brackets with glue and wood screws. Drive one or two screws down through the top and a single one, at an angle, through the bracket and into the leg.

Plant stand (not for sitting)

Top = 1½″ × 10″ × 14″
Leg = 1½″ × 8″ × 10″
Foot = 1½″ × 4″ × 10″

1″ squares

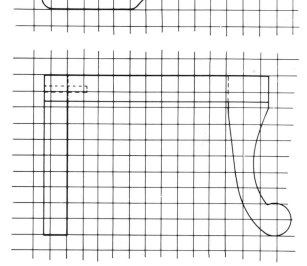

½″ D. × 3″ dowels

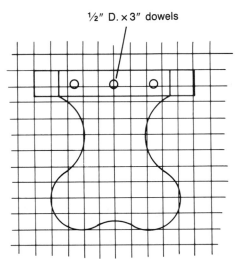

Fig. 13-24. These profiles indicate the components that you need for the plant stand. Put the rear leg in place before drilling holes for the dowels. Let the dowels project a bit so you can sand them flush after the glue sets.

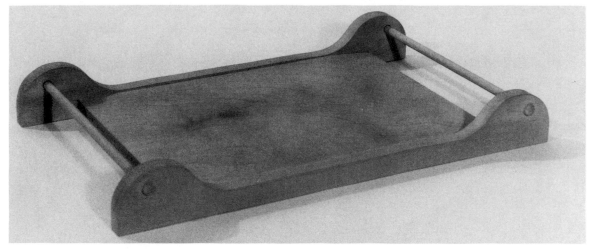

Fig. 13-25. Sides of the serving tray can be 1½-inch-thick material which you then resaw to produce duplicates, or you can produce them by pad sawing. In either case, drill holes for the dowel handles before sawing.

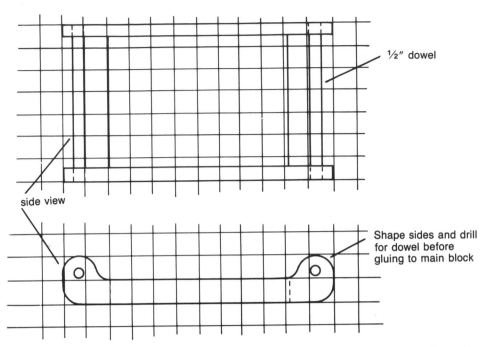

½" dowel

side view

Shape sides and drill
for dowel before
gluing to main block

Fig. 13-26. Serving tray details are shown here. Squares can be 1 inch or larger, depending on how large you want the project to be. The base can be cabinet-grade plywood or solid wood.

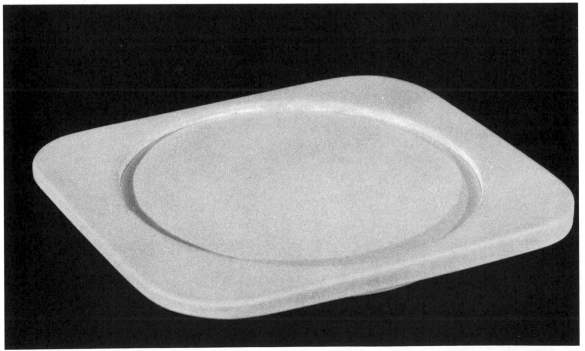

Fig. 13-27. You can make the tray with raised lip from a flat board by using the special bevel-sawing technique.

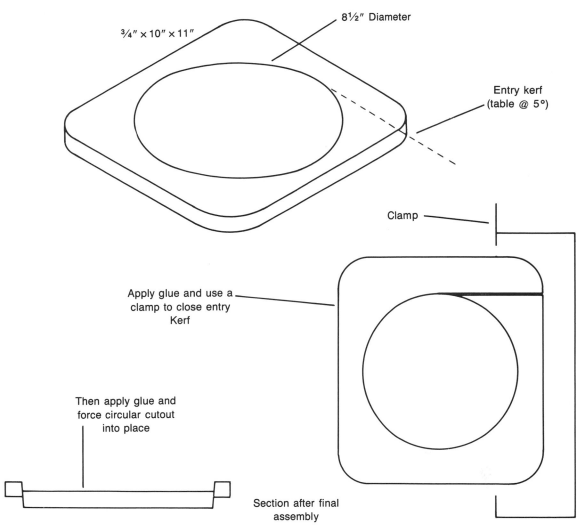

¾" × 10" × 11"

8½" Diameter

Entry kerf
(table @ 5°)

Clamp

Apply glue and use a
clamp to close entry
Kerf

Then apply glue and
force circular cutout
into place

Section after final
assembly

Fig. 13-28. You can fill the entry kerf that is required for bevel sawing the circular cutout with a slim strip of wood, or simply pull it together with a clamp.

You can carve by hand with a small gouge, but a router, equipped with a round-end bit, will make the job go faster and easier. Make straight, outline cuts first by using a clamped strip of wood as a guide. Then move the router in a rather haphazard fashion to provide the texture between the straight cuts. Adjust the projection of the router bit to about ¼ inch for the straight cuts and about ⅛ inch for the irregular ones.

PATIO NAPKIN HOLDER

This project prevents breezes from distributing napkins haphazardly (Figs. 13-33 and 13-34). The weight—just a wooden bar—moves vertically in slots that are in the side pieces so that various thicknesses of napkins will stay in place.

Fig. 13-29. All the wood used for the Spanish-style table is 2 inches thick. If the material isn't on hand in a local lumberyard, you can order it or you can substitute 1½-inch stock, which is more commonly available.

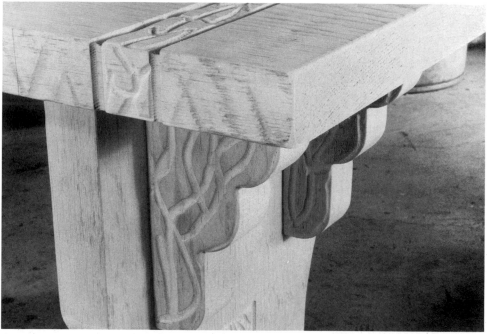

Fig. 13-30. Carving lends authentic detail to the Spanish-style table. Tool marks on the exposed edges of components add to the motif. One way to accomplish this technique is not to sand away entirely the washboarding left by the band-saw blade.

Fig. 13-31. You can do the carving by hand with chisels, but it will be easier to do with a portable router. Make straight cuts first by guiding the router along a clamped strip of wood. Then move rather haphazardly between the straight cuts.

Since the base is only 6 inches wide, you can form outline cuts for the grooves on the band saw by working with the stock on edge. Remove the material between the cuts with chisels. You can adopt the procedure for any project that calls for grooves so long as the width of the work is not more than the band saw's depth of cut. When the idea won't work, form outline cuts by hand with a backsaw. Of course, you easily can form grooves and dadoes when a table saw or radial arm saw is available.

THREE PROJECTS FROM ONE PIECE OF STOCK?

The idea is to view "waste" pieces of material as potential projects or project components. The bud vase, flower urn, and basket, all emerged from one piece

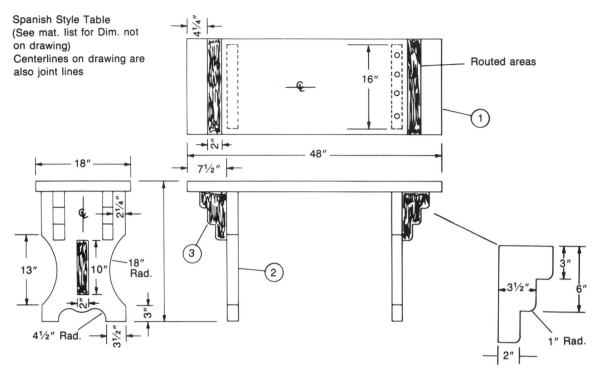

Spanish Style Table
(See mat. list for Dim. not on drawing)
Centerlines on drawing are also joint lines

Routed areas

Fig. 13-32. This drawing shows construction details for the Spanish-style table. Assemble the top to the legs and then add the brackets.

Table 13-7. Materials List for Spanish-style Table.

Key	Part	No. of Pieces	Size (in Inches)	Material
1	Top	2	2 × 10 × 48	Pine
2	Leg	4	2 × 10 × 24	Pine
3	Bracket	4	2 × 5 × 9	Pine

of material. The base stock can be solid or composed of individual pieces that are glued together. Creating a block offers the opportunity to use contrasting wood for an interesting effect. The starting piece can't be thicker than the machine's cut depth, but width dimensions can vary. The projects shown in Figs. 13-35 through 13-43 are examples; variations are possible.

The basic procedure is as follows. The first step is to make a circular cut to produce a solid cylinder. The second cut, also circular, results in a ring and a solid core. Cut the core on its diameter and saw each piece to produce two semicircular forms and two half-cylinders. The illustrations supply construction details for the example projects and suggest additional, interesting touches.

Fig. 13-33. This project for the patio keeps napkins in place when breezes tend to do otherwise.

Patio Napkin Holder

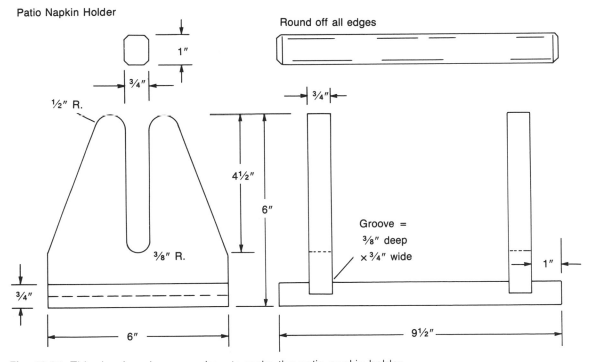

Round off all edges

1″

¾″

½″ R.

¾″

4½″

6″

Groove = ⅜″ deep × ¾″ wide

⅜″ R.

¾″

1″

6″

9½″

Fig. 13-34. This drawing shows you how to make the patio napkin holder.

275

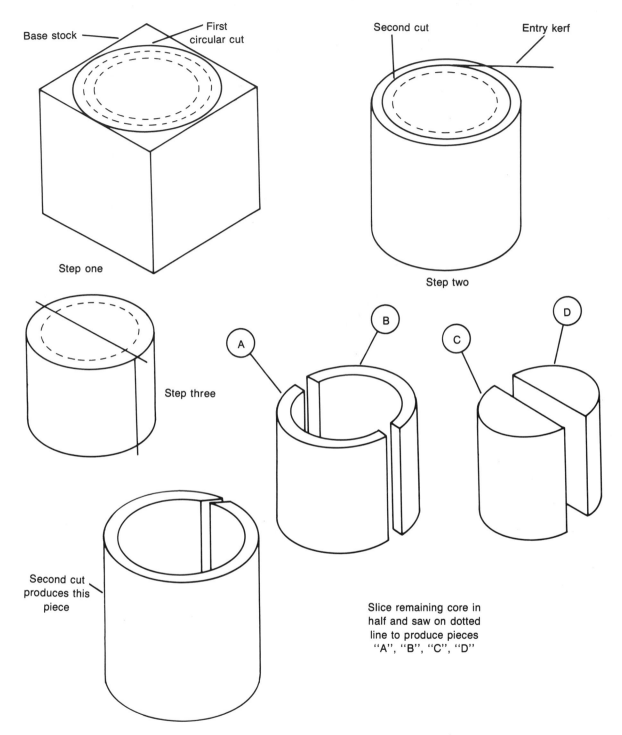

Base stock — First circular cut

Step one

Second cut — Entry kerf

Step two

Step three

A

B

C

D

Second cut produces this piece

Slice remaining core in half and saw on dotted line to produce pieces "A", "B", "C", "D"

Fig. 13-35. Follow these steps to get a variety of project components from a single piece of stock. The only waste is from the first circular cut.

276

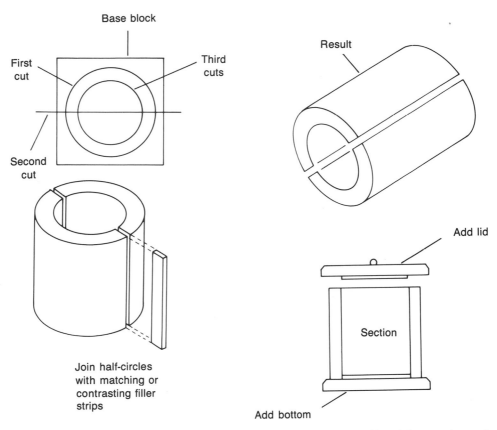

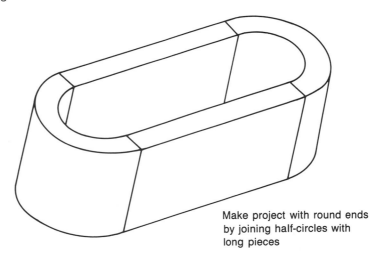

Fig. 13-36. You can make a round project by sawing a cylinder in half and then cutting out semicircular parts that you glue together. Adding contrasting filler strips in the joint provides an interesting detail.

Fig. 13-37. Join half rings like this to form long projects with round ends.

Fig. 13-38. Solid, semicircular core pieces were joined to make the bud vase. Drill a center hole for a water container which can be a test tube or something similar.

CUTTING BOARDS AND SPATULAS

Kitchen accessories like cutting boards and spatulas, or spreaders, are snap jobs for a band saw. Actually, you should give more thought to material selection and design than to the sawing, which is pretty straightforward. Hard maple, birch, and wood species like teak, are good selections for this type of project. It's wise to avoid open-grain wood like oak since surface pores can collect food particles.

You can make cutting boards from solid pieces or from base stock formed by laminating contrasting wood. Use a waterproof glue when laminating and be sure mating edges are straight and square so joint lines will be barely visible. (See Figs. 13-44 through 13-48).

The project should be super smooth so you will need to do a good deal of sanding. Finishing consists of applications of mineral oil which you apply almost like a French polish. The first application is generous and allowed to penetrate before you

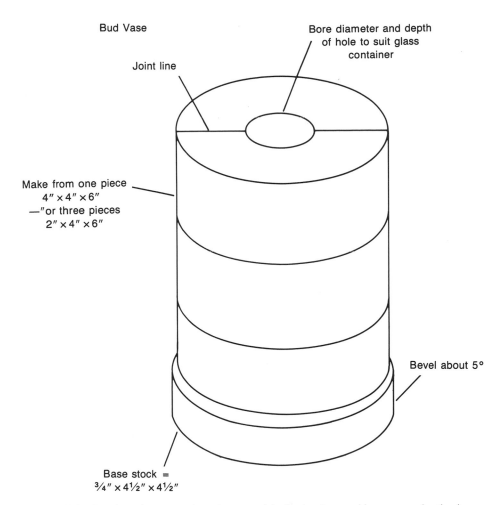

Bud Vase

Joint line

Bore diameter and depth
of hole to suit glass
container

Make from one piece
4″ × 4″ × 6″
—″or three pieces
2″ × 4″ × 6″

Bevel about 5°

Base stock =
¾″ × 4½″ × 4½″

Fig. 13-39. This drawing shows you how to assemble the bud vase. You can make the base stock out of solid material or by laminating separate pieces.

wipe the excess off with a lint-free cloth. Several other applications follow with enough time between them to allow for drying. Stop when you feel the wood won't take anymore, but continue with mineral oil applications about once a month. DO NOT use any type of cooking oil for finishing since it probably will turn rancid.

BAND-SAW SCULPTURES

Compound sawing, the technique that you use to produce furniture components like the cabriole leg, is what makes band-saw sculptures possible (Figs. 13-49 through 13-53). Draw side and top profiles of the figure on adjacent sides of the stock. After you produce one profile, return waste pieces to original positions, by tack nailing or by using tape, and do the final cutting on the adjacent side. This procedure results in a rudimentary figure in the round that you can, if you wish, detail further by hand, working with carving chisels or a small hand grinder, sandpaper, and the like.

Fig. 13-40. The flower urn utilizes the semicircular rings. Narrow strips separate the rings. Prepare these strips so the grain runs vertically.

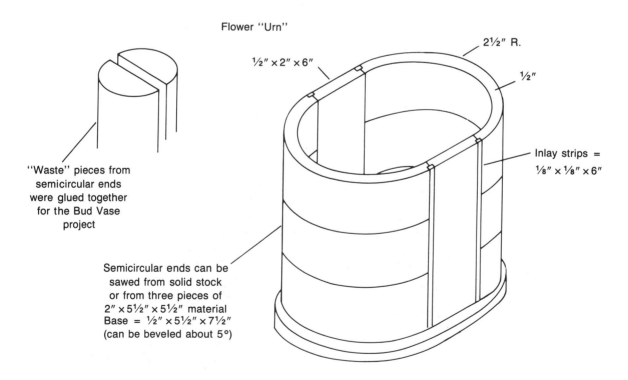

Flower "Urn"

2½" R.

½" × 2" × 6"

½"

Inlay strips = ⅛" × ⅛" × 6"

"Waste" pieces from semicircular ends were glued together for the Bud Vase project

Semicircular ends can be sawed from solid stock or from three pieces of 2" × 5½" × 5½" material Base = ½" × 5½" × 7½" (can be beveled about 5°)

Fig. 13-41. This drawing shows you how to assemble the flower urn. The inlay strips are optional. Cut the shallow kerfs for the strips, if you decide to add them, on a table saw after you completely assemble and sand smooth the body of the project. Work with a miter-gauge extension to which you can clamp the work for each of the cuts.

Fig. 13-42. The first circular cuts produce a full ring that requires only that you glue the entry kerf and clamp it closed, or fill it with a slim strip of wood. The full ring was used to make this basket project.

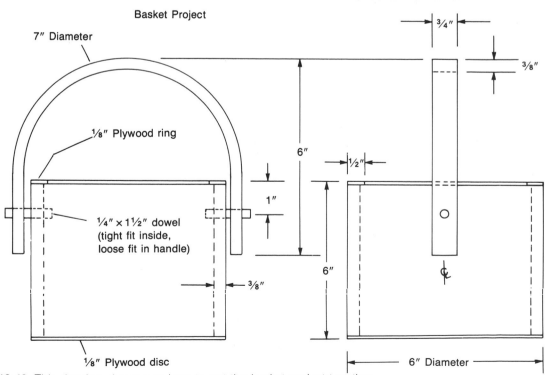

Basket Project

7" Diameter

1/8" Plywood ring

1/4" × 1 1/2" dowel
(tight fit inside,
loose fit in handle)

1/8" Plywood disc

6"

1"

3/8"

3/4"

3/8"

1/2"

6"

6" Diameter

Fig. 13-43. This drawing shows you how to put the basket project together.

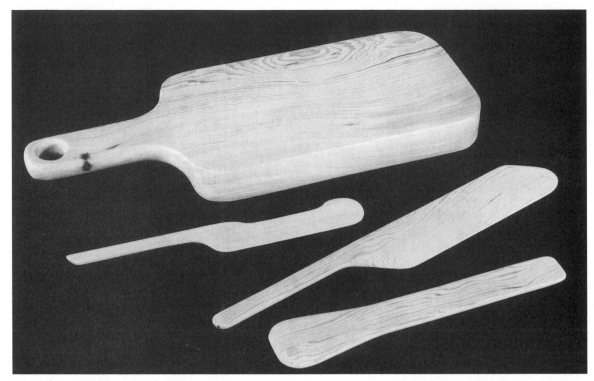

Fig. 13-44. Kitchen accessories like cutting boards and spreaders are quick jobs for a band saw.

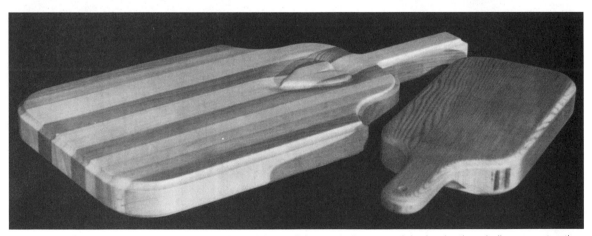

Fig. 13-45. You can make cutting boards from solid material or use a base stock by laminating similar or contrasting strips of wood. Laminating is recommended for large boards to guard against warpage. Note the carved heart. You can add details like this, but not where you will be cutting. Add details to edges by using a portable router.

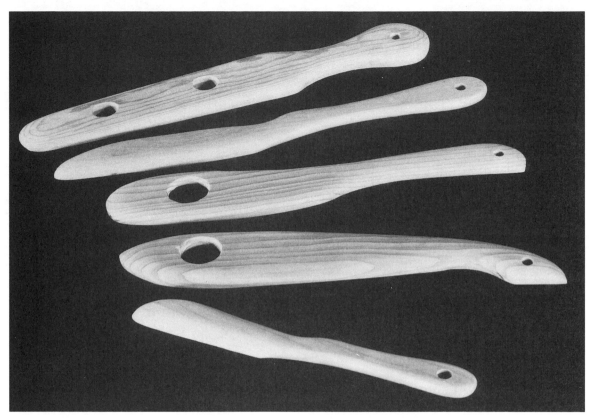

Fig. 13-46. Holes through spatulas that you use for stirring are wise since they allow the tools to move more freely through liquids.

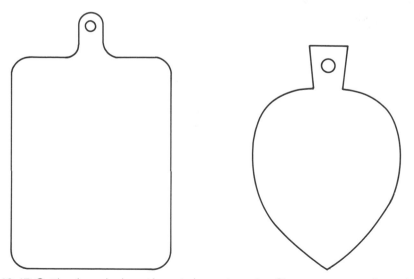

Fig. 13-47. Cutting boards do not have to be rectangular. Choose a square dimension to suit the size of the project you wish to produce.

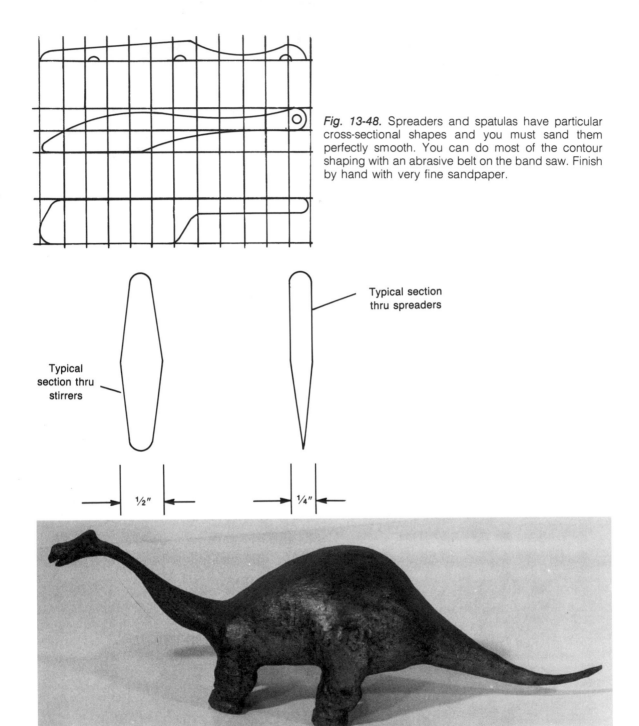

Fig. 13-48. Spreaders and spatulas have particular cross-sectional shapes and you must sand them perfectly smooth. You can do most of the contour shaping with an abrasive belt on the band saw. Finish by hand with very fine sandpaper.

Typical section thru spreaders

Typical section thru stirrers

½"

¼"

Fig. 13-49. Band-saw sculpturing is possible on the band saw because the tool allows compound sawing. The shape that emerges after sawing is rudimentary, but you can do further modeling with hand tools or a small power tool like a hand grinder.

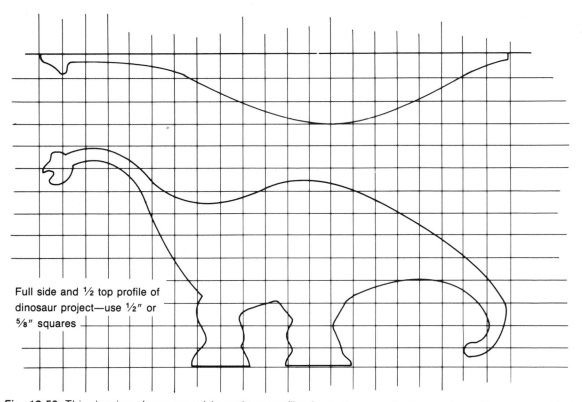

Full side and ½ top profile of dinosaur project—use ½″ or ⅝″ squares

Fig. 13-50. This drawing shows you side and top profiles for a dinosaur. Do the sawing with a narrow blade that has many tpi.

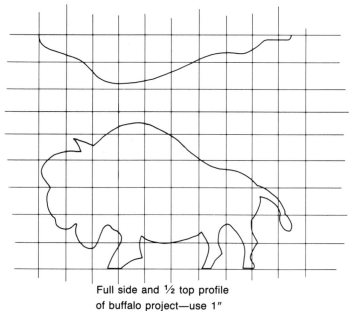

Full side and ½ top profile of buffalo project—use 1″ squares

Fig. 13-51. Here is a design for a buffalo project.

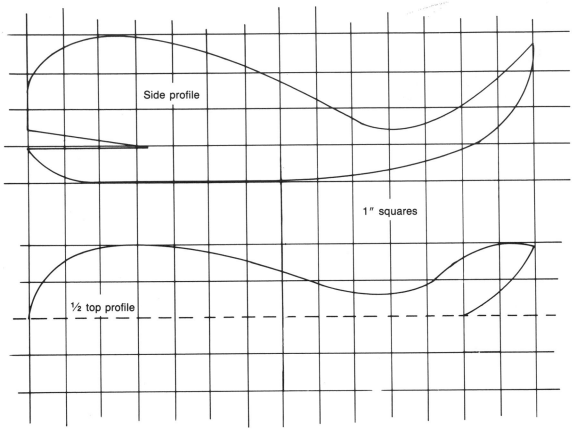

Side profile

1″ squares

½ top profile

Fig. 13-52. This drawing shows you a whale project.

An interesting variation would be to saw only the side profile and then to resaw to get duplicate pieces. You can mount these on backing boards as plaques, or you can mount them on the wall as a running design—a nice idea, say, for a child's room.

ANTIQUED TRINKET BOX

Bevel-cut pieces form the body of the box that you assemble with glue. You can use temporary staples or a band clamp, if available, to hold the parts together until the glue sets.

Antiquing consists of applying plastic wood to all surfaces with a small, stiff brush (Figs. 13-54 and 13-55). When the application is dry, sand the surfaces lightly with sandpaper wrapped around a wooden block. This procedure will result in a kind of stucco texture. Being a bit careless with the sanding so tiny portions of the wood will show through adds to the effect. You can add color using a flat paint, followed by an application of satin-finish varnish.

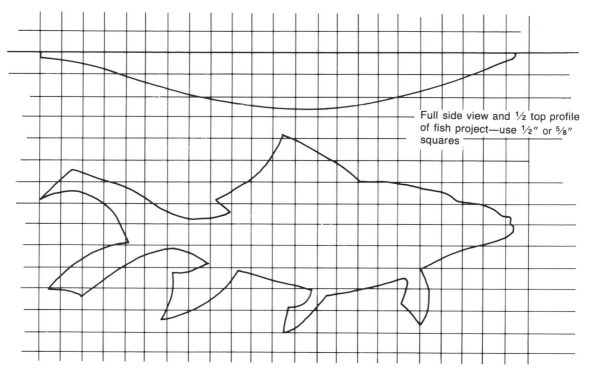

Fig. 13-53. For the fish project, you do not have to make it in the round. Cutting only the side profile in thick stock and then resawing will produce identical pieces.

Fig. 13-54. You can produce the hexagonal body of the trinket box by assembling bevel-sawed sides. Antiquing consists of plastering all surfaces roughly with wood dough and then sanding high spots. The result will be a stucco-like texture.

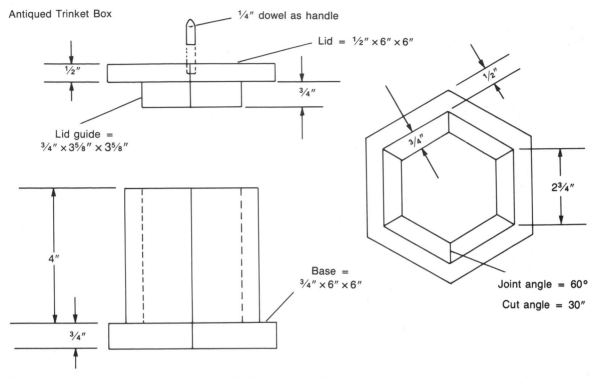

Antiqued Trinket Box

¼″ dowel as handle

Lid = ½″ × 6″ × 6″

½″

¾″

Lid guide =
¾″ × 3⅝″ × 3⅝″

½″

¾″

2¾″

4″

¾″

Base =
¾″ × 6″ × 6″

Joint angle = 60°

Cut angle = 30″

Fig. 13-55. Here are the construction details for the trinket box.

MAGAZINE RACK

To make the sides of this project, tack nail two pieces of wood and then saw the profile (Figs. 13-56 and 13-57). Keep the pad intact until after you have drilled the holes for the dowels. The best assembly procedure to follow is to connect the sides with the dowels, and then add the bottom.

DESIGNS FOR SHELF BRACKETS

Use the enlarging-by-squares method, with suitably-sized squares, to draw the pattern in the size you need for this project (Fig. 13-58). A French curve and a circle template or compass will be very helpful when you are connecting location points. Don't forget that you can use pad sawing or resawing techniques to supply duplicates.

BAND-SAWED LETTERS

You can produce interesting letters and numbers by following the patterns that are offered (Figs. 13-59 and 13-60). The only problem with the band saw is that you can't form the inside of figures like "0" or "zero" or "Q," not unless you make a lead-in cut to get to interior areas. An alternate method is to supply the voids by boring holes before or after you saw profiles.

When you need two or more of the same letter or number, do the initial sawing on thick stock that you can resaw to get duplicates.